AMERICAN

The American Indian and

GENESIS

the Origins of Modern Man

Jeffrey Goodman, Ph.D.

SUMMIT BOOKS/NEW YORK

SUMMIT BOOKS and colophon are trademarks of Simon & Schuster.
Designed by Eve Kirch
Manufactured in the United States of America

1   3   5   7   9   10   8   6   4   2

Library of Congress Cataloging in Publication Data

Goodman, Jeffrey.
American genesis.
Bibliography: p.
Includes index.
1.   Indians—Origin.   2.   Man—Origin.   3.   Man,
Prehistoric.   I.   Title.
E61.G75   970.01   80–18652
ISBN 0–671–25139–2

*To my little Indians, Joy and Robin,
and to the proud natives of this land.*

Contents

I would like to acknowledge the help of the late Oswald "White Bear" Fredericks, Stephen Haines, Anna Jefferson, Maggie McGuire, Jane Smith, Martha Sowerwine, and special thanks to Diane Cleaver.

AMERICAN GENESIS

1

Modern Man's World Debut

... the Calico excavations have ... added a greater dimension to American prehistory. It [the project] has opened the
door to a new era of research and has brought into the
realm of feasibility the concept of a Stone Age man in
America and of an American Paleolithic culture.

— Louis S. B. Leakey,
Pleistocene Man at Calico, 1972

A range of lofty mountains with icy glacial fingers reaches out
from snow-choked valleys. The valleys give way to a wide, gently-
sloping plain dotted with a variety of trees including oak, pine,
and spruce. The floor of the valley is covered with high grass
which bends in the steady breeze blowing down from the mountains. Over the horizon, three figures are striding into view.

They're tall, lean, well-muscled men. Their skin is light brown
in color, their hair long and black. Their sure-footed, confident
strides make them a natural part of the landscape as they head
toward their camp at the foot of the mountain in a dense stand of
trees. Broad cheekbones and hawk noses indicate they are Indians.

Two of the men are carrying a stout, straight branch between
their shoulders. Hanging from it is a hundred-pound chunk of
meat—the hindquarters of some massive mammal. Part of the
hide is still attached to the animal's frame. The long silky hair on
the hide testifies that somewhere close by the men killed and

butchered a woolly mammoth, a giant with twelve-foot tusks, standing more than fourteen feet high and weighing more than eight thousand pounds.

The stillness of the scene is pierced by raucous "honking" as a flight of Greater Canada geese head south on their fall migration. The two men carrying the branch acknowledge the geese by waving their sharp stone-tipped spears. The third, a youth, laughs and motions for the geese to come closer so that he might shoot one with his bow and arrow. The geese ignore the men, wheeling their way south, their cries dying in the distance.

The three hunters soon reach their fall hunting camp. For the last two months they have lived in tents made of hides stretched across stout frames made of mammoth ribs. Their permanent home is five hundred miles to the south in the eastern plains of Colorado. As soon as the hunters drop their prize, two women kneel down with tools made of caribou bone which they use to remove the remaining hide from the meat.

The three hunters join a group of men in listening to one of their band who recently returned from a treacherous seven-year round-trip journey on foot to a far distant land (known today as the French Riviera). The brave traveler holds up a simple map of the landmarks for the journey which he carved into stone. There is talk of how all the members of the clan might go there someday.

The sun is setting fast and several women are grinding a wild grain, perhaps corn. There are some ponies grazing near the camp, feisty equines the Indians sometimes ride.

At first glance, this scenario doesn't seem at all fantastic, except for the Riviera trip. It seems a reasonable picture of the early American Indians, or Paleo-Indians as archaeologists call them. But in fact, this scenario or something like it has generated some of the most fascinating speculation and reconsideration in the world of archaeology in quite some time, because a scene like this took place at least 50,000 years before generally accepted archaeological thinking says it should have—at a time when, the

This scene depicts Paleo-Indians killing a mammoth in Arizona 12,000 years ago. Mammoth remains with the spear points that killed them have been found at many southwestern sites. *Museo Nacional de Antropologia, Mexico*

theory goes, man shouldn't have been in North America at all.

Until a few years ago, scholars would have said such a scene could have happened no more than 12,000 years ago. But now it is clear from growing archaeological evidence that it could have taken place over 70,000 years ago. During the past five years, a startling new rush of archaeological discoveries, new dating techniques, and the recognition of hitherto unknown tool manufacturing techniques show that the Indians were in the Americas much, much earlier than suspected—as early as 500,000 years ago. These astounding discoveries have thrown off all our accepted notions of the way North America and perhaps the world evolved.

Up until now, archaeologists and anthropologists firmly believed that: (1) several million years ago, *Homo habilis*, the first clear ancestor on man's lineage, appeared in Africa; (2) approximately one million years ago, *Homo erectus*, a more advanced form, appeared in Asia, Africa, and Europe; (3) about 180,000 years ago, "near men" called Neanderthals dominated Europe; and finally, (4) fully modern man, our direct ancestors, appeared in Europe 35,000 years ago, spreading into Africa and Asia and eventually reaching North America 12,000 years ago. Since, according to this scenario, there were no fully modern men anywhere in the world 70,000 years ago, these new American discoveries, mostly from North America, point to the astonishing thesis that men like ourselves, subspecies *Homo sapiens sapiens*, made their world debut in the Americas, instead of in Europe. The proverbial Garden of Eden may have been in North America in southern California, and from this Garden the first fully modern men may have ventured forth bearing cultural and technological gifts to the rest of the world.

New information has come from far below the earth's surface, from depths of fifteen to sixty feet, much deeper than the few feet usually dug by archaeologists in the Americas. Steam shovels working on housing sites, steep rain-etched gulleys, and exploratory shafts have penetrated a thick earthen veil to offer a glimpse of these ancient times. Buried under the virtually unexplored geological strata of the American continents may be a message for all of mankind: a saga of our true origins—the saga of who man is and where he has come from.

Ironically, ten years ago the famed Dr. Louis Leakey stood alone when he suggested that there was an ancient prehistoric bounty to be found in the Americas. The theory that modern man first appeared in the Americas is quite a new theory, a turnabout in archaeological thinking. Until recently, it has been an accepted fact that successive waves of nomadic Asian hunters unwittingly wandered across the now submerged Bering Land Bridge—the land corridor which connected Asia to Alaska in glacial times—to populate a new continent and become the first American Indians.

But now it seems more likely that if the first modern men did cross the Bering Bridge to settle in a new continent, they traveled from the Americas to Europe and Asia. A startling pattern has emerged: Many innovative types of artifacts such as advanced spear point styles, specialized bone tools, grinding tools, and the bow and arrow appear to have been used by New World craftsmen in North America many thousands of years before Old World craftsmen in Europe, Asia, and Africa used them. The sequence of artifact dates indicates that the Paleo-Indians radiated out from their southern California base and traveled in three different directions: north to the Old World, east to the Atlantic states, and south to the southern tip of South America.

The American Indians may have even been responsible for the sudden appearance of cave-dwelling Cro-Magnon man in Europe, one of the most celebrated moments in mankind's history. For decades, archaeologists have known that rather suddenly, 35,000 years ago, the crude Neanderthals were replaced throughout Europe by fully modern Cro-Magnon man. A culturally sleeping Europe was awakened overnight. Some scholars have even described this changeover as a sudden "invasion." Where our direct ancestors, Cro-Magnon man, came from and where our distant cousins, the Neanderthals, went has remained a mystery. The American Indians may provide the answer.

American Indians, who migrated to Europe, may have been the Cro-Magnons. We now know that tools unique to Cro-Magnon men who lived in Spain, first appeared in the American Southwest. From a site in Lewisville, Texas, a spear point which is exactly like unique spear points used in Spain 20,000 years ago dated to (was found to be) more than 38,000 years in age. From five different California sites, scientists have found five different fully modern skulls, resembling Indian and generalized Indian/European skulls, all bearing dates older than the oldest of the European Cro-Magnon sites. One skull from Sunnyvale, California, near San Francisco, dated to 70,000 years ago, a date twice as old as the oldest fully modern skull from Europe. The fact that American Indians now predate modern man's appearance in Europe by at least 35,000 years may explain why these first Europeans, called Cro-Magnons, appeared with an already highly developed and sophisticated art style, which included painting, sculpture, and carvings. Skulls dating from 7,000 to 20,000 years ago found in Japan and in Chinese caves which bear a marked resemblance to Indian skulls may well be the remains of Indian settlers, who also took their skills to Asia as well as to Europe.

Going one step further, we can even consider the possibility that many of man's greatest cultural and technological achievements, which include the manufacturing of pottery, plant and animal domestication, mathematical concepts, calendrics, astronomy, and sophisticated medical knowledge first appeared in the New World instead of in the Old World.

The notion that the American Indians may have been the very earliest true men does not surprise the Indians; their legends have said so all along. The Hopi Indians of northern Arizona teach that "three worlds" existed prior to the one in which we now live. During the first of these three worlds, the Hopi say, their ancestors were highly advanced, they had domesticated corn and animals. They say that this first world was eventually destroyed by fire, the second world was destroyed by ice, and the third world by water. To the Hopi, these worlds existed in the San Francisco mountains, the mountains outside of Flagstaff, Arizona. These worlds at least make geologic sense. The destruction of the Hopi's third world by water may correspond to the inner-mountain basin damming and flooding that took place approximately 25,000 years ago in the Flagstaff mountains. The destruction of the second world by ice could represent the glacial activity that took place in the peaks approximately 100,000 years ago. And the destruction of the first world by fire could represent the volcanic activity that took place in the mountains approximately 250,000 years ago. A recent archaeological discovery in the area gives added support to Hopi myth. At this dig I have discovered the oldest known geometrically engraved stone in the world, an engraving two to three times as old as similar engravings made by Cro-Magnon man. While engravings of reindeer and bison catch the eye, geometric engravings usually have a much greater significance. Abstract engravings have been found to correlate with phases of the moon or movements of the planets, or to be records of sacred (esoteric) religious information.

Thus, as with the story of creation and the flood in the Bible, the basic elements and sequence of Hopi legend could be correct. If so, archaeologists must wonder what previously unconsidered monumental events took place in the Americas so long ago, events which led to modern man's first appearance.

2

Lost Tribes and Sunken Continents

Certain errors are stations on the way to truth.
—Robert Musil to C. W. Ceram,
The First American, 1972

The American Indians have been one of the world's most misunderstood, maligned, and persecuted races. For almost one-half million years, the Indians have developed a dizzying diversity of widely different cultures represented by over two hundred mutually unintelligible languages in North America alone. How and when they got to America and began their diversification is one of the most intriguing and most debated puzzles in history. It is a debate fraught with emotions that has involved not only scholars and laymen, but whole organizations, nations, and even religions. This debate has pitted professors, priests, physicians, psychics, mystics, lawyers, businessmen, artists, and even a Senator and a President of the United States (Thomas Jefferson) against each other.

The host of more or less fanciful theories on Indian origins put forth over the past four hundred years exemplifies a still-discernible tendency to draw large, often misrepresentative conclusions about Indians from an inadequate store of facts. The recent wave of new discoveries in the Americas shows how deeply all of these theories underestimated the great age of Indian origins and great importance of those origins to modern man's world distribution and development.

In 1492, Christopher Columbus set sail from Italy planning to circle the globe and bring back spices from India. But instead of reaching his goal, Columbus accidentally discovered (or rediscovered) the New World and its natives. The day Columbus set foot in the New World was the day the Western world got off on the wrong foot concerning Indian origins. Columbus, believing that the natives he met were East Asiatics, promptly and permanently dubbed them "Indians," initiating a series of misconceptions about the first Americans that lasts to this day.

Sadly, the Church at first didn't consider the "Indians" to be human beings, since the Bible made no mention of a "redskinned" people. The Biblical account of creation only described the three continents of Europe, Asia, and Africa, each occupied by the offspring of Noah's three sons who survived the flood. From Shem, given the Semitic land, came the Arabs, Hebrews, and Syrians; from Ham came the Libyans, Egyptians, and Africans; and from Japheth came the peoples of Europe and Asia.

Eventually the Church granted that the Indians were human. In 1512, Pope Giuliana della Rovere, Julius II, officially declared that the New World's Indians were true descendants of Adam and Eve and thus must have come from the Old World's Garden of Eden. Pope Julius was reassured in his declaration by the fact that the Indians believed in the immortality of the soul.

The Spanish called the Indians "*gente colorada*," which means "colored people" as opposed to "white" Europeans. But since *colorado* also means "red" in Spanish, the dubious term "redskin" came into being. The Indians, of course, actually have a wide range of skin color.

After the Spanish explorers reached the Pacific shore of the new land by 1519, Columbus's error in geography was recognized. The realization that another vast sea lay beyond the western limits of America led to immediate speculation regarding the origins of these numerous "red" tribes. Had the Indians always been natives of this new continent? If not, when did they come and how? And did they all come from the same place?

The question of origins was an open one until 1702, when Cotton Mather, the influential preacher from Boston, the spiritual father of the Salem witch trials of 1692, made his own proclamation on the question. He asserted that the Indians had not migrated by any normal route, but that the Devil in person had brought these Red Men to America! Mather's dictum reflected the low regard most colonists had for the Indians.

After Mather, the focus of inquiry into Indian origins was directed at how these people fit into God's creation as it was outlined in the Bible, the sole true authority. Many of the earliest explorers and historians accounted for the Indians as descendants of the "ten lost tribes of Israel."* In those days, ancient Hebrew tribal practice as described in the Old Testament was about the only well-documented primitive way of life. Parallels between the Indians and the Hebrews included marriage within the tribe, marriage by purchase, animal sacrifice, lunar and ritual calendars, first-fruit ceremonies, purification rites, fasting, food taboos, flood myths, and circumcision. Links of all kinds were cited. One savant saw a connection between Mexico's mighty Aztecs and the early Hebrews. The Aztecs, it was pointed out, started as a small tribe of nomads who had only one cherished possession—the

---

* William Penn, Quaker religious leader and founder of the Quaker colony of Pennsylvania, said of the Indians of Pennsylvania: "The natives are generally tall, well built, and of singular proportion; they tread strong and clever, and mostly walk with a lofty chin. . . . Their eye is little and black, not unlike a straight looked Jew . . . and the noses of several of them have as much of the Roman. . . . For their original, I am ready to believe them to be of the Jewish race—I mean of the stock of the ten tribes—and that for the following reasons: first . . . ; in the next place, I find them to be of the like countenance, and their children of so lively a resemblance that a man would think himself in Duke's Place or Berry Street in London when he seeth them. But this is not all: they agree in rites, they reckon by moons, they offer their first-fruits, they have a kind of feast of tabernacles, they are said to lay their altars upon twelve stones, their mourning a year, customs of women, with many other things that do not now occur." (William Penn, Letter of August 1683.)

wooden image of their god wrapped in a bundle, which was carefully guarded by four priests and carried on all the tribes' wanderings. This was seen as a direct link to the early Hebrews, who carried their Ark of the Covenant through the wilderness of Sinai.

The Old Testament (II Kings 15:29 and Isaiah 36–37) tells how in 721 B.C., ten of the twelve tribes that comprised the ancient Hebrew Kingdom were conquered and carried away by the King of Assyria. It was said that some of these conquered tribes began to wander across southwest Asia, their activities and movements disappearing from history. It was argued that some of these tribes found their way to America and fathered the Indian civilizations, best exemplified by the impressive ancient cities in Mexico. Proponents of this theory spent little time trying to explain how and by what route these "Lost Tribes" could have made such a great journey.

This Lost Tribe theory was championed and furthered in a widely-read book about the northeastern Indians published in 1775. The author, James Adair, a literate Indian trader with headquarters in Savannah, Georgia, seized upon a collection of linguistic resemblances as added evidence of Israelite origins. But Adair only presented coincidental similarities (in word sounds and word meanings), not structural similarities. Adair said that during Indian first-fruit ceremonies the natives chanted the mystic phrase, "*Yo Meschica, He Meschica, Va Meschica.*" He argued that the first syllables of these three terms formed the name Jehovah and the rest of each term was clearly Messiah. When Adair heard the Indians chant "*Schiluhyu, Schiluhe, Schiluhva,*" he found Jehovah in the *last* syllables, and identified *Schiluh* with the Hebrew word *Schiloth*, which means "messenger" or "pacificator."

Hebrew scholars have pointed out that while the ten tribes were "lost" to the Jewish nation, they weren't geographically lost at all, since they were to a great extent absorbed by other peoples in that part of Asia. Nonetheless, this theory had its fervent adherents and still has. Among the better known were Esra Stiles, president of Yale, and Edward King, the Viscount of Kingsborough. After completing his studies at Oxford, King, the young English nobleman, was elected to the House of Lords, but soon renounced his seat to devote himself to full-time study of the Mexican manuscripts and archaeology with which he had become obsessed. King spent his entire fortune in publishing a series of luxurious volumes (1835–37) pertaining to the Mexican antiquities and the Lost Tribes, only thereafter to be sent to a Dublin debtors' prison where he died at the age of forty-two. As we shall continue to see, the warring theories about American Indian origins have played on a fierce battleground; the casualties have been heavy.

A related, though not materially improved, theory concerning Indian origins is to be found in the tenets of the Morman religion. The Mormons are most earnest in these beliefs, which are taught in special courses, placed in their Articles of Faith, and given a prominent role in their Bible. They do not believe that the ten Lost Tribes migrated to America. Rather, the Church of Jesus Christ of Latter Day Saints teaches that there were two other Israelite migrations to America. This information was revealed in 1827 to the founder of the Mormon religion, Joseph Smith, by "Moroni," an angel, or "resurrected personage," upon gleaming gold plates in a hieroglyphic script. Smith could read these plates only by peering through two miraculous stones. In about three months' time, Smith dictated his translation to various scribes, this translation becoming the Book of Mormon. It was said that the angel Moroni eventually carried the plates off to heaven. The Book of Mormon, published in 1829, details how America was first settled by a tribe of Israelites called Jaredites, who came direct from the confusion at the Tower of Babel as described in Genesis. These Jaredites were supposed to have come via boats, landing on the Gulf Coast of Mexico and founding a number of centers such as Monte Alban and La Venta, but after a series of calamities, they were destroyed in the Second Century B.C. Then the Book describes a second Israelite migration to America, again by boat, led by a man called Lehi. Lehi and his followers, the argument goes on, came directly from Jerusalem about 600 B.C., and after their arrival quickly split into two groups, the Nephites and the Lamanites. The Nephites are said to have built the great pre-Columbian sites of Central America and the Andes (such as Tikal and Teotihuacan, outside Mexico City, with its famed Pyramids of the Sun and Moon) and to have died out about 324 A.D. The Lamanites are said to have become a nomadic agricultural people who continued in "degenerate condition" and who became the ancestors of the familiar North American Indian tribes. The Mormons also say that the Mexican-Maya god Quetzalcoatl-Kukulkan and Christ were the same being, noting how this god is depicted in Indian art as a person crucified. They say that Jesus Christ visited the Americas and walked and taught among a number of different Indian tribes after his resurrection.

There is no hard evidence to support the Mormon story.* In the days of Joseph Smith, there was no way of dating the founding of the great Central and South American pre-Columbian sites, but today we know these sites are much older than the Book of Mormon allows. In 1975, Dr. Norman Hammond of the Cambridge University found evidence at a new site named Cuello that dated the Maya, the prehistoric Indian group who lived in the magnificent sites on Mexico's Yucatan peninsula, back to 2800 B.C. The Book of Mormon attributes these sites to their second Israelite migration, which didn't take place until 600 B.C.; Hammond's findings actually date the Maya further back in time than

---

* The New World Archaeological Foundation, affiliated with Brigham Young, the Mormon university in Provo, Utah, and mainly funded by Mormon donations, carries out excavations in Mexico among the prehistoric ruins they believe the different Israelite colonies founded in the Americas. Brigham Young's large department of archaeology publishes its own Bulletin about the results of their research. Mormon archaeologists politely resent the fact that non-Mormon archaeologists and anthropologists will not take the Book of Mormon seriously. The Mormon archaeologists believe that the Book of Mormon is an authentic historical document and that archaeology will eventually fully substantiate their beliefs about the Indians. But archaeology today, as in the days of Joseph Smith, still does not have such supporting facts.

the Mormons' first Israelite migration. In 1970, Dr. Stuart Struever, an archaeologist from Northwestern University, digging
twenty feet down in a cornfield in Illinois at a site called Koster,
showed that North American Indians weren't "degenerate" when
he discovered that permanent Indian cities with plaster walls and
sophisticated architecture date back to at least 6000 B.C. To the
Mormons' credit, however, there is a growing body of evidence
that people from different parts of the Near East, as well as the
Far East and Africa, may have visited Mexico on different occasions in ancient times.[1]

In July 1977, the 3.8 million worldwide Latter Day Saints'
membership was shaken by an attack on the authorship and authenticity of the Book of Mormon itself. Howard Davis and three
other freelance researchers said they had evidence that the book
is a hoax.

Stored in the church's Salt Lake City archives are some of the
pages of the original manuscript of the Book which Joseph Smith
translated from the gleaming tablets. Among these are twelve
pages written by a single unknown hand. Davis and his group say
that these unattributed pages were literally taken from an unpub-
lished manuscript on the origins of the Indians written by Solo-
mon Spalding, a Congregational minister who died in 1816, fourteen years before the Book of Mormon was first published.
Spalding's manuscript was supposedly stolen from a Pittsburgh
publishing house by a preacher who gave the papers to Smith.

Davis and his associates were led to their discovery when they
learned of the arguments made by an early Mormon who had left
the faith, disillusioned by the similarities between Smith's scrip-
tures and the missing Spalding novel. Davis and his colleagues
gave photocopies of the twelve pages from the Mormon archives
and known specimens of Spalding's writing to three handwriting
experts. Working independently, and kept uninformed of any tie
to the Book of Mormon, all three experts determined that the
same man had written both sets of documents. Officially, the
Mormon Church remains unruffled and is welcoming researchers
and handwriting experts to Salt Lake City to study the original

documents. "We still declare that the Book of Mormon is precisely what we have always said it was—a divinely revealed scripture of ancient American people," a church spokesman said.[2]

While the early explorers, early historians, and the Mormons had and have the Indians coming from Israel (the "Israelite origins" theory was at its height of fashion in the 1700s), many other theories have also been put forward. Dr. Robert Wauchope of Tulane University, a former president of the Society for American Archaeology, says that in the late eighteenth and early nineteenth centuries, classicists saw Carthaginian-Phoenician traits in the art, architecture, language, and religious and political structure of the Central American Maya, the Aztec and pre-Aztec civilizations of Mexico, and the Inca and other high cultures of the South American Andes. But then, with the spectacular archaeological discoveries that occurred in Egypt, a rash of writers became convinced that our American prehistoric ruins were merely remnants of Egyptian colonists. The similarity between the Pyramid of the Sun in Mexico City, the Mayan pyramid-shaped temples, and the Egyptian pyramids is cited in support of their argument. While the Phoenicians or Egyptians may have influenced the characteristics of American civilization to some as yet undetermined degree,* these theories really say nothing about the much earlier actual origins of the Indian.

During the nineteenth century, many of the simplistic parallels —the legends and isolated traits and customs—which were thought to be peculiar to just the Indians and the Israelites, Phoenicians, or Egyptians were found to occur in many other groups; for example, sacrifices to gods, and lunar and ritual calendars were found among the Abyssinians, Zulus, Burmese, and Malays. The independent invention of such traits was recognized as an alternative to explaining them only by historical connections.

What the Indians themselves had to say about their own ori-

* See Chapter 1, pages 16–21.

gins was largely ignored. Interestingly, many Indian myths did refer to visitors from strange lands, but these visitors were supposed to have come long after the Indians were well established in the Americas. For example, Mayan mythology describes two different sets of legendary visitors, one white-skinned, the other black-skinned, who both arrived by boat from across the great sea which lay to the east. (In fact, it was the Aztecs' trusting anticipation of the return of the white-skinned visitors that led to their defeat by the Spanish Conquistador Hernando Cortez.) These fabled visitations came long after the Mayas had begun building their ornate temples and palaces; they have nothing to do with Mayan origins, which began, the myths said, "worlds" earlier. The Indian myths that the Anglos have been able to gather so far remain incomplete, but it is clear that for the most part they refer to the various Indian groups originating or "emerging" in the Americas. Of course, we must also keep in mind that different Indian groups may have had different origins.

During the twentieth century, the boldest and most imaginative combatants in the quest of fixing the origins of the Indian entered the arena: a fervent group arguing that the first Indians were survivors of the Lost Civilizations of Atlantis and/or Mu. This last theory, which at times has been the most popular of all, is particularly difficult to debate since these alleged great civilizations are supposed to have flourished on continental remnants that have since sunk beneath the sea, the last remnant disappearing some 11,000 years ago, a time which provocatively corresponds with a sudden rise in world-wide sea level.

The concept of Atlantis goes back to Plato (427–347 B.C.). In two of his dialogues, the *Timaeus* and the *Critias*, Plato tells the story of Atlantis "not as a mere legend" but as historical fact, as a "veritable action." According to these dialogues, Solon, an esteemed statesman who lived about two centuries before Plato, heard about Atlantis from Egyptian priests who possessed written records concerning this large island continent. Despite Plato's claims, there is a serious debate about whether Plato was indeed relating fact or only fiction. Unfortunately, the manuscript of Solon's poem "Atlantikos," which is referred to in the Greek historian Plutarch's "Life of Solon," has vanished.

Plato described Atlantis as "the heart of a great and wonderful empire," the home of the "noblest race of men which ever lived." Plato said it was an earthly paradise, with mighty mountains, fertile plains, navigable rivers, rich mineral deposits, a large thriving population, golden-roofed cities, and mighty fleets and armies for invasion and conquest. Plato wrote that Atlantis lay "beyond the Pillars of Hercules" (Straits of Gibraltar), that this "island was larger than Libya and Asia put together," and "from the island you might pass through to the opposite continent [America?] which surrounded the true ocean." Nine thousand years before Solon, the island was wrenched by "portentous earthquakes and floods . . . and it was swallowed by the sea."

Atlantis's sinking "nine thousand years" before Solon (639–559 B.C.) comes to 11,600 years ago—which is precisely the date determined by eminent oceanographic geologist Dr. Cesare Emiliani of the University of Miami for the last worldwide flooding. Emiliani based his findings on borings in marine sediments, which led him to the conclusion that "at the time of maximum flooding about 11,600 years ago, the sea level was about 40 meters [130 feet] below the present and must have been rising very rapidly." Emiliani himself asked if "this is a mere coincidence or was there really an Atlantis? . . . one cannot exclude that some submarine plateaus exposed when sea level was 40 meters below the present and supporting some sort of civilization might not have been flooded 11,600 years ago, with its inhabitants rafting away . . . his [Plato's] brief description fits admirably the Bahamas-Caribbean-Gulf area. . . ."[3]

That Emiliani indicated the Bahama-Caribbean area as a potential locale for Atlantis made one group of Atlantis advocates ecstatic. Edgar Cayce, the American whose psychic healing talents have been acknowledged by many, and whose prophecies have been studied by researchers from many different scientific disciplines, in 1940 predicted that a small part of Atlantis would rise again in 1968 to 1969 near the small island of Bimini in the Bahamas area of the Caribbean. And in 1968, parts of what appeared to be submerged walls or roads and possibly some buildings *were* found in the Atlantic near Bimini. While this has been a great comfort to many believers, critics have argued that the stone configurations may not be roads and walls but rather natural patterns, and that if they are buildings, they are part of a Maya-like settlement and thus much too recent in construction to have anything to do with an Atlantis. Radiocarbon dating of ancient sea levels in the Bahamas indicates that this possible Bimini site only dates from 4000 B.C., which is well after the date Plato and Cayce gave for Atlantis.

While work has been going on in the Bahamas, Soviet scientists have searched for the eastern portion of Atlantis in the area of the mid-Atlantic ridge, near the Azores, islands created by submerged mountain peaks breaking the ocean's surface. Led by Dr. N. F. Zhirov, whose book *Atlantis: The Basic Problem* enjoyed great popularity in Russia and Europe during the late 1960s, these Soviets believe a large land mass dropped out of the bottom of the Atlantic in this area within the last 50,000 years.

On April 3, 1979, Professor A. A. Aksyenov, director of the Soviet Oceanology Institute, reported that the Soviets may have found remnants of the Lost Continent. His recent expedition found ruins and a horseshoe-shaped group of flat-topped mountains three hundred to six hundred feet below the surface of the ocean west of Gibraltar. He said "the geologists think it is quite possible that this horseshoe was a rather large archipelago that submerged as a result of geological unrest." He added that underwater "pictures show quite vividly lines of brick or stone walls and fragments of wide steps." A second, more careful expedition is being planned; Aksyenov commented that "the Atlantis problem belongs to the category of centuries-old secrets that with the rapid progress of oceanology can be uncovered very soon and quite possibly in an affirmative way."[4]

Others have sought Atlantis near Spain, Sweden, North Africa, Brazil, Russia, and Sri Lanka. Dr. Angelos Galanopoulos, the

Greek archaeologist quoted in *National Geographic* Magazine, has drawn attention with his claim that he could prove "once and for all" that the "real" Atlantis was the sunken island of Thera in the Aegean. To try and clinch the case for Galanopoulos, Dr. Jacques-Yves Cousteau has made a two-million-dollar year-long search in this area. But unfortunately, Thera is not in the "real ocean," which was the Atlantic to the ancient Greeks. Thera is also much too small and dates to a much too recent archaeological time to fit Plato's story. But Dr. Galanopoulos counters criticisms with the too neat formula that the otherwise meticulous Plato was off by a factor of ten on both of these points. Thera is just 11 miles wide; the capital of Atlantis, according to Plato, is 110 miles wide. Thera was destroyed in 1000 B.C., while Plato said Atlantis was destroyed in 10,000 B.C. Galanopoulos explains these differences by saying that the Greeks confused the Cretan symbol for 1000 (-ϕ-) with the one for 10,000 ($\oplus$).

The argument over whether Atlantis was fact or fiction and whether the Indians are descendants of the people who lived there provokes fierce controversy to this day. Over five thousand books have been written on Atlantis and new ones come out each year. While there is no reason to call off the search for Atlantis, the suggestion of fraudulence that has characterized some of Atlantis's proponents over the years has certainly aggravated things and brought emotions to the fore. Plato wrote about a people as civilized as the time allowed; with ships, writing, domesticated plants, and domesticated animals, quite an advanced enough group for their day (at least 9,600 B.C.) since archaeologists don't officially date (i.e., recognize) such advancements before 4000 to 6000 B.C. Not content with mere precocity, however, Atlantis's many advocates have also been prone to ascribe to the Atlanteans every manner of invention from space ships to laser rays to mind control and even the creation of life itself.

The most fertile imaginations have had free rein in describing Atlantis and their ancient wonders and ways. German philosopher Karl Georg Zschaetzsch argued that Atlantis was the ancient homeland of the Aryan race, who were originally all blond-haired, blue-eyed vegetarians. But Zschaetzsch said Atlantis was destroyed because the Atlanteans became alcoholics. (This theory was a favorite with Hitler because of its racist slant and its puritanical theme.) Novelist W. Scott-Elliot said he could prove that the Atlanteans had battleships, telepathy, subhuman manlike creations to do their bidding, and priestesses in transparent silk gowns. Perhaps this last circumstance explains why of all the theories of Indian origins, only the Lost Continents have attracted so much attention from artists, poets, fiction writers, and moviemakers. For example, H. P. Lovecraft freely borrowed many of Scott-Elliot's ideas to make his horror stories more convincing, best selling novelist Taylor Caldwell wrote an Atlantean saga called *The Romance of Atlantis*, and Hollywood made three adventure movies on the subject in the 1960s, taking great pains to recreate convincingly the sinking. And where these groups have left off, cranks have pushed things to the extreme. Mystical organizations such as the Rosicrucians, Theosophists, and Anthroposophists have shrouded the issue of Atlantis in an esoteric world view.

Rudolf Steiner and Madame Blavatsky, two revered Theosophists, talked about the cosmologic scheme of human evolution, with its seven root races and seven epochs of history where within each epoch there are seven subracial periods. They talked of how the Atlantean epoch, or the fourth, preceded the present Aryan epoch and how each epoch goes through definite set cycles before giving birth to the next. To these mystics' organizations the Atlantean origin of the American culture is gospel.

Even more enigmatic and mystical than Atlantis is the Lost Continent of Lemuria, more commonly known as Mu; it has, of course, been argued that the Indians are descendants of this lost land. Mu was supposed to have been a continent, even larger than Atlantis, that sank in the Pacific. It was supposed to have covered an area from Easter Island to the Carolinas, from Hawaii in the north to the Cook Islands in the south, with the existing mountainous Polynesian islands the tallest peaks of this now-sunken land mass. According to adventurer Colonel James

Churchward's announcement in 1931, this continent had sixty-four million inhabitants and an advanced civilization that predated that of Atlantis, a civilization "in many respects superior to our own and far in advance of us in some important essentials which the modern world is just beginning to have cognizance of."[5] Also, according to Churchward, the creation of man took place on Mu, with Mu later planting colonies in the Orient and in North America. Following a rather familiar pattern, he based these assertions on a number of clay tablets only *he* had access to. Churchward said he discovered these tablets when, on a trip to monasteries in India and Tibet, he persuaded a priestly friend to show him some secret tablets which had lain untouched in vaults since time immemorial; these turned out to be the "genuine records of Mu." The tablets were inscribed in a dead language Churchward believed to be the original tongue of mankind, and it required two years of study before he could translate these "Sacred Inspired Writings." After this, Churchward says he translated 2,500 corresponding tablets discovered many years later by William Niven in Mexico. The Mexican tablets happily filled in the many details lacking from the Oriental tablets. Churchward explained the crudeness of subsequent stone-age archaeological remains by stating that "Savagery came out of civilization, not civilization out of savagery." His books on Lemuria were quite popular.

The Rosicrucians, Theosophists, and Anthroposophists were quick to incorporate details about Mu into their complex mythology of Atlantis. The Lemurian epoch was one where matter was not quite solid yet, and where man "was guided more by internal perception than external vision." It was also in Lemuria that woman was created from man. Steiner said that "the first subrace of Atlanteans developed from a very advanced part of the Lemurians who had a high evolutionary potential."[6] Madame Blavatsky told how some Lemurians were as tall as twenty-seven feet and how the main preoccupation of the Lemurians was philosophy rather than food and clothing. Steiner and Blavatsky said colonists from Lemuria and Atlantis became the first Indians, with later Indians subscribing to the Lemurian "reverence" for the earth.

In 1977, retired space scientist Sepp Blumrich said he had traced the Indians' origin to a lost continent in the Pacific, the point of view that was championed by Churchward. This was not Blumrich's maiden voyage into esoteric space; in 1973, Blumrich, then at NASA's Marshal Space Flight Center in Alabama, amazed his compatriots with his theory that the "visions of God" recorded by the prophet Ezekiel in the Bible were really an account of the landing of a spaceship. He outlined this revelation in a highly speculative book, *The Spaceships of Ezekiel*. Now he contends that the Indians of North America, as well as the Aztec and Mayan civilizations of Mexico and Central America, came from a lost continent in the Pacific that sank as the South American land mass rose, some time before the sinking of Atlantis. He adds that some of the survivors traveled to their new lands by air, since this ancient civilization had the power of flight.

The advocates of the Lost Continent and Lost Tribes theories never compared their theories with Indian myths and beliefs. If the Atlantis and Lemuria devotees had taken the trouble, they would have found to their delight that some Indian groups speak of their arrival in the Americas by ocean voyages from now sunken islands in the ocean. For example, the origin legends of some Hopi clans, Arizona Pueblo Indian groups directly linked to the prehistoric Anasazi or Basketmakers, relate that during their fourth world they came from the west, crossing the sea on boats from one "stepping-stone," or island, to the next until they reached the mountains of the California coast and moved inland. They say these islands then broke up and sank beneath the sea.[7] The myths of the Dakota, Sioux, Mandans, Delaware, and Iroquois refer to an island in the Atlantic Ocean "towards the sunrise" which sank. The Mandans say that a tribe of white men lived there.[8] The Okanagans of northern Washington and British Columbia also talk about a "lost island" in the ocean.[9]

Close examination of Indian myths, however, reveals a saga of greater complexity than the simplistic stories put forth by these groups of enthusiasts. Indian myths tell us emphatically that the Indians are not just one homogeneous racial group. On the contrary, the various Indian groups have had different racial origins, originating in or reaching the Americas in different ways, and at different times.

Some Indian groups say that they originated or were created in the Americas, usually by emerging from within the earth. Others say that they came from islands in the Pacific or Atlantic, surviving some great flood or catastrophe. Conspicuously missing in all the known myths are any stories that bear the slightest resemblance to the notion of a Bering route; none seem to describe an arduous journey from Asia across the ice and snow of the North. In all these myths it is clear that the Indians believe they have been here for a very, very long time. Many Indian groups say their cultures rose and fell several times, and that they have been visited by "foreigners" on various occasions.

Within some tribes there are a number of different clans, usually designated by their own symbol or totem—for example, Bear, Antelope, Sun, and Water clans. Tribes such as the Hopi believe that not all the clans had the same origin. The Hopi tell how different clans have come from different places and have joined the tribe at different times, some clans being many times older than others. The Hopi also make it clear that the exact details of their origins are known only to priests who have been initiated into certain secret societies.[10]*

It's amazing how many people, dismissing or ignoring Indian legend as mere superstition, still cling to much wilder explanations of their own devising. To the Mormons, there are Israelite origins; to the mystic organizations and occultists, there are Lost Continent origins. Surprisingly, these varied explanations have not competed with one another too militantly. Supporters of Carthaginian-Phoenician origins have also approved Israelite

---

* Some early archaeologists followed clues gleaned from Hopi and Zuni myths to a rich payoff in archaeological sites. The genetic, linguistic, technological, cultural, and archaeological evidence that supports some Indian myths will be discussed in detail in chapter 10.

movements to America, and some Egyptianists are quite willing to recognize Lost Atlantis. The Rosicrucians and Theosophists accept both Atlantis and Mu.

Little attention has been paid to the Indians' own accounts of their origins. But while remaining oblivious to what the Indians have to say, all seem at least to be united against a common foe: academia.

3

The Beloved Bering Bridge

The archaeologist may find the tub but altogether miss Diogenes.

—Sir Mortimer Wheeler,
Archaeology From the Earth, 1962

During the first half of the twentieth century, while the Lost Continent theories captured the public's imagination, the academic world began to study the American Indian in earnest. In this period the scientific discipline of anthropology and its subdiscipline, archaeology, became established in departments at universities and colleges across the United States. In contrast to the dubious and frivolous proclamations from the Lost Continent advocates, the academic world took a very conservative view of Indian origins, maintaining that man was a relative newcomer to the New World, a position it generally adheres to even now. I strongly disagree with this viewpoint; it embraces a set of misconceptions about Indian origins based on sound conservative turn-of-the-century wisdom that is clearly inadequate today. The discoveries of each decade over the past seventy years show that academic skeptics have consistently underestimated the antiquity of the American Indian and his role and contributions in the origin and development of modern man.

By the early twentieth century, archaeologists had clearly established that man and his cousins lived and evolved in Europe and Asia amid the coming and going of four different ice ages (that is, from 1,000,000 to 10,000 years ago). With each successive ice age, the prevailing hominids became more technologically advanced. Building fires, fashioning clothing of animal skins, and living in caves and other shelters, they learned to survive the crippling cold. With increasingly sophisticated tools and weapons, they lived by preying upon the reindeer and woolly mammoths that roamed across the entire continent. In time, the accepted theory states, long after fully modern man appeared, Mongoloid (east Asian) hunters wandered up through Siberia and crossed over into the virginal New World in the Bering Strait area.

The Bering route theory comes of distinguished parentage: Thomas Jefferson first authored this theory. In his *Notes of Virginia*, published in 1781, Jefferson wrote about an Indian burial mound he excavated and how he believed the Indians came from Asia by way of the far north.

The Mongoloids were readily accepted as the Indians' forefathers chiefly because of what the great naturalist Alexander von Humboldt described as a "striking analogy between the Americans and the Mongol race." (!) Early physical anthropologists such as Ernest Albert Hooton of Harvard confirmed von Humboldt's analogies; Hooton's book *Up From the Ape*, published in 1946, noted that the Indians supposedly all exhibited a Mongoloid wash of features which included dark hair and eyes, medium brown skin, straight hair, a relative absence of facial or body hair, and wide cheek bones. The Eskimo, the last migrant to arrive, was pointed to as the most Mongoloid in appearance, with his smooth forehead, marked eyelid folds, infantile nose, and yellow skin.

But these early physical anthropologists made serious mistakes and exclusions in their analyses. All Indians, of course, do *not* look alike. There is tremendous physical variation among the Indians, variations which hint at origins as varied as suggested in Indian mythology. If Indians are of Asian origin, why are their blood types, which indicate mankind's genetic relationships, and their dental forms so different from the blood types and dental forms of the Chinese and Japanese? How can we explain the characteristic convex "hawk" nose common to many Indian groups? (See, for example, a profile of Sitting Bull.) Prominent noses are virtually unknown among East Asians; they have conspicuously flatter facial profiles than American Indians. And, finally, why are the American Indians' languages so varied and so different from European and Asiatic languages? An English-speaking person can understand Chinese no more than an Arizona Hopi could talk with a Creek from Georgia.

Scoffing at the great ages ascribed to the Indians' ancestors by Lost Tribe and Lost Continent theorists, mainstream archaeologists led by Dr. Ales Hrdlicka, who was headquartered at the U.S. National Museum (part of the Smithsonian Institution) in Washington, D.C., where he was curator from 1909 to 1941, argued for a relatively recent arrival, one not more than 3,000 years ago. The possibility of an ice age or glacial man having lived in the Americas was out of the question. They said man couldn't have entered North America until well after the last ice age, which ended 10,000 years ago, because the great ice sheets that once blanketed much of North America had to melt first. They noted how many of the animals contemporary with the last ice age had become extinct before man entered the New World. It was also believed that the first arrivals crossed the fifty-six miles of the Bering Strait by boat, a reasonable supposition within the time frame of the theory, since maritime people elsewhere in the world used boats by 1000 B.C.

Dr. Jesse Jennings of the University of Utah writes in his *Prehistory of North America* that Hrdlicka's "authoritarian and negative stance on matters of early man—that is, an American population earlier than the historic Indian—was so rigorous and so ably defended that for three decades American scholars gave no serious thought to the possibility that the occupancy of the Americas was anything but recent—no deeper than 2,000 to 3,000 years in time."[1]

Hrdlicka also affirmed the unity of the American Indian race, and that it was entirely Mongoloid in origin. He believed that the variations among the Indians were due only to environmental or genetic factors. He also firmly believed that human skeletons more than a few thousand years old had to be very primitive in appearance (i.e., not fully evolved as *Homo sapiens*), a view that was unjustified since fully modern skeletons of great age had already been found in Europe. The first skeleton discovered in North America from deposits from the last glacial age, which lasted from 70,000 to 10,000 years ago, was an apparent drowning victim (1931, Minnesota man). The relic had an appearance much like present Indians, and Hrdlicka quickly attacked the conclusions of the excavator, Dr. A. E. Jenks of the University of Minnesota, claiming Jenks had merely discovered a recent burial of a modern Sioux Indian.

Hrdlicka was significantly challenged not by an archaeologist but by George McJunkin, a cowboy in New Mexico who made a startling discovery that was to make archaeological history. One day in the spring of 1926, McJunkin was riding the range close to the Cimarron River, near the town of Folsom in the northeast corner of New Mexico, looking for lost cattle. McJunkin saw something glistening on the opposite bank near the bottom of a deep arroyo. It was a layer of bleached bones jutting from the bank. Cattle bones were not an unusual sight, but these were twenty feet below the surface of the ground. Fortunately for science, his curiosity got the best of him and McJunkin jumped off his horse and scrambled down the arroyo to dig among the bones with his knife. He quickly uncovered several flint projectile points different from the arrowheads common to the area. These thin points were longer (two inches), had a different shape, and were more carefully made than any he had seen before. The points were leaf-shaped instead of being steeply tapered, the bases were concave instead of straight, and both sides (faces) were grooved almost to the tip (archaeologists call these grooves "fluting"). The bones were different, too: They were more massive than any cattle bones he had seen. Perplexed, McJunkin took some samples and continued his search for the lost cattle.

In 1926, a cowboy found a spearhead between the ribs of a *Bison antiquus*, an animal extinct for 10,000 years—proof that man lived in North America during the ice age. The Paleo-Indian point type used is called a Folsom point. *Denver Museum of Natural History*

Through friends, word of McJunkin's strange find got to J. D. Figgins, the director of the Colorado Museum of Natural History in Denver. The cowboy sent pieces of the bones to Figgins, who was able to identify them as bison bones, not of the modern variety but of a much larger, extinct variety with a horn spread of six feet that had vanished with the glaciers some 10,000 years ago.

Manmade projectile points lying among bison bones which were at least 10,000 years old proved that the early archaeologists were wrong in their belief that man had not entered North America until 1000 B.C. The clear-cut association of stone tools with the remains of one of an extinct animal was considered good evidence of man's presence during these glacial times. Thus, the Folsom discovery provided clear evidence of man's having been a resident of North America during the last ice age. It suddenly made the first Americans at least ten times as old as any archaeologist had dared suspect.

Figgins quickly set off to meet McJunkin and to confirm the find. The systematic excavations which Figgins undertook uncovered more points and more bones. Elated, Figgins showed the evidence to experts at other museums, such as the American Museum of Natural History in New York, but he soon became sadder and wiser. In what has become a characteristic pattern concerning those who have claimed earlier dates for man in the Americas, other archaeologists scoffed at his theories and simply refused to accept that New World man could be so old. Some archaeologists questioned the association of the bones and the points. They said that the association was accidental, that outside influences brought the bones and the points together. It was back to the field for Figgins.

After two more seasons of careful excavation, Figgins was able to find a projectile point "in situ," lodged between two bison ribs. Now there was no question about the authenticity of the association. Telegrams were immediately sent out, inviting the dubious colleagues to see for themselves. Many anthropologists and archaeologists came. Among the visitors to the Folsom site were Dr.

Alfred Vincent Kidder of Harvard University, who had carried out extensive excavations throughout the Southwest, and Dr. Barnum Brown of the American Museum of Natural History. Dr. Frank H. H. Roberts, Jr., one of the most noted anthropologists of the time, summed up the reaction as follows: "Some of the most skeptical critics of the year before became enthusiastic converts. The Folsom find was accepted as a reliable indication that man was present in the Southwest at an earlier period than was previously supposed."[2] On close examination, some of the bones even showed notches and scars from butchering and it was agreed that the points were quite different from those known before. Their size argued that they were spear or javelin points instead of arrowheads.

Archaeologists called the Indians who had hunted the extinct ice-age animals Paleo-Indians. However, even after the Folsom evidence was clear, Hrdlicka had the boldness to decree at a meeting of the New York Academy in 1928 that there could not have been a Paleo-Indian. Years later, in his *American Antiquity* article "An Outline of Early Man Studies," Edwin Wilmsen wrote: "With his back to the wall, Hrdlicka was denying everything to maintain his position that man could be anything, anything at all, but not ancient in America."[3]

Professionals were again shown the way by amateurs who made a key find in 1932 near Clovis, New Mexico, close to the Texas border. Archaeologists from the University of Pennsylvania Museum confirmed the find, and conducted the subsequent excavations. The site yielded the bones of extinct horses, camels, and no fewer than four mammoths, again with distinct spear points in association. Here, too, some of the points were lodged between the ribs of the animals in such a way that there could be no doubt about the contemporaneity of man and animal. The Clovis spear points were different from the Folsom points—longer (up to five inches) and heavier. The more rugged Clovis points were consistent with the Clovis hunters' pursuit of bigger game. Instead of pursuing bison as the Folsom hunters did, the Clovis hunters' target was the woolly mammoth, an ancient elephant

who stood as high as twelve feet at the shoulder with great curv-
ing tusks ten feet long, tall enough to look into a second-story
window. Approximately 12,000 years ago, during the wetter glacial conditions, the now high and dry plains around Clovis were
dotted with lakes and ponds. Extra large and now extinct varieties of mammoth, horse, camel, and sloth called megafauna
abounded.

In addition to the points, other stone artifacts were found at
the site. These included a smaller point, a knife, a hide scraper,
and several flakes, i.e., small fragments of material removed from
a larger stone (core) which are used to make other artifacts. Two
polished, tapered cylindrical bone shafts—which seemed to have
been used as projectiles—were also found, lying by one of the
mammoths.

Most important, though, the Clovis points were found *beneath*
layers of earth containing Folsom points, indicating that they
were greater in age, pushing man's New World residency back
still farther, to 12,000 years ago. But the line was drawn here. In
1948, one of America's leading anthropologists, Alfred Kroeber of
the University of California at Berkeley, wrote: "It may be said
that in the opinion of most Americanists, ethnologists as well as
archaeologists, the first human immigrants arrived in the Western
Hemisphere in late Pleistocene times [late glacial]. The meagerly
known Clovis, Folsom and similar cultures . . . represent this early
level of culture. . . . If anything earlier than Clovis and Folsom
existed in America, it has not been found."[4]

The Folsom and Clovis findings rekindled interest in the question of how man had actually entered the New World. Most
experts again, incorrectly, supported a Bering Strait-northern
entry route at this new and much earlier entry date, satisfied that
Old World man already knew how to brave the cold of a northern entry route in the glacial period of 12,000 years ago. Some
archaeologists and geologists correctly pointed out that at this
time man did not need to paddle or sail across the Bering Straits,
or to make his way over the hazardous winter pack ice; he could
have simply walked across on dry land! For during the last ice

These eight Paleo-Indian points of the Clovis type were used to kill a mammoth almost 12,000 years ago near Naco, Arizona. Points of exactly the same type have been found in Cro-Magnon sites in Spain. It now seems that this point type appeared in America almost 20,000 years before it appeared in Europe. *E. B. Sayles, Arizona State Museum*

age a land bridge existed between Asia and Alaska. (This point conveniently explained away the question of whether man had an advanced enough maritime technology to cross the fifty-six miles of open sea in the Bering Strait area where the Asian and American continents are closest together, or if man could have carried enough food with him if he had tried to cross the hazardous pack ice which occasionally fills the Strait in the winter.)

As the glaciers of the last ice age (the Wisconsin, which extended from 70,000 to 10,000 years ago) approached their peak, billions of gallons of water that would normally have been in the oceans were locked up in ice. The absence of this water lowered sea level by over 300 feet, more than enough to turn the shallows of the Bering Strait (even today only 140 feet deep) into a broad bridge of land connecting the two continents. Geologists have made correlations of sea levels, ice accumulations, and land-bridge width during the last two ice ages (the Wisconsin and the Illinoian, from 260,000? to 170,000 years ago), so it is known when the bridge existed, as well as when conditions were best for man to cross it. Although this bridge was last exposed from 23,000 to 8,000 years ago, geologists believe it was also exposed from 35,000 to 27,000 years ago, as well as 170,000 years ago, with the possibility of a fourth exposure 70,000 years ago.[5] Probably there were exposures of the bridge even earlier than 170,000 years ago, but not enough data has been collected to fix actual dates.

GLACIAL PERIODS OF THE PLEISTOCENE EPOCH IN NORTH AMERICA

	years ago
Recent epoch	10,000 to present
Pleistocene epoch	1,000,000 to 10,000
Wisconsin glacial period (Interglacial stage)	70,000 to 1u,000
Illinoian glacial period (Interglacial stage)	260,000? to 170,000
Kansan glacial period (Interglacial stage)	? to 430,000?
Nebraskan glacial period	1,000,000 to ?

During times of exposure, where the Bering Sea now exists there was a broad land, called Beringia by geologists, some one thousand miles wide when the ice sheets were at maximum size. During some of these exposures, ice age animals moved freely across the so-called Bering Bridge. It is generally accepted that across this causeway the ancestors of the modern horse, camel, wolf, fox, and woodchuck—all of which evolved in the Americas —migrated to Eurasia; whereas the mammoth, bison, musk ox, deer, elk, and moose, which are Eurasiatic, migrated into the

Americas. Climatologists say that the conditions around the bridge at times of exposure were cold and damp and often overcast. This produced a treeless tundra vegetation that was particularly lush because of its recent emergence from the fertile sea. Streams, lakes, and bogs abounded. From Alaska's muck, paleontologists have recovered the packed and jumbled remains of mammoths, reindeer, bison, moose, and musk ox, indicating that game was very plentiful at these times.

Based on the availability of the Bering Bridge and the ecological circumstances associated with it, archaeologists have put forth a scenario to explain Indian origins.* In this scenario, bands of nomadic Asiatic hunters 12,000 years ago are said to have traveled up into Siberia following the wandering big game herds of mammoths, bison, and reindeer. These Asians eventually became well adapted to the local conditions. Not only was the big game their main source of food, but the animals' hides provided their clothing and covering for their tents, which were framed with mammoth bones or sticks. As the animals moved into the new verdant range of Beringia, the Asian hunters followed and themselves migrated from the Old World into the New World. Most likely in autumn, many of the Beringia herds retreated to their winter range in Alaska, bringing the hunters with them.

The tundra would have provided exceptional forage for the large herds of animals, the theory maintains, allowing their population to increase. As these hunters moved south of Canada, they would have encountered animals who had never been hunted before, animals extremely vulnerable to their weapons.

In this scenario, only thirty to a few hundred individuals are held to have crossed the bridge at different times over a period of a few thousand years (10,000–8000 B.C.), rapidly moving south and east around the edges of the ice.† Shortly after they entered,

---

* I do not subscribe to this scenario, and in the next chapter I shall discuss my reasons why.

† Note that the scenario does not include the distinctly more Mongoloid ancestors of the Eskimos and the Athapascan Indians (Navajo, Apache) who are said to have come over in some relatively late migrations just 5,000 to 6,000 years ago.

the path of retreat back to their homelands was cut off due to the melting ice, the rising sea level, and the subsequent submersion of the bridge. Their big projectile points, like those found at Folsom and Clovis, were well suited for bringing down the big game animals they encountered everywhere. In the space of a few thousand years, these few migrant tribes thrived in the rich new land and exploded into a population of millions, scattering themselves from the Bering Strait to the southern tip of South America. For example, according to archaeologist Dr. Vance Haynes of the University of Arizona, a single tribe of only 30 mammoth hunters could in just 500 years increase to a population of 12,500. Geologist Dr. Paul Martin, also of the University of Arizona, working from a computer simulation, says that from a tribe of 104 individuals in just 345 years a population of 590,000 could be reached, a growth rate I consider much too steep. The rapid population explosion from several different migrant groups is also used to account for the multiplicity of Indian languages and cultures and racial variation.

The "Virginal American Megafauna," the plentiful and massive big game which had never encountered human predators, is taken as the food base for this unbridled population explosion. In the southwest, these migrants would have also encountered beaver as big as bears and even larger and more helpless ground sloths with their incongruous small heads topping elephant-sized bodies. In fact, this intense big game hunting tradition or specialization is often given as the reason for the extinction of the megafauna at the end of the last geologic epoch, the Pleistocene (see chart, page 50) which began 1,000,000 years ago and ended 10,000 years ago. It was characterized by four separate glacial periods: the Nebraskan, the Kansan, the Illinoian, and the Wisconsin, which was the last. Dr. Martin, the champion of this theory, calls it "Pleistocene overkill." Martin describes these skilled hunters, swiftly moving southward, as virtually "invincible" predators who killed many more animals than they actually needed with their main hunting method of using fire to create stampedes and driving entire elephant and bison herds off cliffs. Martin pictures an initial prehistoric blitzkrieg wherein a postulated 300,000 hunters in North America wipe out 100 million gigantic animals in 300 years.[6]

This academic scenario, like the other theories about Indian origins, doesn't correspond with Indian myth. Instead of the ancient origins Indian myth indicates, only a relatively recent origin is put forth. Instead of having the Indians originate in the Americas or ocean islands as they themselves say, only a single Asian origin is attributed to all the tribes. And instead of the cultural ups and downs noted in Indian myths, a single and steady increase in population and culture up until the time of European contact is assumed.

During the 1930s, 40s, and 50s, more than a hundred sites came to light where Paleo-Indian artifacts were found in situ with the bones of extinct elephants, camels, horses, or bison. In 1939, Marie Wormington of the Denver Museum of Natural History, summarizing the existing knowledge of the early hunters, wrote a book of just 80 pages, listing 92 references. Eighteen years later, in 1957, this book (*Ancient Man in North America*) jumped to 322 pages, and listed 586 references.

In the late 1940s, the radiocarbon method of dating was developed; for the first time, archaeologists had a way to get almost exact dates on the glacial sites.

The radiocarbon dating technique was invented by Willard Libby of the University of Chicago, a scientist who had worked on the creation of the atom bomb during World War II. Radiocarbon dating consists of measuring the amount of the radioactive isotope of carbon, C-14, present in a once-living organism. Radioactive carbon is created in the atmosphere as cosmic rays bombard nitrogen atoms. This radioactive carbon is taken in by plant life during photosynthesis and by animals that feed upon the plants. All living organic matter contains radioactive carbon in the same proportion. Upon death, C-14 intake ceases and the radioactive carbon present begins to decay back to nitrogen at a

The archaeological sites upon which the very conservative "12,000-Year-Old Latecomer" Indian origins model is built. Until recently, these were the oldest sites available for study.

fixed rate. It is therefore possible to determine that after a lapse of a specific period of time the amount of radioactivity in a substance will be reduced to exactly one-half, after a lapse of an equal amount of time to one-fourth of its original level—and so on. This first period—about 5,570 years—is called the half-life. While the radiocarbon dating technique has been criticized based on variations in the amount of C-14 in the atmosphere in the past, the technique has been repeatedly proven accurate to within 10 percent. By measuring the amount of radioactivity left in animal bones and ancient plant material found at early sites, it has been possible to go beyond relative dating based purely on geological strata and get "absolute" dates as to when these animals were slain or died. For the first time it was possible to speak with some certainty about when the first Indians reached the Americas.

Radiocarbon dating showed that the Clovis mammoth sites dated to approximately 12,000 years ago (10,000 B.C.) and the later Folsom bison sites to approximately 11,000 years ago, with many other sites clustering around these dates. When the floodgates were opened, there seemed to be a veritable log jam of early sites from 10,000 to 12,000 years in age. Why?

Radiocarbon dating quickly helped archaeologists seemingly tie together the loose strings of the origins scenario. In addition to the log jam of dates from 10,000 to 12,000 years in age, the major unanswered questions dealt with how the migrants crossed the tremendous ice field that must have blocked their way to the south after they traveled over Beringia's tundra. While eastern Siberia, Beringia, and central Alaska were unglaciated, the Cordilleran ice cap covered the Canadian Rockies from Vancouver to eastern Alaska. And the Laurentide ice cap covered most of the rest of Canada and much of the northern United States. These two huge glacial formations merged at the foot of the Canadian Rockies, formidably blocking entry into the western United States. Radiocarbon dating also showed that 12,000 years ago a brief warm period within the last ice age known as the Two Creeks Interstadial caused a marked glacial retreat. It was, incorrectly, believed that this retreat created an ice-free corridor between the up-until-then coalescing Cordilleran and Laurentide ice sheets. If such an ice-free corridor existed at this date, it would have let the hunters (supposedly confined until then to central Alaska) enter the western United States, where big game abounded. Since 12,000 years ago is precisely when Clovis points were believed to have made their sudden appearance in the western United States (an observation which has since been shown to be in error), it was convenient for conservative traditional archaeologists to tie these two events—the opening of an ice-free corridor and the first appearance of Clovis points—into a neat wrap-up of their current scenario. Dr. Vance Haynes, who postulated the dramatic population explosion, used radiocarbon dating to fix the subsequent extinction of the elephants at about 11,000 years ago. While Haynes was correct in his dating of this extinction, he was not on firm ground when he said that "the rapid increase in the number of mammoth-hunters could easily be one of the main reasons why these animals became extinct in North America sometime around 9000 B.C.; leaving the succeeding Folsom hunters with no larger prey than bison."[7]*

In the 1950s, unaware of the flaws in their reasoning, most archaeologists used radiocarbon dating to support and reinforce their story of a land bridge during the last glacial period, of an ice-free corridor (10,000 B.C.), the first appearance of man in the Americas (10,000 B.C.), the extinction of the mammoths (8000 B.C.), and the rapid spread of sites and growth of population across North America and down to the tip of South America.

The official establishment view about Indian origins seemed to ring truer than ever. Harvard's Dr. Gordon R. Willey, considered archaeology's foremost spokesman at the time, put it best in 1966 in his major synthesizing work, *An Introduction to American Archaeology*: "The oldest radiocarbon dates for archaeological discoveries which demonstrate, beyond any doubt, man's presence in the New World fall in the range of 10,000 to 9,000 B.C."[8] Dr. Haynes, in a November 1969 article in *Science* entitled "The Ear-

---

* I will support this critique in the next chapter.

liest Americans," added that "after 40 years of searching, little positive evidence for earlier occupation of the New World has been found."[9]

By the late 1960s, the question of Indian origin according to the archaeological establishment was a closed one. But was it?

4

The Bridge Starts to Sag

Despite 50 or more years of search in the Arctic for evidence of man's passage across the Bering land bridge [from Asia to America], no reasonable evidence has been found either in Asia or in Alaska as to the tools, stone, bone, or wood which the first men carried.

—Jesse Jennings,
Prehistory of North America, 1974

By the middle of the twentieth century, while the consensus scholarship firmly embraced the Bering Bridge/ice-free corridor immigration of Asians into the New World, a few dissenters had noted that the evidence for the theory was circumstantial, and highly suspect at that. There was, in fact, not one piece of direct evidence to support the Bering Bridge route theory. Increasingly, geologists, biologists, and meteorologists indicated that the ice-free corridor was not the idyllic yellow brick road to the Americas it was supposed to be, if it indeed was available to early man at all. Embarrassingly for advocates of the theory, many sites didn't seem to fit the official scenario for one reason or another. Plank by plank, almost immediately after its general acceptance, the Bering Bridge route theory began to look questionable, but to its fervent adherents some sort of bridge was better than no bridge at all.

If man used the Bering route to enter the Americas, one would expect him to have left some evidence of his passing somewhere along the lengthy route. If the route was much of a thoroughfare, one would expect that the different bands built and abandoned many hunting camps along the way, just as present-day migrant hunters, such as the Eskimos, do. But despite many intensive searches, no artifacts or archaeological sites of appropriate age have ever been found on the land areas which adjoin the now sunken Bering Bridge in Siberia or in interior Alaska, which has always been ice-free, and no evidence has come from the entire six hundred and twenty-five mile expanse of the ice-free corridor leading down from Alaska across the Yukon and into the United States. In fact, the closest site of enough age comes from Lake Baikal in Siberia, over two thousand miles from the Bridge. The Lake Biakal site dates to 20,000 years ago, a date much too early to have much relevance to the traditional archaeological entry scenario.

Dr. Paul Martin, the scientist who theorized that intense big game hunting led to the extinction of the megafauna, was not perturbed by the lack of tangible remains to mark man's use of the Bering route. He believed it to be only natural, since relatively few people rapidly passing through a vast amount of territory, as described in his scenario, would have left but scant traces. But in answer to Martin, Dr. Richard MacNeish, Director of the Robert S. Peabody Foundation for Archaeology in Massachusetts, brings up the many sites we now have dating to 12,000 years ago and older from the United States and South America which show that man was not quite so invisible at this time in the New World. Dr. Jesse Jennings of the University of Utah is disappointed with the findings at Lake Baikal because the tool complex found there is unlike the tool complexes of the Folsom or Clovis hunters. In fact, there are no recognizable tool complexes in Siberia or Asia that match the earliest American complexes, and there is not a single recognizable ancestral tool form in Siberia and Asia known to have been earlier than any American tool forms. While the Clovis and Folsom tool types may remain undiscovered along the rapidly-traveled route, they nevertheless should have contemporaneous and visible counterparts in Siberia and Asia.

Realizing the importance of finding some direct evidence of

man's using the Bering route, a desperate effort was recently made to correct this long-standing embarrassment. In September 1976, the National Parks Service and the National Geographic Society announced that they were sponsoring a search in central Alaska for evidence of early man. A sum of six hundred thousand dollars was committed to a three-year search. Initial explorations and excavations were to begin at Dry Creek, a wooded, green area just north of Mount McKinley National Park and about seventy-five miles south of Fairbanks. Eight other dig sites in addition to Dry Creek were initially proposed. To date, no success has been reported.

In the absence of direct evidence, mainstream archaeologists have pledged their allegiance to a northern entry route on indirect evidence, on their interpretation of a group of supposedly interlocking facts. This selected group of facts includes: (1) the availability of the Bering land bridge, (2) the Clovis and Folsom sites, (3) the occurrence of a warm period which would have brought about the opening of an ice-free corridor, (4) the sudden disappearance of the megafauna, and (5) the rapid spread of sites down to the tip of South America soon after entry. All these events are said to have taken place between 10,000 and 8000 B.C., and advocates of the northern entry route theory rely on the apparent correspondence of these key phenomena. But these events need not correspond at all; their similar dates may only be coincidental. Moreover, it is likely that many of these events may not be facts at all. Some may never have happened. The Bering Bridge may not have been the great causeway it is supposed to have been.

The picture of man and beast teeming across the bridge has been questioned by many. Dr. Arthur Jelinek of the University of Arizona, one of the world's leading archaeologists, said at a special conference on the Paleo-Arctic in 1971 that the only fact the experts present were certain of was that the woolly mammoth and the sage antelope were common to both sides. Jelinek says there is no evidence for herds of reindeer or other animals wandering across the bridge. The stormy and cold weather which hung over the bridge area seems to have been a deterrent to travel. Froelich Rainey, an archaeologist who worked at the University of Alaska during the 1940s and 1950s, has pointed out that "Northwestern America and northeastern Asia, under present climatic conditions, together form one of the most formidable barriers to human communication one can find anywhere in the world,"[1] and things can hardly have been nicer in the crucial period. Even the woolly rhino, one of the hardiest animal travelers of those times, Jelinek says, didn't make it across. The absence of significant numbers of migrating animals in the Bering area would take away one of man's major incentives for crossing the bridge—and under glacial climatic conditions, such a journey needs all the incentive it can muster.

It also turns out that the extinction of the megafauna may not have been at the hands of man. The real culprit may have been the climate. Ten thousand years ago, while these animals were disappearing, the Americas were undergoing significant climatic changes. The harsh glacial freeze was giving way to a milder and warmer climate. In the mountains and plains of western America, the many shallow lakes and marshes and the forests and heavy foliage which the megafauna depended on disappeared. Some archaeologists believe that instead of "overkill" by man, this climatic and vegetational change can be invoked to explain the disappearance of the megafauna. After all, not all the big game animals disappeared, just those of megasize who possessed megaappetites. For example, while the giant-sized *Bison antiquus* disappeared, *Bison bison*, a model more modest in size and appetite, took its place and survives to this day.

The Bering route scenario requires man to have moved from Beringia to South America much too rapidly, inexplicably rapidly. At the very tip of South America, by Tierra del Fuego and the treacherous Straits of Magellan, there is the Fells Cave site which dates to 8700 B.C. This implies that it only took man 1,300 years to make the 8,500-mile-long journey from northernmost North America to southernmost South America, in the process crossing and adapting to the extremely different climatic and ecological zones, and negotiating the formidable barriers of the Central American jungles and the towering South American mountains. Instead of "walking" or "strolling," it seemed that man had literally to "race" to make the journey. Dr. Louis Lorenzo of the National Anthropological Institute of Mexico has suggested that Asians walking into this hemisphere cannot be credited with possessing an awareness of "manifest destiny which enabled any one group to set track records for the course from the Bering steppes to Patagonia."[2]

There is something mysterious about why such struggling bands of lost or nomadic hunters forsook the animal supermarkets at their mercy and gave way to the impulse to march ever southward. Why didn't the Eskimos, the latest prehistoric immigrants to America, possess this impulse, instead of acclimatizing themselves to the harsh rigors of the Arctic?

The rapid appearance of Paleo-Indians on both the east and west coasts of the United States shortly after entry is also perplexing. For example, the Debert site in Nova Scotia dates to 8600 B.C. and the Bull Brook site in eastern Massachusetts is dated at 7000 B.C. Dr. K. R. Fladmark of Simon Fraser University notes that the known distribution of early archaeological sites in the New World does not match that expected from an initial population from the Bering route. Fladmark says, "If the initial population moved southward through a mid-continental corridor, one would expect that the oldest sites would occur closest to the southern ice margin, there would be a perceptible temporal gradient from north to south, and that movement into peripheral areas such as . . . the Pacific Coast would show a secondary-temporal gradient with decreasing age from west to east. In fact, the available evidence reflects no such gradients."[3]

Most damaging to the northern route scenario is new meteorological evidence that if man did successfully cross the Bering Bridge 12,000 years ago, an ice-free corridor across the huge ice fields—in some places almost two miles thick—that lay to the south of the Bering Bridge might not yet have been available for man to pass through. Recent research showing that the

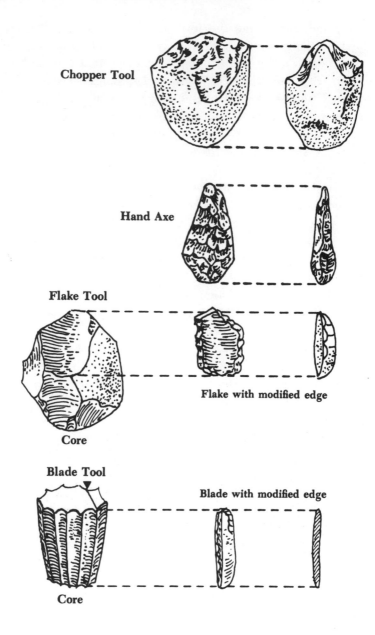

Chopper Tool

Hand Axe

Flake Tool

Flake with modified edge

Core

Blade Tool

Blade with modified edge

Core

Basic stone tool types.

625-kilometer-long ice-free corridor was not open until *well after* man was already in the New World comes from Dr. Reid Bryson, head of the University of Wisconsin's Department of Meteorology. Recognizing that many people were generalizing about the timing of glacial events in the northwest to suit their fancy, since there were few actual dates pertaining to when this long corridor opened up, Bryson went to work under a National Science Foundation grant in 1964. Bryson hiked into the field and for the first time dated many of the deposits left by the different glacial movements in the area. The radiocarbon dates Bryson got pointed to a very disturbing circumstance: that it was not until just 8,000 years ago that the ice-free corridor opened up—4,000 years too late to make the Bering route scenario work. Bryson even doubts that man could have used the corridor very soon after it opened. "Assuming that the structure of Arctic air then was like Arctic air now," he says, "air moving into southern Alberta and the plains . . . should have been about 20° colder after the corridor opened than before."[4] So instead of a lush passageway into North America teeming with animals, there may well have been a corridor with more miserable meteorological conditions, lower temperatures, and stronger winds than those encountered on top of the ice sheet itself. And if for some reason men tried to brave these chilling conditions, what could they have eaten? To pass through the 625-kilometer corridor would take fifty days if man traveled a very brisk 14 miles a day, or 3 miles per hour based on an eight-hour day; at this rate of travel, it is unlikely that he could have carried a fifty-day food supply.

Bryson's bluntness and lack of regard for archaeological gamesmanship seem to have alienated many archaeologists from his findings, as shown by the conspicuous absence of comment on his work in papers by archaeologists discussing the Bering route.

Supporting Bryson's work, however, archaeologist Dr. Alan Bryan of the University of Alberta, in Canada, says that "there is a congruence of evidence from several lines of research which suggest that the ice barrier did not disappear until 8,500 or 9,000 years ago."[5] And the specific location of a possible five-hundred-mile blockage of the corridor even at this date has been identified by V. K. Prest of the Canadian Geological Survey.

Further support for Bryson's findings comes from Dr. Fladmark. Fladmark expresses worry that his fellow archaeologists "seem satisfied" with the notion that the first early men in the Americas used the ice-free corridor "despite the lack of agreement over the age of the opening of the corridor." Expressing a scientifically ecumenical point of view, Fladmark maintains that "a wide range of data suggests that a mid-continental corridor was not an encouraging area for human occupation," if it was even habitable at all. Fladmark notes that topographic depressions such as valleys act as traps for dense cold air and have significantly colder temperatures than the surrounding area, so like Bryson he believes that the temperatures were extremely low in the corridor. He adds that there is evidence that extensive lakes of melted ice in the corridor, in addition to glacial blockages, would have presented man with added obstacles. Moreover, Fladmark notes, pollen and biological studies give no evidence for useful plant or animal communities in the mid-portion of the corridor, so that the "dining" opportunities in the corridor, at most, could have only been a "feeble reflection of Beringia."[6]

Thus, the available data at best is quite equivocal as to whether an ice-free corridor was inhabitable or even existed at a time early enough to fit the Bering route scenario. Traditional archaeologists are left with the question that if man couldn't walk into North America before 8,000 years ago, how else could he have already been in the Americas 12,000 years ago?

Chagrined by the major flaws in the Bering route scenario, a few establishment archaeologists put forth alternative entry routes. The first serious proposal came in 1963 from the late Dr. E. F. Greenman, a highly respected anthropology professor at the University of Michigan and the curator of the university's museum. A bit desperate for an explanation, Greenman argued that man reached the New World *from Europe* by canoe. While archaeologists weren't able to find parallels between Paleo-Indian artifacts and artifacts from Siberia or Asia, Greenman (who had a detailed knowledge of both Paleo-Indian artifacts and the artifacts of Europe) was startled by the many similarities he discovered between Paleo-Indian and European artifacts. This led him to postulate the theory that during Europe's Upper Paleolithic cultural period (35,000 to 12,000 years ago) men from France and Spain traveled to North America by crossing the Atlantic in "Beothuk," unique deep-water skin canoes. He noted how evidence for these unique canoes and a number of Upper Paleolithic art designs and artifacts are clustered on opposite sides of the North Atlantic. In a rather lengthy article to support his arguments, he presented an imposing catalog of trait parallels. The parallels he cited were based on actual objects or cave paintings and they included: certain boat and house types, pendants, design motifs, representations of animals, projectile point types and stylized pictographs. He proposed Newfoundland as the point of entry, with subsequent migrations to the southwestern United States, including portions of Mexico.[7]

Before Greenman's article, several French archaeologists had at least noted similarities in skull shape between Europe's Cro-Magnon man and Indians such as the Sioux, Huron, Iroquois, Cherokee, and Delaware. But American archaeologists immediately attacked Greenman's theory. They took a dim view of Paleolithic man crossing the treacherous, ice-choked Atlantic by skin boat, and they noted "the lack of evidence for ocean-going boats in the world at such an early time." Greenman's theory was taken as a tolerable weak moment at the close of a career that had otherwise been distinguished.[8]

Despite evidence suggesting a bold ocean journey and the doubts raised regarding the possibility of an ice-free corridor, the Bering route entry was still adhered to by mainstream conservative archaeologists who tried to adjust their arguments to support the northern entry concept. After man crossed the Bering Bridge and found his way blocked by ice, the arguments went, man could have inched his way south by hugging the coast and foraging along the beaches. At that time, the coast was along the narrow continental shelf that was exposed at the same time as

Beringia. Some criticized this route, citing the danger of the deeply gouged fjords of the northwest coast where the sea washes against sheer cliffs, and the great ice lobes that reached into the sea during glacial times. These objections were countered with the idea that these Paleo-Indian hunters had used small boats to navigate the difficult stretches.

Upset by the many drawbacks of an interior route, Dr. Fladmark has revived and championed this idea of a coastal entry for man into the Americas and argued for earlier entry dates. Fladmark believes that man could easily have moved along the coast until he reached the unglaciated shores of Oregon and California, and then dispersed to different parts of America. Fladmark says that this marine environment should have provided a plentiful food supply with sea fish, shell fish, sea mammals, migratory water fowl, and spawning salmon. Fladmark admits that direct evidence for such a coastal entry is lacking, but he is quick to point out that the fact that no cultural deposits predating 7000 B.C. have yet been found on the outer coast is not surprising. He says this is due to postglacial submergence of the continental shelf and the beaches that would have been inhabited during entry. Even though these areas are now out of sight, according to Dr. Fladmark, we should not ignore their potential role in America's prehistory.[9]

Fladmark may indeed be right in calling for much earlier entry dates, but his argument based on possibly submerged evidence is not scientifically satisfying (shades of Atlantis). Bryson, the meteorologist who seems to have closed the ice-free corridor, also sees troubles with a coastal route. He argues that a coastal route would be treacherous because the meteorological conditions along the coast and the edge of the melting ice sheets would be even more forbidding and colder than those above the ice sheets or within the corridor. Besides bitter cold, the coastal migrants would also have had to contend with a floating obstacle course of icebergs and avalanches breaking from glaciers that extended into the sea, and dense fog resulting from the cold air off the glaciers meeting warmer air rising from the ocean. One must wonder what reason man could have had for making that particularly arduous journey along the coast into the New World.

Even more incriminating evidence against the generally accepted Bering Bridge entry route theory emerged when it became clear that findings at many sites were challenging the sanctity of the 10,000 B.C. entry date, the "official" date for man's first appearance in the New World. These new sites suggested much earlier dates, but since they didn't yield beautifully fashioned pressure flaking points such as the Clovis and Folsom sites had, they were immediately suspect. Instead of spear points these sites contained very crude chipped stone tools such as choppers, scrapers, and simple stone flakes. A much more primitive manufacturer was pictured, and to some, the crudeness of these materials indicated that they weren't made by man at all, but by nature imitating man via such natural processes as thermal flaking from frost and heat and from rocks tumbling in streams or down hills or being ground up in mud flows, though there weren't any studies to support this contention. There simply were no scientific grounds for contending that nature could fashion stones in a way indistinguishable from man. Many of the "nature made it" theories were far-fetched. This led one of the authorities in the field to say that "certain archaeologists wouldn't accept any really crude and early stone tools even if they somehow saw the tools being made with their own eyes."[10] Once it was clear that early dates were involved, these "pre-projectile" materials, which would unquestionably have been classified as artifacts at less ancient, and therefore noncontroversial, archaeological sites, were arbitrarily rejected. Some archaeologists who had initially supported the materials from particular sites changed their opinions, rejecting them after very early datings were obtained. Emphasizing the ambiguities associated with these seemingly technologically less advanced "pre-projectile" complexes (also called chopper-scraper complexes), it was easy for scholars to sidestep them.

The historical emphasis on an ice-free corridor entry led most researchers to "assume unquestioningly" that big game hunting cultures with their characteristic spear points provided the base for all later American Indian cultures. It was accepted as a postulate that only big game hunters were technically advanced enough to make the difficult journey to the New World. If a "pre-projectile" technology existed in the Americas, this brought with it the possibility that tools independently evolved in the New World from simple choppers to sophisticated bifacial points, and this in turn opened the door to even earlier entry dates.

Gordon Willey commenting on the possibility of such a pre-projectile cultural horizon said, ". . . the numerous instances of chipped stone tool complexes whose typology and isolation from technologically more advanced implements suggests the possibility of great age. These have been found in all parts of the hemisphere." But Willey notes that he and other archaeologists remained unconvinced, believing that the data were not strong enough.[11] Dr. Jesse Jennings summed up the case regarding a pre-projectile horizon when he wrote that "Most archaeologists reject or even ignore the matter." Jennings says that many archaeologists rejected the idea because the typology of the implements would require an immigration to the New World during the middle of the last ice age (mid-Wisconsin, c. 28,000 B.C.) or before the last ice age even began (pre-70,000 B.C.).[12]

Thus, the powerful hint the pre-projectile sites provided to man's antiquity in the Americas went ignored. Such early dates would mean that archaeologists would have to face head-on all the misconceptions in the generally accepted view of Indian origins, and few were ready to accept such a challenge. On the other hand, the new geological and meteorological research was raising strong questions about the belief that early man used an ice-free corridor to enter the New World 12,000 years ago. The time was ripe for the discovery of much older sites and new origin concepts. Incontestable evidence was not long in coming.

5

Sinking the Bridge

Data have been presented on site after site with dates and geological context telling of occupations earlier than Clovis.
—Herbert L. Alexander, in
Early Man in America, 1978

I sense that most conservative thinkers, on the basis of the evidence reported from widely separated localities . . . are now willing to concede that man probably entered America during a major interstadial of the Last Glacial (at least 25,000 years ago).
—Alan Bryan, in
Early Man in America, 1978

Early Man Confirmed in American 40,000 Years Ago.
—*Science News*, March 26, 1977

Off the coast of southern California opposite the city of Santa Barbara, lie three small islands: Santa Cruz, San Miguel, and Santa Rosa. The three lie like jewels in the shimmering Pacific sea. Recently, a treasure was discovered deep beneath Santa Rosa.

Santa Rosa has never had much development or disturbance by man. The family that owns the island has confined its activities to leisurely cattle ranching and making the otherwise unpopulated island a wildlife sanctuary. The commotion of the twentieth century has never reached the island.

On a beautiful fall day in 1975, John Wooley, a member of that family, and his fiancée, Charlene Haupt, were exploring a deep gully nestled in the barren "badlands" area of the island. A curiously red patch of earth caught their eye and after investigating, they telephoned Dr. Rainer Berger, a UCLA archaeologist and geophysicist who had been studying the island. What was discovered and subsequently carefully uncovered singlehandedly strikes down the orthodox view of the Indian as a latecomer in the Americas, and furthermore, stretches the Bering route scenario to the breaking point.

Eighteen months after that phone call, Science News, the weekly newsletter of the Association for the Advancement of Science, carried in bold headlines the announcement of this key discovery made on Santa Rosa. They reported: "Conclusive evidence that man was present in North America at least 40,000 years ago . . . has been confirmed for the first time by carbon-14 dating."[1] This is a date more than three times greater than the generally accepted 12,000-years-ago entry date. Berger's expertise in radiocarbon dating confirmed an already proposed view of ancient habitation on Santa Rosa that had been previously put forth in 1956 by archaeologist Phil Orr of the Santa Barbara (California) Museum of Natural History. From another site on the island, Orr had collected four samples of burned bone which gave an average radiocarbon date of 30,000 years ago.

Mother Nature, in the process of fashioning a deep gully on Santa Rosa, had exposed what some scientists, attracted by the plentiful mammoth bones on the island, had been combing the island for since the turn of the century: an ice-age "pit barbecue" where man roasted and ate the dwarf woolly mammoths that had roamed the island long ago. Berger says the hearth itself seems to be a giant pressure cooker. Berger feels that after killing the dwarf elephant (about the size of a bull), the hunters lined the bottom of the pit with wood slabs which they set on fire. Then they wrapped the meat in plant leaves and placed it on top of the burning wood. Next, they placed more wood on top of that, set it on fire also, and covered the pit with rock, leaving the meat to cook for twelve to twenty-four hours, or however long it takes to make an elephant roast tender. (Berger further whetted appetites when he reported that at Santa Rosa he has since found more new sites of likely great age that he has yet to excavate.) Twenty-seven feet below the ground surface, the burned soil of the reddish-colored fire pit exposed by the gully contained not only the remains of a butchered and roasted mammoth but also the crude stone chopping tools used to cut up the unfortunate pachyderm. These hand-sized tools made of chert and basalt clearly show pieces flaked away to provide sharp cutting edges. Berger has shown these tools to experts from around the world who have confirmed his view that the instruments were shaped and used by humans.

Most important, though, analysis by Berger, a specialist in radiocarbon dating methods (he once was an assistant to Willard Libby, the inventor of radiocarbon dating) showed that four chunks of charcoal also dug from the pit had no measurable C-14 left in them. Since it takes 40,000 years for an object to lose all of its measurable C-14, the site has to be at least that old.

Berger's announcement that 40,000-year-old bones had been discovered on Santa Rosa shook the foundations of the archaeological community. It was, in fact, the straw that broke the camel's back for the Bering Bridge scenario. Berger had been studying the island for over twenty years hoping to make just such a find.

The quiet island of Santa Rosa stands as a testimonial to the stubbornness of dogma. Since the turn of the century, it had been common knowledge that a wealth of archaeological evidence lay in various sites on the island. The lengthy dossier arguing for early human habitation there featured:

1. Concentrations of mammoth bones; most notably, specimens with their heads missing or smashed in, both indicating a peculiarly human style of slaughter.
2. Mammoth skeletons whose bones were separated, with ribs and vertebrae missing, indicating that man had butchered these specimens and carried off the choicest parts.
3. Deeply buried areas of burned clay containing charcoal,

a combination indicating the presence of an intelligent fire-builder. Some of these hearths also contained mammoth bones, like Berger's barbecue pit.

4. Finds of large numbers of abalone shells miles inland, in beds that also contained mammoth bones, indicating a strictly human willingness to put out extra effort for the pleasure of a two-course meal.

5. Many isolated finds of crudely chipped stones, tools of the chopper and scraper types; one such stone had been found in a burned area along with mammoth bones. These indicated a human presence but of a seemingly less technologically developed culture than that of the Clovis and Folsom hunters.

Taken together, these lines of evidence did not mesh with the "latecomer model"; conservative professionals, therefore, took them apart, rejected them one by one, and refused to acknowledge man's presence on the island. Burned mammoth bones, bashed skulls, and disarticulated ribs were taken as mere curiosities; the crude stone tools as accidental works of erosion. Here the reasoning was entirely Jesuitical: The stones could not be considered man-made tools, since if they were, they would represent the first documented pre-projectile culture in the New World, an early level of stone age technology the field agreed had never existed here.

The "hearths" of burned clay were held to have been naturally burned; if they contained plentiful charcoal, they became "naturally burnt wood rat nests," even though biologists say there have never been wood rats on the island.

Such determined rationalization of a theory at the expense of visible evidence hardly serves to build confidence in a system of science. Just before Berger's conclusive discovery, a few archaeologists, such as Jennings, began feeling pangs of conscience and gave Santa Rosa a "Scotch verdict," a resounding *maybe*.

With Berger's discovery, the existence of so-called pre-projectile type tools in the New World was also confirmed. Since crude stones of this type were found in a man-made hearth, with a butchered elephant, there was no question that man and not nature had fashioned them. But, as some feared, this finding does not necessarily mean that there was an entire pre-projectile cultural horizon in the New World corresponding to the Middle Paleolithic period in Europe, nor that tools independently evolved in the New World from simple choppers to technically more advanced projectile points.

Tools do not the man make. There is no need to assume that all very crude stone tools or pre-projectile type tools are very old and could only have been made by biologically primitive men. While more sculptured tools like Folsom and Clovis points have only been made by biologically modern man, biologically modern man may also make crude chopper-type tools. For example, biologically modern, present-day Australian aborigines typically use chopper-type tools and even unmodified pieces of stone. What the Australian aborigines are after is a stone with the proper edge angle to do the job at hand, such as skinning or woodcutting. They could make more elaborate tools, but they don't choose to. Once biologically modern man is on the world scene, tool types best reflect cultural style and economic activity. Makers of choppers or pre-projectile types of tools are not inherently older and less knowledgeable than makers of projectile points. In many instances, the chopper tools from a site may only be a partial sample of the full complement of the artifacts possessed by the people who made them. Instead of using stone projectile points, for example, makers of chopper tools may have used fire-hardened wooden tips for their spears.

This raises the question of how the first Americans truly lived. Was it a life of constant nomadic big game hunting, or did these progenerators also gather fruits, nuts, and edible plants? Were choppers used to split open bones for their marrow or to crack open shellfish like the abalones found on Santa Rosa? Some of the earliest crude tools collected resemble grinders. Did the first Indians already know the secret of how to grind certain grains into meal and bake it?

It is hard for archaeology to recreate the ways a people truly lived unless the entire culture is frozen in time. The ashes from Italy's Mount Vesuvius froze ancient Pompeii, just as a giant mudslide in the early 1500s entombed Ozette, an Indian whaling village in Neah Bay, Washington. At these rare sites, everything that was happening on a particular day has been perfectly preserved. A balanced view is presented of the people's life-style. At Ozette, a coastal cliff collapsed covering several communal cedar houses in a sea of mud, encapsulating the village for four and a half centuries. Thousands of household items, tools, weapons, and elaborate carvings were preserved. There were harpoons, bows and arrows fitted with wooden points, fishhooks, ceremonial clubs, looms, sleeping platforms, and figures of thunderbird gods. Even perishable items like clothing, baskets, and food were found. A unique carved-cedar dorsal whale fin studded with seven hundred sea otter teeth has puzzled the excavators. Dr. Richard Daugherty of Washington State University, who is currently directing the Ozette excavations, said the Makah Indians who lived at Ozette had an incredible degree of sophistication. Art permeated every facet of life. This art was tied to their very definite religious beliefs.

When it comes to the first Indian, little survives the ravages of time. Elaborately carved wooden items, clothing, or basketry would not survive to the present at a site as old as Santa Rosa if the people had them. Was Santa Rosa the permanent home of the early barbecuers, or only a place visited by hunters who lived elsewhere, like Manhattan when the Dutch landed? And while "kill sites" such as the Clovis and Folsom sites tell us what and how some early Indians hunted, we know little of their social life and nothing of their religious beliefs. We have no "living sites" from the earliest of Indians. From the shells at Santa Rosa, we now know that nomadic big game hunting was not the only economic activity and not the only way of life for the earliest of the American Indians. But this peek at the early Santa Rosans' technology says nothing of their ideology. What could a chopper say about their beliefs and life goals? Could you imagine an archaeologist excavating the loincloth of a sixteenth-century Tibetan monk and then coming close to recognizing the essence of this monk's ascetic culture? The Santa Rosa discovery is extraordinary in that in one undisturbed, deeply buried site unequivocal evidence for man's activities (fire building, tool making, and elephant hunting) and plentiful material for the absolute dating (C-14) of these activities are found in an area just ten feet wide and six inches deep. It is hard to comprehend how unceremoniously items found in this small space overturn the drawers full of artifacts, museum displays, and textbooks that scholars claim represented the true essence of American Indian origins.

Berger says Santa Rosa "clinches the argument that human presence and evolution [in North America] go back much further than we thought. . . . It can be safely said today that man's entry into the new world occurred at least 40,000 years ago."[2] In one grand moment, Santa Rosa reminded scholars that they had missed 28,000 years (40,000 B.C.–12,000 B.C.) of American Indian prehistory, and that their theories of American Indian origins demanded reconsideration. What happened during those missing years?

We get a glimpse of the nature of the Paleo-Indians' world from a 10,000-year-old burial ground found in an eroding stream bank in northern Colorado. Archaeologists from the University of Colorado excavated this site at Gordon Greek in 1963. The body of a biologically modern woman, resembling a present-day Indian, was found buried in a small pit. The ancient Indians who buried their comrade, tightly flexed the body and placed it on its left side with the head to the north. The pit and the body were coated with red ocher. Two unused stone knives, two scraping tools, a hammerstone, two incised animal bones, and four elk teeth which seemed to have been torn from a necklace were buried with the woman. Charcoal and bones found in the pit indicate the cremation of some animal before the pit was covered over. Drs. David Breternitz, Alan Swedland, and Duane Anderson, who conducted the excavation and studied the materials, have concluded that the burial circumstances show there was a strong belief in an afterlife at this early date. Painting the deceased with red ocher is frequently associated with ceremonial burials and a belief in an afterlife. The incised bones, the unused tools, the broken and perforated elk teeth, and the animal cremation all seem to be offerings. An "elk tooth complex" is well known among the religious practices of the Historic Plains Indians.[3] This burial therefore indicates great time depth to a number of the cultural-ideological practices of the American Indian. (If the person buried had been a medicine man or shaman, I would guess that some crystals would have been found as well as some pollen from particular herbs. Historical Plains Indians had deep beliefs in the efficacy of crystals and herbs for healing. A medicine man would use the crystal to help him "see" and diagnose the illness and the herbs to cure the illness.)

In 1977, a deep sulfurous sinkhole called Little Salt Spring, near Sarasota, Florida, gave us yet another look at the cultural range of the Paleo-Indians. Ten thousand years ago, while the Indians of Gordon Creek buried their dead in red ocher, the Indians of Sarasota ceremonially wrapped their dead in swamp grass and sank them in the spring. A fortuitous combination of water chemistry and controlled temperatures has preserved with uncanny perfection organic artifacts that would otherwise have deteriorated. Besides the skeletons, dated as 10,000 years in age, a wooden mortar, wooden boomerangs, and a projectile point made of antler have been found. The boomerangs were quite a technological surprise.[4]

In 1973, an archaeological site called Koster, in a cornfield along the Illinois River, was equally surprising by providing evidence that New World man had been leading a leisurely life and had been building permanent settlements with plaster walls for more than 8,000 years in the fertile Illinois River Valley, i.e., long before the Egyptians built the pyramids or the ancient Britains erected their monument at Stonehenge.[5]

The current stereotype of the first Indians as brazen savages obsessed with killing elephants who over the millennia became civilized is very misleading. Maybe the first Americans were very gentle and religious people who over the millennia lost their omnipotent knowledge of nature and fell from grace as their myths recount.

Can we safely project back some of the activities found 10,000 years ago at Gordon Creek, Colorado, or Little Salt Spring, Florida? Cave paintings from modern men who inhabited Europe 35,000 years ago indicate that these men were already socially organized and caught up in ceremony, shamanism, and a belief in an afterlife. What surprises remain to be uncovered in the Americas? Were the first Americans less advanced or more advanced than their European counterparts? From the evidence of the Santa Rosa site alone, it is no longer clear which branch of modern man came first.

In fact, the Santa Rosa site could be even more than 40,000 years old. All that is known for sure is that it is *at least* that old. Since the charcoal from the hearth had no C-14 remaining in it and it is off the radiocarbon scale, the site could just as well reach back another 20,000 years, as some archaeologists have already speculated.

This speculation is supported by the logistics of having to use a "northern door" to enter the Americas. If man was in the Americas at least 40,000 years ago, by virtue of the circumstances controlling the availability of the Bering route, he would have to have entered even earlier. Like commuters following a tight time schedule to reach their destination, the first American immigrants would have had to reach the Bering area at a time when sea level was low enough to expose the Bering land bridge, so they could cross it. Then they would have had to transfer quickly and move south at a time when an ice-free corridor through Canada was also traversable. In other words, the Bering Bridge and the ice-free corridor had to be more or less simultaneously available; the existence of one without the other would not permit entry. There weren't many periods in time when both were available. We have already learned that both were definitely available about 8,000 to 10,000 years ago. Geologists say that the other known exposure of the Siberian-Alaskan land bridge within the last ice-age was from

35,000 to 27,000 years ago,[6] but even this appearance of the bridge does not go back far enough for Santa Rosa.

Dr. Jeffrey Bada, a young geochemist at the Scripps Institution of Oceanography (University of California), says, "We know that sea level was low enough to allow the formation of a land bridge about 140,000 years ago, and perhaps also about 70,000 years before the present."[7] Thus, the Santa Rosa evidence indicates that man may have been in the Americas not just 40,000 years ago but as far back as 70,000 or even 140,000 years ago.[3]* Unfortunately, we know very little about the availability of a corresponding ice-free corridor in those areas, and the opening and closing of the ice-free corridor at these very early dates. It may be that the bridge and the corridor were never open together earlier than 8,000 to 10,000 years ago. This would argue well for the basic elements of the Indians' own origin myths—much earlier origin dates and New World origins—which do not correspond at any point with the "exodus" constructed for them by archaeological orthodoxy.

Two types of relics are readily accepted by archaeologists as evidence of man's presence at the earliest of ancient sites: the classic "stones and bones," stone tools and human fossils or skeletal remains. Human fossils are the more emotionally satisfying of the two types of evidence, perhaps because they are much scarcer than stone tools. For a believing archaeologist, stone tools are so many beads in a rosary; a human bone is a fragment of the true cross. Such sanctifying evidence would be immensely powerful support in calling for the total revision of all previous theories on an issue. So, while Berger has found clear-cut stone tools at Santa Rosa, he would also like to find human bones. He believes that human remains are buried on the island and he hopes to discover them as he continues his diggings.

One can't help but wonder what these most ancient Americans looked like. Did they look like the Indians of today, like Asians,

---

* It will be shown in later chapters that neither the 70,000- nor the 140,000-year old exposure is old enough.

like crude Neanderthals or Europe's Cro-Magnons, or like some unknown entities from space or a possibly lost continent? Ironically, the answer to this intriguing and crucial question became available just before the question was asked.

As Rainer Berger toiled in the soil of pristine Santa Rosa, Dr. Jeffrey Bada was at work 180 miles to the south in San Diego. His project, the development of a new absolute dating technique which ranged far beyond the 40,000-year practical limit of C-14 testing, led to the unmasking of America's pre-40,000-year-old inhabitants. The sequence of events, plot twists, and ironies associated with this unmasking are incredible enough to challenge the most elaborate Hollywood fantasy.

The impetus for Bada's work came from Dr. George Carter, now a geography professor at Texas A & M University. From 1934 to 1938, Carter was Curator of Anthropology at the San Diego Museum of Man. While in San Diego, Carter spent much of his time exploring for and studying local archaeological sites, and reached the heretical conclusion that man was in the New World *before* the start of the last glacial period (the Wisconsin, which began approximately 70,000 years ago), and perhaps even by the beginning of the third glacial period (the Illinoian), which is dated to over 170,000 years ago. Carter based his extraordinary claims on ancient charcoal residues he presumed to be man-made hearths, and on rocks chipped into crude pre-projectile tool-like forms which he had found together at a site he called Texas Street, named for the street that crossed over the San Diego River near the site.

Carter's assertions were held up to unalloyed ridicule by other scientists when he first published them in 1949. His ideas were dismissed as preposterous: Nature, not man, had set the fires that left charcoal in an ancient stratum; nature, not man, had chipped the stones into a random resemblance to crude tools. His findings were pejoratively dubbed "Carterfacts," and they were always good for a professional chuckle.

Nevertheless, Carter held fast. In particular, he kept in mind several Paleo-Indian skulls he had examined at the Museum of

Man which came from what he believed were very old geological contexts. Carter was perplexed by the fully modern appearance of these skulls. These skulls and other human fossils were excavated between 1926 and 1929 from sites close to the museum by M. J. Rogers, an archaeologist who worked for Scripps. In the 1920s, no absolute dating techniques were available, and following the bias of the time it was "guesstimated" that the modern-looking skeletal material was only about 7,500 years old, even though Rogers, the excavator, felt that the materials could be of very great antiquity. Rogers' suggestion and Carter's protestations aside, the human fossils were stored away and the sites ignored. Ironically, while archaeologists searched, sifted, and sweated over the next forty years, they didn't realize that some of the most vital evidence concerning Indian origins already resided in one of their museums.

When radiocarbon dating came into use during the 1950s, the San Diego bones still couldn't be dated since this technique consumed almost one pound of bone and would destroy the very evidence it was to confirm. Further, the carbon-14 technique could only date items back to 40,000 years, a rather modest date for Carter's prehistorical scenario. But in 1973, Carter heard about the new dating technique developed by Bada, a technique consuming only a fraction of an ounce of bone that could reach back as far as one million years, and decided the time had come to put his precious skulls to the test. They had been lying virtually undisturbed in storage for over four decades in the San Diego Museum's laboratory, only ten miles south of Bada's laboratory at Scripps.

Bada's absolute dating technique measures a natural process of change called racemization. Racemization entails a kind of chemical clock built into living things which ticks on in their remains after death. In principle, the test is similar to the radiocarbon dating technique. Racemization dating is based on the fact that the amino acids in plants and animals have a geometric property that causes them, in crystal form, to rotate polarized light waves to the left. When the organisms die, however, the amino acids, at a constant rate, gradually racemize or change their geometry to a mirror-image configuration in which the light is rotated to the right. The time for complete reversal in the direction of light rotation is a long one; it can take up to several hundred thousand years for certain (aspartic) types of amino acids. The specific time period required for total change and the corresponding rate of change must be calculated for the particular environment the remains being dated are found in. The easiest and surest way to determine these factors for a particular area is to calculate them from the amount of racemization present in remains from the same area whose age is already known. Thus, by measuring the ratio of lefthanded to righthanded amino acids in a given fossil, and determining the local racemization rate, Bada and his colleagues can determine its age and go far beyond the limits of radiocarbon dating.

Excited over the prospect of a real verdict on the skulls, one that could reach as far back in time as his own vision of Indian presence in California, Carter contacted Bada and got him to date the skeletal remains unearthed so long ago by Rogers.

For the San Diego skulls, Bada first determined the local racemization rate from a radiocarbon-dated skull dug up in nearby Laguna Beach (see chart, page 85), then made the test that rocked the archaeological world.

Bada stated that his racemization dating of the two San Diego skulls from the two separate sites made "an air-tight case" for man's being in the San Diego area at least 50,000 years ago and "therefore refuted the generally accepted theory" that man first populated North America only 12,000 years ago. One skull dated to 44,000 years ago and the other to 48,000 years ago.[8] (These datings also confirmed Dr. Rogers' long-ignored belief that they were not only very old but also of approximately the same age.) Bada concluded that man had to be at least 50,000 years old in the Americas because of the familiar problem of entry. Though man was in San Diego 48,000 years ago, because of glacial movement he could have used the bridge only either 140,000 years ago or possibly 70,000 years ago.

The 48,000-year-old skull* came from a sea cliff at Del Mar close to the San Dieguito River mouth just six miles to the north of Scripps. The skull, a mandible, and ribs were found in 1929, eroding at the base of this sea cliff. Del Mar man had been purposefully buried in a midden, a refuse heap of sea shells discarded by ancient man. From the Del Mar skull it can be seen that this most ancient San Diegan was physically as fully evolved as present-day San Diegans. Most important, he looked more like a modern-day Indian than an Asian. Unfortunately, the opportunity to excavate and discover artifacts which might have given us a glimpse at Del Mar man's mode of life is forever lost; continued erosion and tidal action have now totally destroyed the site.

The 44,000-year-old skull (frontal fragment)† came from a site in La Jolla approximately three miles south of the Scripps. Rogers was called to this site in 1926 when a steam shovel working on a development project began unearthing human remains. The skull itself was found in place six feet below the ground level from a stratigraphically old horizon. Fortunately, this site remains partly intact. Crudely made stone tools still abound on the nearby ground surface. The site is in a wealthy residential neighborhood, in the backyard of the Chancellor of the University of California at San Diego, on a narrow strip of land between his swimming pool and the edge of a bluff overlooking the ocean. The circumstances seem to emphasize in a symbolic way how readily available such information has been to academia. New excavations under the guidance of Dr. Gail Kennedy of UCLA have already begun at the La Jolla site and the initial results, which include the discovery of a new skeleton dating to 20,000 years ago from a younger deposit, clearly support Bada's datings.[9]

When Bada's report on his work was published on May 17, 1974, in the prestigious magazine *Science*, not many archaeologists were ready to lionize him.[10] Berger's discovery at Santa

* Lab #SDM [San Diego Museum] 16704.
† Lab #SDM 16742.

ASPARTIC ACID RACEMIZATION AGES FOR SEVERAL
CALIFORNIA PALEO-INDIAN SKELETONS*

General Location	San Diego Museum (SDM) Number	Radiocarbon Age (Years Ago)	Aspartic Acid Age (Years Ago)
Bones from near Los Angeles, CA			
Laguna skull	—	17,000	—
Los Angeles skull	—	23,600	26,000 (control)
Bones from near San Diego, CA			
Del Mar femur	16704	—	48,000
Del Mar skull	16704	—	47,000
La Jolla	16742	—	44,000
Cliffs north of Scripps	16740	—	39,000
Cliffs north of Scripps	16724	—	27,000
Batequistor Lagoon (near Oceanside)	16706	—	45,000
Cliffs north of Scripps	19241	6,700	6,000 (control)
La Jolla	18402	5,000–7,500	6,000 (control)
Bones from near San Jose, CA			
Sunnyvale skeleton	—	No radiocarbon left	
ulna } skull }	—	40,000	70,000?
Stanford Man I	—	7,200	6,000 (control)

* Adapted from Bada and Helfman in *World Archaeology*, 1975.

Rosa was still a year away, and talk of 40,000- to 50,000-year-old dates for man in the Americas was dismissed by those still largely committed to man's being a latecomer to the Americas. Some complained that this new dating technique was not yet proven. Other archaeologists attacked head-on and said it had to be "faulty." For a classic example, Dr. Robert Heizer, now retired from the University of California at Berkeley, said he found the

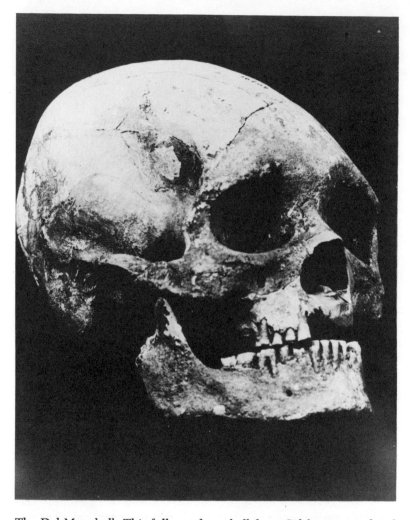

The Del Mar skull. This fully modern skull from California was dated
to 48,000 years ago by Dr. Jeffrey Bada, a chemist at the Scripps Institution. It is older than any fully modern skull recognized from Europe,
Asia, or Africa. A new study at UCLA called it "proto-Caucasoid" in
its racial affinity. *San Diego Museum of Man*

dates produced by Bada's racemization suspect simply because "they're too old."[11]

"When we first published this in *Science*," Bada says, "I was very naive about the emotional reaction from scientists [archaeologists]."[12] The reaction of geologists, physicists, and chemists who reviewed Bada's methods was unanimous in its praise.* Skeptical archaeologists ignored the fact that when Bada dated the two skulls he also successfully dated two controls, an ancient skull from Los Angeles and one set of human leg bones from San Diego. The ages of these controls had been determined by radiocarbon dating as 23,600 and 5,000 to 7,500 years ago and the racemization technique gave the *same* datings. Bada's prior and subsequent racemization datings of bones from African and European sites, including some beyond the carbon-14 limit, have also agreed well with dates derived by radiocarbon and other methods. Most recently, Bada dated the Santa Rosa site and got agreement with Berger's radiocarbon dates. In a *New York Times* interview, Bada said, "I don't see why the [racemization] technique should work everywhere else in the world but not here."[13] How could the racemization dating technique be right in controlled tests and in so many other instances and be wrong when it comes to the two 50,000-year-old skulls from San Diego?

Since his report in *Science*, to further test the reproducibility of his results for California, Dr. Bada has gone on to date other Paleo-Indian skeletons from that state. He found three other examples of fossil hominids from California (see chart, page 85) with ages of 39,000 years or more, making for a total of five.† If there is safety in numbers, five different California locations cer-

---

* In 1973, Bada was the recipient of the Golden Plate Award presented by the American Academy of Achievement for his work with dating fossils. He was also named as one of the eight "Young Builders of America" in the February 6, 1976 issue of *U.S. News & World Report Magazine.*

† In a special release sent out by the Scripps Institution in 1979, Dr. Bada is quoted as saying that the controversy over his dates for man in California "hinges on the belief that modern man first appeared in Europe about 35,000 years ago in the form of Cro-Magnon man. . . . But that theory is certainly under fire today."

Dr. Jeffrey Bada and the Del Mar skull which has greatly extended man's antiquity in North America. Bada developed the new chemical test used to date the skull—aspartic (amino acid) racemization, which is like radiocarbon dating. *Union-Tribune Publishing Co.*

tainly provides it. His racemization tests of radiocarbon-dated control skeletons continue to bolster the case for his technique. These particular controls (Stanford man and SDM 19241) had radiocarbon dates of just 5,000 to 7,000 years ago, and Bada's racemization gave correspondingly low dates. Further, these newer racemization results, as reported in *World Archaeology*, were independently reproduced by a NASA lab which began using the technique. This confirmation was especially important because the Sunnyvale skeleton (see chart, page 85) gave the remarkable date of 70,000 years. This skeleton, which had no radiocarbon left in it, was excavated near San Jose by Dr. Bert Gerow of Stanford University in 1972. While Bada has noted that his technique would tend slightly to underestimate the age of very old skeletons, Bada remains cautious about the 70,000-year-old Sunnyvale date, considering it "less reliable than the southern California bones, due to the lack of a suitable radiocarbon dated bone to use as 'calibration' sample."[14]

Bada and Berger, with their mutually supportive findings, have powerfully and fatally damaged the late-entrant model of man's appearance in the New World. They have opened up a whole new vista in America's past.

6

A Parade of Sites—The Bones
Don't Lie and Cultural Surprises

About fifty excavated sites have yielded eleven human
skeletons, more than a thousand artifacts, and three times
that many bones of extinct animals. From the evidence, we
have obtained more than fifty radiocarbon determinations
earlier than 12,000 years before the present.
                    —Richard S. MacNeish,
              in *American Scientist*, June 1976

Evidence from a number of archaeological sites distributed
in the western part of the hemisphere from the Yukon into
South America now indicates a *minimum* possible date of
40,000 years ago for the earliest entry of man into the
North American continent.
                    —Ruth Gruhn, in *Annals of the New
              York Academy of Sciences*, 1977

The theory that men migrated to North America from Asia and
that ideas diffused to North America from Asia no longer suffices
to explain the origins of the American Indian and his culture. And
the dramatic new findings of Drs. Bada and Berger in California
don't stand alone in making this point.

A rapidly mounting collection of ancient human bones and
artifacts from sites across the Americas helps strike down the
Bering route migration scenario—the so-called "latecomer"
model. No less than twenty-eight verified sites (see chart, page
95, and map, page 94) testify to the great antiquity of man in the
New World. None of these twenty-eight sites is farfetched—the

type where slight threads of evidence for great antiquity are counted as conclusive. On the contrary, all the sites listed here have been endorsed in scholarly papers by at least three different professional archaelogists who are currently teaching at universities and colleges. With improved dating techniques in the future, some sites on the list may prove to be even older than is now thought.

There is a rapidly mounting number of professional archaeologists who no longer accept the traditional archaeological version of Indian origins. They believe we are just now beginning to discover and realize the great antiquity of the American Indian. In their papers and journals, they are talking about "early-early" man instead of "early man." While these dissenters are mostly younger archaeologists (whose names for the most part will be associated with the listing of sites which shall follow), those far in time from Hrdlicka's day, there are also many older archaeologists among the dissenters, who for a long time stood quite alone in their beliefs. Among them are some of the world's most distinguished archaeologists—for instance, Dr. Louis Leakey (whose dramatic entry into American archaeology will be detailed in Chapter 7) and Dr. Richard ("Scotty") MacNeish, the director of the prestigious R. S. Peabody Foundation for Archaeology in Andover, Massachusetts. MacNeish is a past president of the Society for American Archaeology and a winner of the coveted A. V. Kidder Award (1971), a triennial award presented by the American Anthropological Association for eminence in American archaeology. (Archaeology didn't take Scotty to their bosom for his championing of earlier dates; in fact, he set tongues wagging in 1969 with his claims based on a site he dug in Peru. MacNeish believes that man entered the New World "some 70,000±30,000 years ago."[1] But regardless of the reputations of their champions, the sites can speak for themselves in the plain language of stones and bones.

The brief commentary that follows is divided into sites where the key element of proof has come from human bones and those where the key element is from artifacts; in some cases, of course, both bones and artifacts have come from the same site. All the sites mentioned are at least 14,000 years in age, well clear of the traditional 12,000-year entry date. Considering these sites with the new confidence gained from Berger's Santa Rosa dating, an entirely different picture of America's past begins to emerge.

Early Human Bones Sites

Up until the very recent wave (1974–   ) of discoveries and redatings, archaeologists had relied on the following pitifully sketchy trove of human skeletal material from the Americas.

1. An undated pelvis found discovered in 1846 lying close to mammoth bones in Natchez, Mississippi.
2. Texepan man, a 10,000-year-old skeleton discovered in Mexico City in 1949.
3. Midland man, a skull estimated to be 10,000 years old, discovered in Texas in 1953.
4. The skeleton discovered in 1963 in Gordon Creek, Colorado (see pp, 77–78), radiocarbon dated to 9,700 years ago.
5. Fragments of three human skulls found in 1964 in southeastern Washington, referred to as Marmes Man, dated 11,000 years old.
6. Several skeletons almost 10,000 years in age discovered in 1977 in Little Salt Spring, Florida (see page 78).

But now the Del Mar (48,000 years) and La Jolla (44,000 years) skulls, and the four other California sites dated in 1974 by Bada as being 27,000, 39,000, 45,000, and 70,000 years in age have turned things upside down for conservative archaeologists, and the following six sites add to the dilemma.

Taber (Site #6 on the chart [page 95] and reference map)

In 1963, the fossil bones of an infant were found at Taber, Alberta, Canada, by geologist A. MacS. Stalker. The bones were weathering out of a bluff sixty feet below prairie level under glacial deposits. Radiocarbon-dated organic material in adjacent

Bering Straits
and Bridge Area

14

10

13

Laurentide
Ice Sheet

Cordilleran
Ice Sheet

Ice free
corridor zone
Blocked most
of the time

6

7
25

1

20

5

9

—, 16

22

2, 3, 4, 8, 15, 18

19

17

26

23

11

21

27

SITES THAT SHATTER THE "12,000-YEAR-OLD LATECOMER"
INDIAN ORIGINS MODEL*

Number	Site and Location**	Human Remains (H) or Artifacts (A)	Date (Years Ago)
1	Sunnyvale, California	H	70,000?
—	"Black Box"	H	50,000+
2	Del Mar skull, California	H	48,000
3	Oceanside (San Diego Museum Number 16706), California	H	45,000
4	La Jolla skull, California	H	44,000
5	Santa Rosa Island, California	A	40,000+
6	Taber, Alberta, Canada	H	40,000+
7	American Falls, Idaho	A	40,000
8	Cliff North of Scripps, (San Diego Museum Number 16740), California	H	39,000
9	Lewisville (and Frieshenhahn and Malakoff sites), Texas	A	38,000+
10	Dawson City, Yukon, Canada	A	38,000+
11	Otavalo, Ecuador	H	30,000+
12	Sheguiandah, Ontario, Canada	A	30,000
13	Tanana Uplands, Yukon, Canada	A	29,000
14	Old Crow, Yukon, Canada	A & H	29,000
15	Cliffs North of Scripps (San Diego Museum Number 16724), California	H	27,000
16	Los Angeles skull, California	H	24,000
17	Tlapacoya, Mexico	A	24,000
18	Scripps Campus, California	A	22,000
19	Yuha Desert, California	H	22,000
20	McGee's Point, Nevada	A	22,000?
21	Pikimachay Cave, Peru	A & H	20,000
22	Laguna Beach skull, California	H	17,000
23	Muaco, Venezuela	A	16,000
24	Meadowcroft Rockshelter, Pennsylvania	A	15,000

(*Continued*)

(Continued)

25	Wilson Butte, Idaho	A	14,500
26	Taima-Taima, Venezuela	A	14,400
27	Alice Boer, Brazil	A	14,200

* Adapted from Krieger (1964), MacNeish (1976), Lorenzo (1978), and Bryan (1978).
** See text and appendix for multiple references to each site.

---

overlying beds was approximately 35,000 years in age and Stalker believes that the remains might be as old as 60,000 years.[2]

Otavalo Skull (Site #11)

Near Otavalo, Ecuador, north of Quito, an Indian died in a crushing fall into a thirty-foot-deep fissure in the ground. Dr. David Davies of the University of London has conducted a number of different dating tests on the Indian's skull which indicate that it is at least 30,000 years old.[3]*

Los Angeles Skull (Site #16)

In 1936, the mineralized cranium of a fully modern skull was found thirteen feet below the surface near Los Angeles, California, by workmen excavating a storm drain. Mammoth bones were found at the same depth nine hundred feet away. The skull went undated until the development in the late 1960s of collagen dating, an improved radiocarbon-dating technique. In 1970, Rainer Berger of the University of California at Los Angeles (UCLA) showed that the skull was at least 23,600 years old.[4]

Yuha Man (Site #19)

In 1972, a nearly complete fully modern human skeleton was found in the Yuha desert of California's Imperial Valley by a

---

* Professor J. H. Fremlin of the Department of Applied Radioactivity, University of Birmingham, England, has obtained a 25,000-year-old date on aragonite crystals found in the skull. Confusion has resulted from a collagen radiocarbon date of just 2,500 years obtained at Birmingham, but they also obtained a date of 28,000 years on a skull sample composed of bone and calcium carbonate.

local land developer, Morton Childers. The ceremonially buried skeleton, known as Yuha man, was found lying on its side in a fetal position in an earthen burial mound (approximately nine feet by twelve feet in horizontal dimensions) covered with rocks. Radiocarbon dating of the calcium carbonate material (caliche) deposited on the bones indicated that the remains were at least 22,000 years old, possibly more. At that time, there was a large inland lake, the Salton Sea, in the Imperial Valley.[5]

Laguna Beach Skull (Site #22)

Louis Leakey, who reached fame with his spectacular discoveries of man's earliest known ancestors at Olduvai Gorge in Africa in 1959, made his first inroad into American archaeology via the Laguna Beach skull. In 1967, on one of his lecture tours, Leakey consented to examine a skull brought to him by Howard Wilson, a very stubborn amateur archaeologist who had discovered the skull in 1933. Dr. Leakey recognized that the thick calcium carbonate layer on the skull suggested considerable antiquity and asked Dr. Rainer Berger at the University of California to radiocarbon date the skull; it was at least 17,000 years old.[6]

The 17,000-year-old date was amazing because in 1968 Berger was still seven years away from his unassailable and shattering Santa Rosa discovery, and Bada was six years away from his revolutionary new datings. Up until these new discoveries the Los Angeles man skull (24,000) and the Laguna Beach skull, both dated by Berger using the newly developed and refined collagen-based radiocarbon dating technique, provided the first direct dating of man or his artifacts by a widely accepted dating technique which severely challenged the 12,000-years-ago entry date of the "latecomer" model for Indian origins.

"Black Box" (Site #——)

At the request of those doing the research, the "Black Box" is a site I can't identify. The researchers are from a major university and they are being extremely conservative about announcing their monumental findings. As was the case with the Los Angeles skull, the Del Mar skull, and others, they have applied modern dating techniques to a decades-old discovery previously assumed to be of no special importance. Not far from where Los Angeles man was discovered, six complete skeletons were found in 1924 which were believed to be no more than 5,000 years old. Racially, they looked as if they could be the ancestors of both the American Indian and European Caucasians. While the 24,000-year-old Los Angeles skull was found at a depth of thirteen feet below the surface, these six skeletons lay at a depth of twenty-six feet. The fact of their coming from such a great depth lends credence to the great age which the Black Box researchers obtained for the bones using the racemization dating technique. The skeletons dated to 52,000 years in age! The researchers are presently seeking added confirmation from radiocarbon dating before reporting their findings.[7]

Early Artifacts Sites

While the skeletal sites of the preceding section confirm the great age of man in the Americas, that biologically he was fully modern, and that he seemed to originate in the Americas, a number of other sites yielding only artifacts tell us even more. A wealth of very ancient artifacts from sites discovered in the last decade has begun to put flesh on the bones. We are learning that the first Americans were very different from their generally accepted primitive big-game-hunter stereotype. Instead, the first Americans may have been people as inventive, skilled, and culturally sophisticated as any of us today. They were people who could survive in whatever environment they chose; people who hunted both big and small game; collected shellfish, fish, mussels and snails, seeds, berries and nuts; ground seeds into meal and baked bread; wore fitted clothing; wove baskets and ropes;

carved exquisite tools of bone, used cosmetics, wore ornamentation, buried their dead, made notations, rendered mysterious carvings, and had complex ideological beliefs. Most provocatively, man in the Americas did many of these things long before anyone else in the world did them. While these sophisticated artifacts were being used in America, man in Europe was still in the stone age. Evidence is rapidly mounting that the first Americans were truly kin to the knowledgeable and noble ancestors celebrated in Indian myth.

In addition to Berger's recent discovery on Santa Rosa Island (40,000 +) discussed on pages 71–77, the following sites produced artifacts which substantiate the claim for the great antiquity and complexity of the first Americans. Additional very early sites from the chart on page 95–96 are discussed in the appendix.

Lewisville (Site #9)

Near Lewisville, Texas, twenty miles northwest of Dallas, nineteen hearths were uncovered as a result of earth-moving operations. A chopper tool, a stone hammer, stone flakes, a Clovis point, and burned bones of big and small game animals were found within the hearths. Snail and mussel shells and hackberry seeds showed that red meat was not the only thing on the menu. A burned bone which came from the same hearth as the Clovis point was submitted to the Humble Oil Company Laboratory for radiocarbon dating. An age of at least 37,000 years was indicated. This dating was confirmed by a UCLA radiocarbon date on hearth charcoal of at least 38,000 years.[8]

The real excitement from this site comes from the Clovis point. Long and sleek, glassy obsidian Clovis points, whose cutting power is better than steel, are not supposed to have appeared in North America until 12,000 years ago. If the 38,000-year-old dating for the Clovis point is correct, it vaults the Lewisville site to world prominence, since stone projectile points exhibiting equal skill and sophistication in flintwork are not believed to have been made in Europe and Asia until 20,000 years ago.

Dr. Herbert Alexander of Simon Fraser University, who was a graduate student at the University of Texas in 1958 while the Lewisville site was being excavated, vividly recalls the process by which academic support of new facts fell before the onslaught of theory:

> On a number of occasions, I had the opportunity to listen to faculty and visitors discuss their visits to the site. The opinions voiced at the time were that the hearths were man-made, and the faunal associations [animal bones], valid. Once the dates were announced, however, some opinions were changed and after the Clovis point was found, the process of picking and ignoring began in earnest. Those who had previously accepted the hearths and/or faunal associations began to question their memories.[9]

Shocked archaeologists, skirting libel, suggested that the Clovis point might have been "planted" in the hearth it came from, according to Marie Wormington of the Denver Museum. Arguing against the possibility of a hoax, Wormington points out that "Archaeologists who have worked closely with the individuals involved in the excavation (W. W. Crow, R. K. Harris, and members of the Dallas Archaeological Society) are completely convinced of their integrity and competence." Furthermore, Alex Kreiger of the University of Washington, who saw the hearth before it was excavated, states that "there was no evidence of disturbance in the hard-packed clay surface such as would have been present had an object been intentionally introduced into the hearth."[10] This would also rule out the possibility that the point was tumbled into its location by the earth-moving operations that led to the discovery.

Today, archaeologists such as Alex Kreiger, Herbert L. Alexander, and Richard MacNeish consider Lewisville a valid site with valid dating, but they shy away from or ignore the issue of the far-too-early Clovis point, remaining content to discuss the

Stone carved by the Paleo-Indians estimated to be 30,000–40,000 years old. The carving is one of three found twenty-six feet down in a gravel pit in Malakoff, Texas, with the bones of extinct animal species. *University of Texas Press*

chopper tools and flakes.[11]* If the point is also authentic, the implications are astounding.

Support for Lewisville's dating comes from a mysterious site called Malakoff, just seventy miles away. During the 1930s, geologists and paleontologists from the University of Texas unearthed three very large stone carvings from a gravel pit in a twenty-six-foot-deep zone that also contained the plentiful remains of extinct species of animals attributed to the middle of the last glacial period, approximately 30,000 to 40,000 years ago. The carvings were the only evidence for man's presence at that date—but what evidence!

The three Malakoff carvings were made on sandstone boulders, and were fashioned to represent human faces. For example, on one of the boulders, carved depressions represented eyes, ears, nose, and mouth, and bore holes depicted teeth. The figure was sixteen inches long, fourteen inches wide, and weighed one hundred pounds.[12]

These three figures bring to mind a carving found at Tequixquiac just north of Mexico City at a depth of forty feet, excavated in 1890 by a Mexican naturalist from a zone rich in extinct Pleistocene fauna. The sacrum (part of the pelvis) of an extinct llama was carefully carved and drilled to resemble the face and snout of an animal, probably a coyote. Beds, well above and much younger than the beds the carving came from, have been dated to 16,000 years ago.[13] A dating of at least 30,000 years in age is indicated for the Mexican carving.

Sheguiandah (Site #12)

Sheguiandah is a site located on Manitoulin Island in the north part of Lake Huron in Canada. There is a type of quartzite on the

---

* The Lewisville site has since been flooded by a dam, but in 1978, an exceptionally dry year, the site was exposed. At that time, Dr. Dennis Stanford of the Smithsonian Institution excavated the site and found stone tools and debris which support the original evidence.

island that is excellent material for tools. Twenty-six acres of the island are littered with this quartzite, piled yards deep in some places. Although the ancient inhabitants extensively quarried this material, leaving blocks, chips, and worked fragments possibly for trade, they seem to have subsisted on a diet consisting mostly of fish. This site is yet another that points to Paleo-Indian activities quite apart from elephant-hunting.

Sheguiandah is generally conceded to be at least 30,000 years old, although the site's excavator, Thomas E. Lee, argues for an interglacial date (70,000 +).[14] This concession comes after what Dr. Lee calls a bitter battle with the "establishment." Lee excavated the site from 1951 to 1955, while he was Director of the National Museum of Canada. In the 1950s, few archaeologists believed that a 30,000-year-old American site was possible, and an interglacial site was unheard of. Lee says that he had been warned by one University of Toronto professional to "Go after the Paleo-Indian projectile points, and forget about what is beneath them in the glacial till."[15] But Lee dug deeper. He describes the consequences, not altogether dispassionately, thus (emphasis is Lee's):

> Several prominent geologists who closely examined the numerous excavations in progress during four years at Sheguiandah privately expressed the belief that the lower levels of the Sheguiandah site *are* interglacial. Such was the climate in professional circles—one of jealousy, hostility, skepticism, antagonism, obstructionism, and persecution—that, on the advice of the famed authority, Dr. Ernst Antevs of Arizona, a lesser date of 30,000 years *minimum* was advanced in print by some of the geologists to avoid ridicule and to gain partial acceptance from the more serious scholars. But even that minimum was too much for the protagonists of the fluted-point first-Americans myth.* The site's discoverer was hounded from his Civil Service position into prolonged unemployment; publication outlets were cut off; the evidence was misrepresented by several prominent authors among the Brahmins; the tons of artifacts vanished into storage bins of the National Museum

---

* The Clovis and Folsom hunter sites were believed to be no more than 12,000 years old.

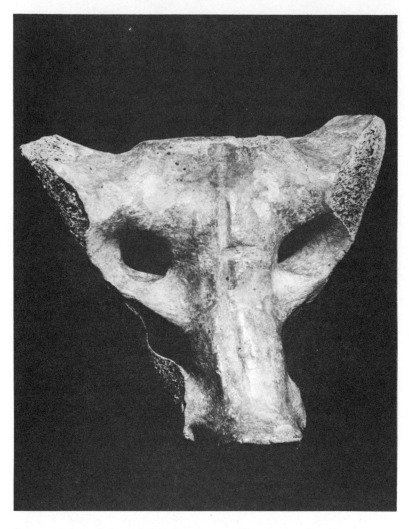

Sacrum (part of the pelvis) of an extinct llama carved to represent an animal. The bone was found forty feet below Mexico City near Tequixquiac. *Museo Nacional de Antropologia, Mexico*

of Canada; for refusing to fire the discoverer, the Director of the National Museum, [Lee] who had proposed having a monograph on the site published, was himself fired and driven into exile; official positions of prestige and power were exercised in an effort to gain control over just *six* Sheguiandah specimens that had not gone under cover; and the site has been turned into a tourist resort. All of this, without the profession, in four long years, bothering to take a look, when there was still time to look. Sheguiandah would have forced embarrassing admissions that the Brahmins did not know everything. It would have forced the rewriting of almost every book in the business. It *had* to be killed. It *was* killed.[16]

Old Crow (Site #14)

The Old Crow flats in the desolate northern Yukon in Canada are marked by a number of different archaeological sites within a valley never reached by glaciation. In 1976, one of these sites yielded the jawbone of a child dating to 29,000 years ago. A number of unique and sophisticated artifacts from several different locations have also been found in the valley.

In 1973, *Science* magazine reported the discovery of a ten-inch-long "flesher" made of caribou bone fashioned in a style still used by present-day Canadian Indians. After an animal is skinned, a flesher is used to remove the meat and fat that still cling to the hide. A cleaned hide could then be treated and made into the warm skin clothing so essential for survival in a cold environment. The Old Crow flesher was perfectly preserved and it could be seen that someone had once whittled this piece of caribou bone into spatulate form and then added a regular series of notches to the working edge, giving the appearance of teeth. (The flesher looks like a back scratcher.)

The authors of the *Science* article, Drs. William Irving of the University of Toronto and C. R. Harrington of the National Museum of Canada, said that the clearly visible whittling marks on the bone showed that the carver had used a very sharp stone tool with a straight working edge. Dr. Richard Morlan, also of the

A caribou leg bone shaped into a hide fleshing tool. Note the serrated tip which gives the tool the appearance of a back scratcher. Found at the Old Crow site in Canada's Yukon Territory, it is 27,000 years old. *National Museums of Canada, Neg. #73-31475 and #73-31474.*

Canadian National Museum, calls the tool "exquisite": the tool's "symmetry and delicate denticulations on the cutting edge bespeak a degree of sophistication in the craft of bone technology which should immediately banish the notion that the ice-age inhabitants of the Old Crow Flats were crude or ignorant or clumsy or primitive."[17]

When this flesher was subjected to radiocarbon dating, it was found to be 27,000 years old. Irving and Harrington averred, "We believe at least three human artifacts from the Old Crow region are between 25,000 and 29,000 radiocarbon years old."[18]

In 1973, archaeologists including Jesse Jennings and Hansjurgen Muller-Beck of Switzerland criticized Irving's and Harrington's conclusion about the flesher and other bone artifacts. These critics suggested that modern-day Indians might have made the beautiful flesher after they found the already-ancient caribou bone, and that the other bones were fractured not by man but by various natural agencies such as stream tumbling or animals. To resolve these questions, Irving commissioned Dr. Robson Bonnichsen of the University of Maine to study the bones. Bonnichsen —a skilled flintknapper—has learned and mastered many of the techniques the ancient Indians used to make stone tools. But little was known of the techniques used to make bone tools, since the use of bone tools was relatively rare in prehistoric times and remains so in modern times. (This may be because a much greater degree of skill and knowledge is required to make bone tools; stone is harder, but easier to fashion than bone.)

Dr. Bonnichsen's work showed that the discoloration and mineralization on the notches etched on the flesher matched that of the rest of the bone. He proved that the exquisite flesher had been fashioned while the bone was still green. Bonnichsen was also able to show that the distinctive fracture patterns on the other ancient bones at the Old Crow site alleged to be artifacts were not the result of natural causes. It was man who had modified these bones. Bonnichsen proved this by producing distinctively similar fracture patterns by various methods of striking fresh, or "green," bone obtained from recently butchered steers

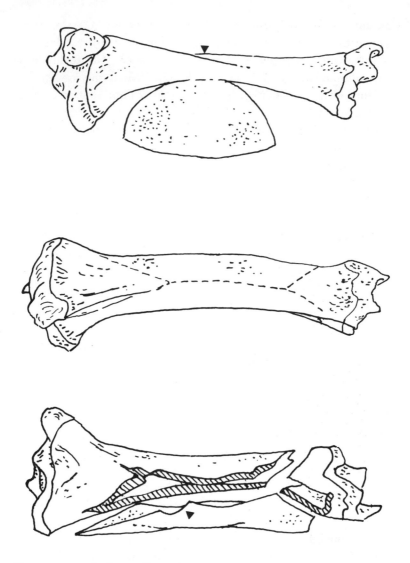

How man cracked open bison bones to get at the tasty marrow inside. Controlled tests show that bones split this way have characteristic spiral fractures. Bones with such spiral fractures have recently been found at the Old Crow site in the Yukon, and they now provide evidence for man's presence in North America during interglacial times, at least 70,000 years ago.

and horses. From his experiments, Bonnichsen was able to recognize in the Old Crow collection a category of boneworking new to archaeology: the use of bone cores and flakes. He showed that mammoth bones with their massive walls had been flaked to produce sharp-edged tools just like stones. These massive bones produced conchoidal flakes similar to those struck from chert or other glasslike stones.

Bonnichsen was able to identify approximately one hundred other bones from the same period which were shaped by grinding and cutting with stone tools. Many of these showed signs of long use from the polish on their working edges. These artifacts, like the flesher, were evenly discolored and mineralized and thus were made and used while still green.

Besides those fashioned into tools, many of the large animal bones found at Old Crow were split open for the tasty marrow inside. The question was, who did the splitting, man, or animal carnivores such as the long-gone dire wolf, who stood six feet high at the shoulder? These split bones had distinct "spiral fractures," where the fracture surfaces formed a spiral around the central long axis of the bone.

Bonnichsen experimented with such features. His work showed that green bone fractures spirally from blows delivered to the bone shaft if the bone is placed on an anvil, or on supports beneath the ends of the bone. These blows usually produce small telltale flakes of bone, which are driven into the center of the shaft at the point of impact. Bonnichsen found clear evidence for these driven flakes on some of the spirally fractured Old Crow bones. Bonnichsen believes that man not only split these bones open for their marrow, but then went on to use some of these spirally-fractured bones for tools, without any further modification. For example, one spirally-fractured bison leg bone exhibits extensive polish and bevelling on its end.

Finally, he discovered that old, already-mineralized bone will not fracture in spiral patterns as fresh bone does. This, along with their even staining and mineralization, proves that the Old Crow bones could not have been fractured by modern Indians; the Old

Crow bones had to be fractured while they were still fresh, approximately 25,000 to 29,000 years ago.[19]

In 1975, as a result of the initial discoveries and Bonnichsen's findings, the Yukon Research Programme was organized to study all phases of human prehistory in the Old Crow region. Since then, over one hundred additional artifacts made of mammoth, bison, and horse bones have been identified, as well as hundreds of bone specimens which were broken by spiral fractures prior to mineralization. These artifacts included a bone awl used for punching holes in hides for clothing and three wedgelike tools made of antlers, similar to those used by northwestern Indians in recent times to split wood. (This is a technique that would be hard to improve upon, as any honest chainsaw owner will testify.)

In 1977, ancient bones that had been fractured while still fresh, including one fashioned into a scraper, were found midway down a high river cliff below a layer of peat dated to 35,000 years ago. Also in 1977, ages beyond the limits of the radiocarbon method were confirmed for two worked bones from a suspected Sangamon interglacial geological context (see chart, page 142), which means that Old Crow man could be as much as 70,000 to 170,000 years old.[20]

The Old Crow sites represent a culture of ancient Indians who used a unique bone tool industry instead of stone tools. In fact, suitable material for making stone tools is very scarce in the Old Crow basin, and it would have been almost impossible to find most of the year when the ground was covered with ice and snow; the use of bone tools there makes a great deal of sense.

The case for these ancients' having been eminently sensible men goes further. Chemical analysis of the bones indicates that they lay in a wet, unfrozen environment for some time. Old Crow man killed and dismembered many of the animals he hunted on the ice of ponds and lakes. When the ice thawed, the bones sank to the bottom and lay among the sediments until recent erosional processes and newly diligent archaeologists began to reexpose them. Now it appears that the ancient Old Crow people, after having killed a tasty varmint on a frozen pond, very efficiently employed the animal's own bones to complete its butchering. "We think of recycling as a modern answer to new problems," says Dr. Morlan, "but these people may have invented the process by butchering their game with the very bones obtained from the carcasses."[21]

The Old Crow people lived in and adapted to one of the most challenging of environments. Considering the great technical skill and knowledge required to meet this challenge, it would be a great mistake to call these very early Indians "primitive." At Old Crow, we get sophisticated bone working at a date (35,000 years old) at least as old as it is found in Europe and Asia. If the most recent find is confirmed by other dating techniques to be interglacial as suspected, then Old Crow gives us bone working at a date (70,000–170,000) more than twice as old as has been found in the Old World.

Tlapacoya (Site #17)

In the late 1960s, two striking, significant radiocarbon dates were obtained from hearths on an ancient beach of Lake Chalco near Mexico City. One hearth dated to 24,000 years ago and the other to 22,000 years ago. Near each of the hearths lay piles of extinct-animal bones and stone and bone tools. Among the artifacts was a long, thin obsidian flake, called a blade, and one obsidian projectile point.[22]

Scripps Campus (Site #18)

The Scripps Campus site at La Jolla is one of a collection of California sites that have profound significance. Among other remarkable points, these sites indicate that the world's first use of grinding stones, a basic and essential step toward civilization, occurred in North America.

The earliest generally accepted date for European grinding tools is 15,000 years ago.[23] Since grinding tools didn't appear until relatively late in European archaeology, scholars concluded that they also were late in the Americas. American archaeologists generally believe that ground stone didn't appear in the New World until 9,000 or 10,000 years ago, but in 1955, George Carter (the man behind Bada's datings), digging at the Scripps Campus site, found a mano, or handstone, in a deposit radiocarbon-dated to 22,000 years ago.[24] This was thought to be an anomaly, but support now comes from the nearby sites which yielded the over-40,000-year-old Del Mar and La Jolla skulls. The original Del Mar site report notes that a sandstone metate was also found on location. The metate came from a position in the sea cliff not too far above, or younger than the skull. And Dr. Gail Kennedy, who undertook the re-excavation of the La Jolla skull site, reported finding a grinding stone dated to 20,000 years ago.[25]

These early datings for American ground stone are reinforced and pushed even further back by several sites which now also become believable as a result of the Del Mar and La Jolla skulls' datings and the Santa Rosa dating. In 1929, D. B. Rogers of the Santa Barbara Museum of Natural History found manos and metates on a raised Pleistocene beach at Santa Barbara. And at Crown Point, six miles to the south of San Diego, engineers also found manos and metates on a raised beach. Based on the absolute dating of similar raised beaches, geologists believe that both of these beach terraces are interglacial; they consider the Santa Barbara beach to be approximately 100,000 years in age and the Crown Point beach approximately 80,000 years old.[26] With the Santa Barbara and Crown Point sites, we get technologically advanced grinding tools in North America over *five times* earlier than in the Old World.

Meadowcroft Rockshelter (Site #24)

Over the last few years (1973 to the present), archaeologists from the University of Pittsburgh, the University of Texas, the Smithsonian Institution, and the Carnegie Museum have joined together to excavate an ancient rockshelter in southwest Pennsylvania, overlooking the Ohio River Valley. As they meticulously peeled back successive layers of earth, they encountered a veritable treasure trove of Indian artifacts. A radiocarbon date of 15,000 years was obtained on charcoal from a firepit from one of the deeper levels. Over four hundred stone items (tools and toolmaking debris) have been recovered from this level. Advanced manufacturing techniques were clearly in use; the assemblage featured long slender "bladelike" items similar to those found at European Cro-Magnon sites. There were also projectile points. And from a slightly deeper level came a radiocarbon date of 20,000 years ago for what is believed to be a basketry fragment. This would be the earliest dated evidence for the making of baskets anywhere in the world. Hackberry seeds were found at the site and the use of hackberry seeds for fruit and grinding for flour and the making of baskets (to collect the harvest efficiently) certainly seem to go hand in hand.[27]

Alice Boer (Site #27)

A steaming jungle seems an unlikely place for Paleo-Indians, but in 1974, archaeologists discovered evidence for their presence at the Alice Boer site at Rio Claro in east-central Brazil. The stone tools found included unique projectile points and blades. A radiocarbon date for the middle occupation levels at the site came to 14,200 years, and Dr. Ruth Gruhn, an archaeologist from the University of Alberta who worked at the site, believes that the earliest occupation level at the site is approximately 20,000 years in age.[28]

To reconfirm the Paleo-Indians' presence in the jungles of Brazil, Dr. Eurico Miller of the Archaeological Museum of the state of Rio Grande Do Sol has been excavating a cave site on the southern boundary of the Amazon Basin. The site is called Abrigo do Sol, or Shelter of the Sun, and shows that sun-worshipping Paleo-Indians lived there at least 12,000 years ago. Chopper and scraper tools and grinding stones have been found at the site.

There are also numerous rock carvings which document the sun worship. For the present, no one knows if these petroglyphs are meaningless graffiti or true symbology waiting to be deciphered. The carvings on the wall and roof of the shelter bring to mind the highly decorated caves of Cro-Magnon man in Europe. Besides depictions of the sun, there are dancing animals, female symbols, and stylized faces which may be images of masks worn by tribal witch doctors.[29]

From this review of key sites—even though it is *not* exhaustive —it can be seen that the evidence for the earliest Paleo-Indian presence lies deeply buried, usually fifteen to sixty feet below the surface. Archaeologists can rarely afford extensive explorations at this depth, and have only recently begun to consider them worthwhile. It is impossible to say how much evidence lies still undiscovered; more than likely, we have only scratched the surface of the truths to be uncovered at these levels. From the recently discovered and dated evidence, it can be seen that modern man walked this continent at least 70,000 years ago, 35,000 years before he "officially" appeared in the Old World. Surprisingly, the earliest of these ancient American sites come not from the far north, as would be expected if a Bering entry route was used at whatever date, but from the south. The coasts and valleys of southern California seem to have been a focal point for very early dates. The fantastically early (interglacial) dates theorized for both bone tools and grinding tools in North America make for a consistent pattern given the very early dates for *Homo sapiens sapiens* in California. In prehistoric Europe, bone tools and grinding tools go hand in hand, both characterizing the presence of fully modern man. Actually, the simultaneous development of these advanced technologies is only to be expected, since many of the same techniques are used to manufacture both—abrasion, shaving, and polishing. These techniques require more imagination and dexterity than the percussion flaking techniques used to make chopper tools, flakes, and scrapers.

The widespread geographic distribution of other ancient sites —in the Yukon, California, Texas, Mexico, and Ecuador—shows that by 30,000 years ago modern man was already well established in the New World. In fact, by 30,000 years ago, it appears that New World *Homo sapiens sapiens* boasted greater cultural and technical range and more diverse interests than his European counterpart. Despite the lack of ideal conditions for preservation as is provided by caves, such as those in southern France, much more skeletal evidence for fully modern man at this early date now comes from the New World than from the Old World.* (This may be a comment on differences in relative population sizes between the Old World and the New World at this time.) While some Paleo-Indians lived in caves, discoveries to date indicate that for the most part they preferred more open territory, and were able to cope with its attendant hazards by building simple structures made of skins, wood, and bones to protect them from the elements.

By 40,000 years ago, New World man was already knowledgeable in all the basic technologies needed to exploit any environment he chose to live in; these same technologies do not appear in Europe until thousands of years later (between 25,000 and 10,000 years ago, depending on the particular technology). By 30,000 years ago, the first Americans had mastered sophisticated projectile points, grinding tools, bone tools, and possibly basketry. The projectile points made the Paleo-Indians deadlier hunters, the grinding tools gave them unlimited food supplies, and the skill of making bone tools gave them access to living areas poor in workable stone tool materials. And while their tools might be considered primitive, bone fleshers and antler wedges are still in use today because they do a better job than readily available steel.

By 30,000 years ago, a number of different economic lifestyles were practiced and the Paleo-Indians were able to live in several climates and terrains—islands, seacoasts, inland lakeshores, deserts, the icy north, the plains, the mountains, and the jungle. While elephants and other big game were often on the menu, so

---

* This in spite of European archaeologists having looked harder for their ancestors than we for ours.

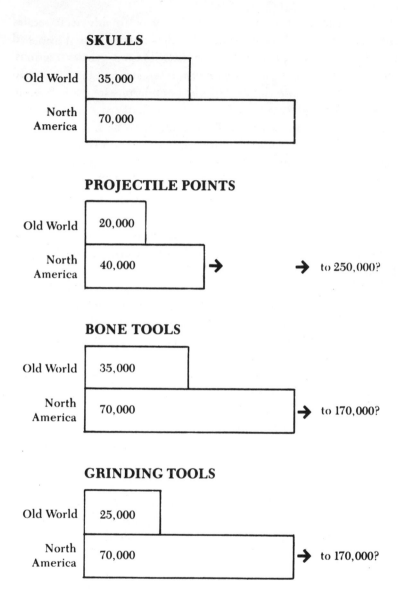

Comparative dates for the appearance of fully modern man and his advanced tool technologies in the Old World and in North America (dates in years ago).

was small game such as duck, prairie dog, and rabbit. There was fishing, and time was taken to gather the bounty of land and shoreline: shellfish, mussels, snails, nuts, seeds, and wild greens. Some of the seeds were ground into meal, and some were stored for a rainy day. Leather clothing was tailored and baskets were woven. These cultures did *not* need to exist from day to day, hand to mouth. Instead, it seems that relatively little time sufficed to meet life's basic needs. This perception of the citizens of the prehistoric world, particularly those living in resource-rich environments, is supported by contemporary studies of South African Bushmen, and of the Tasaday, a recently-discovered "lost tribe" culture living in the Philippine jungles.

There was time for group activities, burying the dead, making carvings on stone (Malakoff) and bone (Tequixquiac), for developing ideological beliefs and religious ceremonies. We get the picture of a knowledgeable people seeking a deeper understanding of the world they confidently inhabited. A model closer to Indian myth begins to take shape, putting to shame archaeology's traditional concept of "poor primitives."

But is this mere speculation? How much can we safely infer from these sites about the activities of these first Indians? How much must we imagine? Our sample of hard evidence comes from a collection of sites which are predominantly "kill" sites instead of "living" or camp sites. Aside from the burials and carvings, there is a heavy emphasis on the big game animals they hunted and the weapons they used, while there is little hard information about their other activities and possessions. A key factor in this sample bias is that the massive bones of these prehistoric animals are relatively hard to overlook. They serve as flags for discovery, while campsites are much harder to find.*

But we can get a glimpse at some of their other activities by looking at one complete campsite, the Lindenmeier site in northern Colorado. Even though the Lindenmeier site is only 11,000

---

* Also, the stones of weaponry and the bones of its victims are infinitely more durable than the materials of the gentler arts of living, which return to the soil in far less than the 30,000 to 70,000 years in question here.

years old, it seems reasonable to project back in time what we have learned from it, as was done with the Gorden Creek burial site, considering the many artifactual ties that connect Lindenmeier with the 30,000-year-old sites. Support for this projection also comes from the recent recognition of the longevity of the La Jollan culture.

At Lindenmeier, Paleo-Indians camped by a pond. There was a long and continuous occupancy, indicated by the presence of both Clovis and Folsom points seventeen feet below the ground surface. Along with these sophisticated projectile points, there were chopper and scraper tools like those from Lewisville and Santa Rosa. Even the "workshop" debris from the places where these tools were made has been found. A number of grinding stones prove that these Indians dined on more than the mammoth, bison, camel, and deer whose remains were found in large piles. The "hammerstones" found at Lindenmeier may have been used to split open these bones for their succulent marrow. Also, as at Old Crow, there were carved bone tools including awls, fleshers, and distinctive spatula-shaped items.

This sampling was probably not fully representative due to disintegration of bone materials. Nevertheless, it is clear that the inhabitants of Lindenmeier were both big game hunters and food gatherers. One can easily imagine the division of labor between male and female. Most likely the females gathered and ground foods while the men hunted and made tools. The range of craftsmanship in tool quality already indicates that there were specialists among them.

The Lindenmeier habitation site has also yielded other types of artifacts, more perishable than those recovered from the earliest sites. There were eyed needles proving they sewed clothes. There was a red hematite bead ornamented with a simple carved design and a smaller undecorated bead of black lignite. This concern for decoration was also shown in such finds as tubular bone beads; several smoothed stones stained with red pigment, thought to be paint palettes; and many pieces of hematite, the source of the red pigment. This red pigment could have been combined with water to make a red paint and applied to hides, or used in its powdery form as facial makeup. Similar evidence for painting comes from the Lind Coolee site in Washington (9,000 years old)—and recall the red ocher-stained burial from Gordon Creek (9,700 years old).

Among the most important of finds at Lindenmeier were three bone disks incised with small lines around their edges. Since these disks were not perforated, it is unlikely that they could have been worn as ornaments; Marie Wormington speculates that they may "represent markers or counters used in some type of game." These disks may have even had some religious significance as similar pieces do to modern day Tasmanians. The Malakoff heads seem to fit here. These last items bring to mind the sense of art, beauty, and shamanistic ritual that characterized Europe's first modern men, the Cro-Magnon, documented and preserved in their magnificent cave paintings, and still found in modern American Indian traditions. A priest adorned with a buffalo headdress and cape is a frequent theme in both traditions.

The great number and the great diversity of American sites at truly early dates calls for entirely new theories to explain Indian origins and to explain how the Paleo-Indians obtained their knowledge of projectile points, bone tools, grinding tools, and basketry well before their European brothers. With Del Mar, La Jolla, and Sunnyvale man dating from 50,000 to 70,000 years ago, we must also ask how this relates to the first appearance of *Homo sapiens sapiens*, fully modern man, anywhere in the world. Was modern man's world debut the result of slow development or the result of a quantum leap inspired from some outside source? Who is to take credit for the technological inventions that let man conquer the environment? These questions are critical because there are now sites which indicate modern man's presence in the Americas over 250,000 years ago! The history of the fully modern branch of the human race must now be rewritten.

7

The Tables Are Turned:
Migration in Reverse—
Indian Settlers in
Paleolithic Europe and Asia

Instead of assuming that the Indians came from the Old
World, he [a European freethinker] could have decided
that they represented the primitive human race from which
he himself was descended.

—C. W. Ceram,
The First American,
1972

Skeletal remains make it quite clear that fully evolved man had
made himself at home in the New World at least 70,000 years
ago—thousands of years before his earliest appearance in the Old
World. As early as 40,000 years ago, he was using the tools and
techniques characteristic of *Homo sapiens sapiens* (projectile
points, bone tools, grinding stones, basketry), while in Europe at
that time, his distant cousin *Homo neanderthalensis* used only
crudely fashioned stones.

Based on the evidence now coming to light, I believe that there
was migration in reverse. Instead of nomadic hunters coming
from the Old World to populate the New World, I believe that
Paleo-Indians from the New World, the first fully modern men
anywhere in the world, traveled to the Old World and woke it
from its sound evolutionary sleep. If the Bering Bridge marked

the route, then the path of migration was from North America to Siberia, Asia, and then Europe.

One of the great moments in mankind's history, celebrated and commemorated in book after book, is the first appearance of modern man (called Cro-Magnon man) in Europe. Cave-dwelling, cave-painting Cro-Magnon man's sudden appearance in Europe is generally considered the first appearance of modern man on a world-wide basis with the possible exception of a slightly earlier debut in the Middle East.* But where did these "invading" Cro-Magnon men come from?

Before Cro-Magnon man appeared 35,000 years ago, Europe was populated by the Neanderthals, low-foreheaded fellows with limited imagination, who represented an evolutionary and cultural dead end. Compared to what was going on in the New World at this time, Europe was a cultural backwater. But with the influx of the biologically fully modern, high-foreheaded Cro-Magnons, the Neanderthals were displaced "overnight" and Europe made a quantum leap forward biologically and culturally.

I believe that the Cro-Magnon men came from the New World, where they had already been living for over 40,000 years, and represent a specific example of the migration in reverse I call for. Similarities in physical appearance, tool types, and the shaman-based religions of both the Paleo-Indians and Cro-Magnon man, noted by a number of researchers, testify to this specific connection. For decades, these undeniable links were regarded only as anomalous curiosities. But now, with earlier datings for the Paleo-Indians in the New World, we can finally see how these links point to the great debt all the peoples and races of the world owe to the American Indian.

---

* Some researchers (such as Dr. Arthur Jelinek of the University of Arizona) believe that modern man appeared in the Middle East a few thousand years earlier than he appeared in Europe. This belief is mainly based on the fact that the earliest widely accepted modern skull from the Old World comes from the site of Skhūl on Mt. Carmel in Israel. The Skhūl skull has been radiocarbon dated to 38,000 years, while the earliest fully modern skull from Europe has only been dated to 35,000 years. But some anthropologists are quick to point out that the Skhūl skull still has some primitive features.

Early on, it was assumed that since no ancestors to modern man were found in the Americas, the Americas had not been involved in the evolution and appearance of modern man and that the Paleo-Indians were externally derived. The remains of ancient pre-men such as *Homo erectus* and the Neanderthals were widely found in Africa, Europe, and Asia, so it was assumed that man had first reached modern biological status in the Old World and eventually migrated to the Americas.

The most generally accepted story of human evolution begins with the Australopithecines, the first clearly to split away from the family tree common to both man and ape. They lived in East and South Africa upward of nine million years ago. It took twenty years (1939-1959) of painstaking work at Olduvai Gorge in East Kenya for Louis Leakey to uncover the remains of "Zinjanthropus," a large variety of Australopithecine. Documenting the existence of this previously unsuspected ancestor was a startling breakthrough. Today there are approximately sixteen known Australopithecine sites.

The Australopithecines were relatively small, weighing just fifty pounds and standing approximately four feet tall; they never mastered a fully upright walk. Their skulls were much cruder, thicker, and smaller than modern man's (approximately 450 cubic centimeters in cranial capacity versus modern man's 1,400 cubic centimeters) and only slightly larger than that of a present-day chimpanzee. They roamed the grassy savannahs of Africa scavenging and preying upon the less formidable animals that teemed all about them. It is not clear whether they had crude stone tools.

Then, approximately 3,000,000 years ago, again in Africa, *Homo habilis* (handy man), the first unquestioned ancestor on man's lineage, appeared. Again, it was Louis Leakey who first discovered this type, in the 1960s, and argued for its unique evolutionary position. Scholars turned a deaf ear to Leakey's arguments, but in 1972, shortly before Louis' death, his son Richard found "Skull 1470," another *habilis*, which proved Leakey right in holding that *Homo habilis* was a valid type. This set in motion a second Leakey-inspired land rush of anthropologists and archaeologists to Africa, resulting in many new discoveries which served to fill in the gaps and to reconfirm Leakey's pioneering discoveries.

Homo habilis was five feet tall and had a much larger skull and brain case (800 cubic centimeters) than Australopithecus. *Habilis* did not have the long, sharp canine teeth characteristic of the apes. There is no question that *habilis* had crudely-fashioned stone tools to aid in his survival. The prominent bony ridges above the eyes, called brow ridges, which anchored the Australopithecines' powerful chewing muscles, were greatly diminished in size, and the general shape of *habilis*'s skull bore a great resemblance to modern man's. In fact, *Homo habilis*'s skull shape was more modern in shape than that of his successor *Homo erectus*.

Homo erectus appeared approximately 1,000,000 years ago. As a result of the skin clothing he learned to make and his discovery of fire, *Homo erectus* was able to move out of his warm African cradle into the colder climates of the world. The remains of *Homo erectus*, sometimes called Pithecanthropines, have been found in Africa, Asia, and even in then-glaciated Europe. There are less than a dozen known sites. Well-known examples are Java Man from Indonesia and Peking Man from Choukoutien in China. Hand axes characterized his tool kit in Europe, and he hunted big game such as mammoths and rhino. *Homo erectus* stood fully upright on a sturdy muscular five-foot frame. His skull was very rugged, with heavy brow ridges. He had no real forehead, and what he did have sloped steeply. *Homo erectus*'s brain size averaged two-thirds (1,000 cubic centimeters) that of modern man. But the walls of *Homo erectus*'s skull were inexplicably thick compared to the thin skull walls of earlier *Homo habilis* and of later fully modern man.

After a long period of time, it is speculated that environmental demands led *Homo erectus* to a higher stage of development, which resulted in the appearance of the Neanderthals (*Homo sapiens neanderthalensis* or *Homo neanderthalensis*) approxi-

Australopithecus

Homo Erectus

Neanderthal

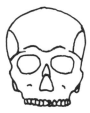

Homo Sapiens

Comparison of skull shapes between modern man and his predecessors.

mately 100,000 years ago. The Neanderthals resembled *Homo erectus* with an enlarged brain case. The Neanderthal skull was thick and rugged with brow ridges (now continuous and arched), a sloping forehead, and large teeth. But the Neanderthal skull was less harsh in general appearance than *Homo erectus*'s and much closer to modern man's. But unlike modern man, the Neanderthal skull vault was still very long and low, and the back part of the skull (occiput) often bulged out in a characteristic bun shape. And as in all pre-modern forms of man, there was still no chin.*

Although their brain size was the same as modern man's, the Neanderthals had many conceptual limitations. The Neanderthal tool kit is still simple: There are no bone tools or ground stone, and there is no art. Most important, the Neanderthals didn't have

---

* Studies which have proposed that the face of Neanderthal was adapted to cold have long gone by the wayside, as have studies which said that the form of the nose was related to climate, where a large projecting narrow nose was supposed to warm the air that comes into the face in cold climates. It seems that many of the facial changes associated with *Homo sapiens sapiens* have no adaptive basis at all, and have a purely aesthetic quality to them. This aesthetic quality is enhanced by the sixteen muscles of expression on each side of modern man's face.

speech and language. This has been confirmed by anatomical studies of the vocal areas of both the Neanderthals and *Homo erectus*. The vast behavioral differences between modern man and Neanderthal man come from the reorganization of the brain. Our high forehead shows that the frontal portion of the brain has been greatly expanded compared to the constricted frontal of Neanderthal and *Homo erectus* brains. The frontal lobe of the brain controls motor skills such as manual dexterity and speech.*

Over forty Neanderthal sites have been discovered, yielding skeletal material from over two hundred individuals. These sites are found from Africa to the Near East and the Far East, but chilly Europe was the Neanderthal's favorite haunt. "One of the surprising aspects of the classic Neanderthal population," says Dr. J. B. Birdsell of UCLA, one of the world's leading physical anthropologists, "is the very low range of variation shown. If you have seen one male skull, so to speak, you have seen them all."[1]

In his theory of evolution, Darwin said that natural selection "can act only by taking advantage of slight successive variations; she can never take a leap, but must advance by the shortest and slowest steps." Thus, due to the Neanderthal's crudeness immediately before the appearance of *Homo sapiens sapiens* in Europe and the Near East, most scientists reject the idea of his having evolved into modern man. The Neanderthals are considered an evolutionary deadend. Instead, another as yet undiscovered branch of *Homo erectus* is believed to have evolved into *Homo sapiens sapiens* approximately 35,000 years ago.

The archaeological evidence linking *Homo erectus* to *Homo sapiens sapiens* is admittedly slight; most scholars believe that *Homo erectus* made this crucial evolutionary transformation to *Homo sapiens sapiens* just once. That is, instead of *Homo erectus* being transformed into *Homo sapiens sapiens* in each of the areas that he inhabited (Europe, Africa, and Asia), this genetic leap probably occurred only in one area, the resulting *Homo sapiens*

---

* Part of the frontal lobe is also associated with drive inhibition, and damage to the human frontal region often produces profound changes in mood and personality.

sapiens then traveling and replacing *Homo erectus* in the other areas ("replacement radiation"). Some scholars, such as F. Clark Howell of the University of California at Berkeley and Bernard Vandermeersch of the University of Paris, believe that *Homo sapiens sapiens* may have appeared in the Mid-East a few thousand years before he migrated into Europe and sent the Neanderthals packing.[2]

In spite of the ideal conditions of preservation in the caves of Europe and the Near East, which have given us a rich horde of ancient skeletal material, no one knows where the Neanderthals disappeared to, nor where the Cro-Magnons came from. There is no trace of Cro-Magnon man before his appearance in the Middle East. The generally accepted story of human evolution falls silent at its crucial moment, the birth of fully modern man.

Many scholars find it hard to see how crude *Homo erectus* could have made the transition directly. Skull-wall thickness is genetically controlled and it would be hard to explain what set of genetic tricks gave *Homo erectus* his thick skull walls, while those of his predecessor (*Homo habilis*) and his successor (*Homo sapiens sapiens*) were thin. This pattern of successive turnabouts stands in direct opposition to the slow and continuous developmental processes Darwin spoke of. Dr. Birdsell says that "It is very difficult to visualize how any of the known forms of *Homo erectus* could have evolved into the grade of *Homo sapiens* during the Middle Pleistocene and later periods. . . . nowhere can it be demonstrated that men of the *Homo erectus* grade did evolve into modern populations . . . modern populations [are] the results of massive replacement radiation."[3] Birdsell, however, like others, is at a loss to suggest where the replacing population may have come from.

Prehistoric France was one of Cro-Magnon man's strongholds, and the cave paintings at Les Eyzies are world-famous. The prevailing view in France today shows even more dissatisfaction with the generally accepted evolutionary picture. French physical anthropologists reject the Neanderthals not only as ancestor to modern man but also as descendant of *Homo erectus*. The French reject as an ancestor to modern man any fossil that differs in form from modern man. They point to some as yet undiscovered "Presapiens" as modern man's direct ancestor, but they do not indicate where this missing link may be found.

Louis Leakey rejected both *Homo erectus* and the Neanderthals as man's direct ancestors. The only known form he accepted for man's family tree was *Homo habilis*, the form seemingly more advanced than its supposed successor *Homo erectus*. Provocatively, he claimed the oddly prematurely-sophisticated blade tools found at Tabun in Israel, a Neanderthal site dating to over 70,000 years ago, as evidence of a visit by already existing fully modern men. Unfortunately, Leakey never said whether or not he derived these "too early" *Homo sapiens sapiens* from the New World, where he believed man had existed for over 500,000 years based on his excavations at Calico Hills, California (see pages 130–40).

While scientists have been at a loss to explain this missing parentage—i.e., where the first *Homo sapiens sapiens* population came from—a valuable tip has come from Francois Bordes of the University of Bordeaux, one of the world's foremost prehistorians. Bordes, referring to human evolution, said that "If someday traces of man dated at more than 100,000 B.C. are found in America, it will be a different matter."[4] I believe Bordes' criteria are fulfilled, that there is ample direct evidence for man in America at more than 100,000 years ago. Recent discoveries in America have opened up new possibilities about the origins of modern man. Dr. Alan Bryan acknowledged this when he stated that biological evolution probably occurred in America. Bryan feels such evolution is necessary to explain "the highly diverse populations of modern American Indians."

Instead of direct biological evolution from some as yet unidentified primitive ancestor, I think the extreme physical variations characterizing modern American Indian groups can be explained by their having been fully modern at least three times as long as Europeans and thus having a longer period of time to develop variations, and also by recent traffic in the Bering Bridge area resulting in interbreeding.

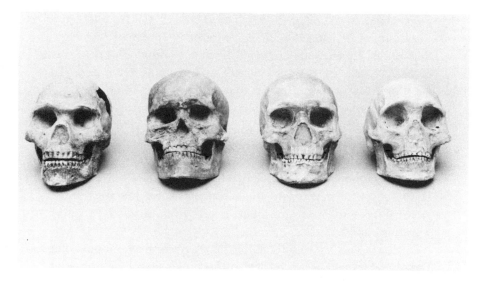

A comparison of replicas of fully modern skulls. *Left to right:* Skhūl V
from Mount Carmel, Israel (35,000 years?); Cro-Magnon from Les
Eyzies, France (30,000); Upper Cave, Choukoutien from Choukoutien near Peking, China (18,000 years); and Shoshone Indian (recent)
from Nevada.

If you recall, the Sunnyvale site (see chart, page 142) was dated
to 70,000 years ago, a new find at Old Crow was interglacial, and
grinding tools were found on interglacial beach terraces at Santa
Barbara and Crown Point, San Diego. These three interglacial
sites could be anywhere from 70,000 to 170,000 years in age.
Other sites at Calico Hills, California; Hueyatlaco and El Horno,
Mexico; Flagstaff, Arizona; Mission Valley, San Diego; Texas
Street, San Diego; and El Bosque, Nicaragua, press harder for the
revision of models for the origins of modern man. The inspiration
for the discovery of these truly early, early sites came from Louis
Leakey when in 1970 he stood virtually alone in suggesting that
there was an ancient prehistoric bounty to be found in the Amer-
icas. Leakey so deeply believed in man's long sojourn in the
Americas that, in conduct quite unbecoming a scientist, he made

a bet about it. In 1965, Leakey bet Dr. Emil W. Haury of the University of Arizona, one of the deans of American archaeology, that within fifteen years he would be able to prove that man was in North America between 50,000 and 100,000 years ago. To most archaeologists, Leakey's ideas about the Americas were heresy, completely unthinkable, but this was the same way archaeologists and anthropologists had once greeted Leakey's ideas about African prehistory—ideas which later proved to be entirely accurate. Now that the fifteen years are nearly up, Leakey's judgment is being vindicated once more—but the story of the years he devoted to the effort illustrates the frustration, political maneuvering, and time delay often needed to effect scientific change.

In 1963, still in the thick of his African explorations, Dr. Leakey was spending a semester at the University of California at Riverside as a visiting professor when Miss Ruth deEtte Simpson, who worked at the San Bernardino County Museum, paid him a visit. She showed him some very primitive artifacts she'd recovered from the Mojave Desert near Barstow, east of the Calico Mountains, artifacts which she believed to be considerably more ancient than her colleagues were willing to consider. Intrigued, Leakey agreed to have a look at the site.

In Pleistocene times, there had been a lake at the foot of the Calico Hills, and built up large, overlapping mud deposits which are now known as the Yermo Fan. Visiting the site area with Miss Simpson, Leakey liked what he saw. He strode rapidly about the area, musing aloud: "Out in front . . . ideal." Ideal, he meant, as a setting for habitation by ancient man.

The ancient lake had provided not only abundant game and plant life, but also suitable material for tool-making in the form of chalcedony, a chertlike rock. Leakey was certain that hard evidence of man's presence was to be found in the immediate vicinity, but he did not like Miss Simpson's original location, where, he felt, the artifacts could have been moved about and redeposited out of their true context by natural forces. He quickly

Louis Leakey and Dee Simpson twenty feet below the surface at Calico Hills, California, excavations. The date for man at the site may reach back as far as 500,000 years ago. *John Kettl, San Bernardino County Museum*

located a more likely area on the fan, drove some pegs into the ground, and announced to an astonished Miss Simpson, "This is where we're going to dig."

With his usual enthusiasm, Leakey inspired the National Geographic Society, who had funded much of his African work, and they gave him money to begin excavations immediately. In November 1964, Ruth Simpson and a crew, mostly from the Archaeological Survey Association of Southern California, began the digging. They dug down three inches at a time, using small hand tools such as mason's trowels, dental picks, shoemaker's awls, and whisk brooms. The original position of each possible artifact was carefully plotted, photographed, and witnessed by at least three people before it could be removed. The "good" specimens were kept aside for Leakey's visits. Only a few met with Leakey's approval as being truly man-made. When the six-to-nine-foot level was reached, "possible artifacts" began to appear in significant numbers. The National Geographic Society then arranged a field conference of experts to decide whether excavations should continue; the answer was "yes, but. . . ." Following the suggestions from this conference, Leakey had three control pits dug to see if comparable finds turned up at random all over the fan. They did not, demonstrating that the location of the main dig had providentially struck a concentration of what Leakey considered to be genuine artifacts which were not present at the other fan locations excavated. This finding was coolly received.

By 1967, the National Geographic Society began to lose interest and Leakey had to raise money elsewhere. The Wenner-Gren Foundation, the Pennsylvania Museum, and various wealthy individuals gave money.

Year after year, Miss Simpson and her faithful crew continued to dig, doing so for a total of six years. During this time a second master pit, forty feet from the first, was opened and both pits were roofed over to afford some protection from the broiling sun and winter snows. A generator was brought in to permit digging at night. In all, they dug one 25-by-25-foot pit to a depth of 20 feet (Master Pit 1), one 15-by-15-foot pit to a depth of 22 feet, one 105-foot-long trench, and one 85-foot-long trench.

In 1968, something really exciting was found, a "feature," a circle of nine medium-sized rocks with smaller ones in between. One of these rocks was cut in half and sent to two separate laboratories (UCLA and the Geophysical Institute of the Czechoslovakian Academy of Sciences) to measure its degree of magnetism in order to determine if it had been subjected to heat. Both labs concurred that the end of the stone which had been pointed toward the center of the "feature" was highly magnetized. In the final analysis, said Dr. Berger of the UCLA lab, "it would appear that in that circular arrangement of stones there must have burned a fire!"[5] In other words, the "feature" was an ancient campfire made by man.

A preliminary report on the excavation at Calico was published in *Science* in 1968, but for the most part prehistorians were not convinced, a situation aggravated by Leakey's calling for an age of at least 50,000 years. One key scientific endorsement came from Professor Clark Howell of the University of California at Berkeley. And in 1969 Dr. Bordes, himself an expert in manufacturing stone tools, visited the site twice and capitulated. Bordes gave his views on tape for the Leakey Foundation's use, carefully distinguishing, according to Leakey's biographer Sonia Cole, "between those specimens which he felt could have been created by nature and those specimens which gave a good indication that man might well have been there at the time of formation of the fan."[6] A few months later at a UNESCO conference on the origins of *Homo sapiens sapiens*, Bordes, who chaired the session, "publicly proclaimed that some of the Calico pieces were artifacts."[7]

Leakey was tremendously popular on the college speaking circuit. He was always greeted with thunderous applause and there never seemed to be enough tickets to go around. In October 1970, Leakey's popularity was professionally affirmed when about a hundred geologists and archaeologists assembled in San Bernardino for a conference to evaluate the results of Simpson's and Leakey's six years of excavation at the Calico site. The gathering was the largest scientific get-together ever to examine the evidence from a single site. One day was spent examining the excavations, one morning listening to papers by Leakey and his staff, and one afternoon scrutinizing over two hundred possible artifacts. The visiting geologists agreed there was no doubt that the site was at least 100,000 years old. Dr. Vance Haynes, then at Southern Methodist University, at a later date said after studying the deposit, "Allowing for the geologic events I have estimated that it [the deposit] is at least 500,000 years old. Most other geologists have reached a similar conclusion."[8] But the extremely ancient dating for the deposit made it more difficult than ever for the visiting archaeologists to accept Leakey's finds as artifacts.

Leakey's case for the artifacts rested on seven main lines of evidence: (1) the anomalous concentrations of flakes found only at certain locations and levels in the fan, especially one concentration that was found near fragments of a mammoth tusk; (2) the selectivity in the material used to make the flakes, the better quality material being consistently used; (3) the presence of flakes of lithic material (jasper and moss agate) that had to be imported into the site; (4) a number of technical arguments concerning the use of several different flake manufacturing techniques; (5) the presence of a nearly spherical stone; (6) the presence of a hearth; and (7) above all, the recovery of several hundred specimens which Leakey accepted as artifacts.

The opposition view, characterized by Dr. Kenneth Oakley of the British Museum of Natural History, argued that the flakes were the products of nature battering stones as they moved downhill, though Jesse Jennings of the University of Utah said that "any one of the flakes . . . would have passed muster as a waste flake in a collection of debitage [flake manufacturing debris]."[9] The flake concentrations and the spherical stone were also considered mere natural accidents, and the selectivity of material was attributed to chalcedony and jasper's inherent fragility. The imported materials were just considered rare local varieties of the plentiful chalcedony. While it was admitted that the magnetic data from the possible hearth were suggestive in the final analysis, the magnetization was attributed to lightning. Though few actually said so out of deference to Leakey's feelings, quite a number of the prehistorians were content to explain away all the data without offering any experimental verification to support their opinions about exactly what nature can and cannot do in the way of flaking.*

---

* Dr. Walter Schuiling, Commissioner of the San Bernardino County Museum and Chairman of the 1970 International Conference at Calico Hills, after reading the first draft of this chapter, wrote me (October 12, 1979)

John Witthoft of the University of Pennsylvania, a specialist in stone technology, had made a study of the materials prior to the conference and concluded that "analysis of the range of lithic material supplies clear-cut evidence for human presence."[10] Witthoft's analysis was based mainly on the distinctive wear marks found along the edges of eighteen specimens, markings from which the trained eye can deduce what type of job the tool performed. But in 1970, edge wear analysis was new to archaeology and few archaeologists were familiar with it, so Witthoft's findings were ignored.

At the end of the conference, most were not impressed with the evidence and only a handful of those who attended were "absolutely convinced" of the existence of Leakey's ancient Americans (one of those convinced was Dr. Robert L. Stephenson, the Director of the Institute of Archaeology and Anthropology at the University of South Carolina). There was also a high proportion of "don't knows"; many felt that more evidence was needed. However, all agreed that the site should be preserved as a model of how prehistoric excavations should be conducted, thanking Leakey for his inspiration for future research.

The site has been preserved, but Leakey never got to do any more work at Calico. Less than a year after the conference, Leakey was stung by several hundred bees in Africa. A less energetic and obstinate man would have been killed, not to mention one who had suffered a severe heart attack only a year earlier. Then came a fall at a conference in San Francisco resulting in a blood clot on his brain. While removing this clot, the surgeon found yet another clot below it. Added to this was a none too successful hip operation, constant headaches, and a series of bladder infections. Still, Leakey subjected himself to the strain of

and noted that some American archaeologists were even openly hostile to Leakey's efforts, apparently for one of the following reasons: "1) a resentment at his getting involved on what they saw as their own "turf", i.e. America; or 2) jealousy growing out of Leakey's ability to get publicity and grant money; or 3) an unwillingness to admit that they had been wrong or premature in making some positive judgments about early man in America in public statements or writings."

the American lecture circuit in an effort to raise money for his far-flung excavations. On October 1, 1972, in London while enroute to America and Calico Hills, Leakey suffered a coronary and died at the age of sixty-nine. It was a great loss for all of prehistory, and the issue of Calico Hills seemed destined to remain unsolved. It appeared that Leakey, the great shatterer of theories, had lost his bet about the age of man in the New World. Even Sonia Cole, a long-time friend who had helped on many of his African digs, wrote Calico off. In her book *Leakey's Luck*, she wrote, "For many colleagues who felt admiration and affection for Louis and his family, the Calico years were an embarrassment and a sadness."[11] In fact, Leakey's wife, Mary, also an excellent archaeologist, didn't accept the Calico materials.

What the Calico collection lacked was one stone tool that was unquestionably man-made—an artifact that no one could dispute. Five years after Leakey's death, Alan Bryan, a professor at the University of Alberta, in Canada, met with Miss Simpson in Vancouver, B.C., and asked to go over the Calico collection she had with her. Bryan searched through not only the "best" pieces which had been shown at the conference, but *all* the chert materials recovered. Bryan's trained eye quickly fixed on one piece that had not been brought out for the conference. One end of a thick chert flake (approximately three inches long and two inches wide) was fashioned into a point! Dozens of tiny flakes had been sequentially removed in one direction from the flake's bulbar surface to form this point, and the entire periphery of the object had also been shaped by flaking. This artifact resembled a graver spur, a characteristic Cro-Magnon tool type used to engrave bone. When this object was later shown to Vance Haynes of the University of Arizona, Calico Hills' severest critic, Haynes quickly agreed that it was a tool. But there was a catch: while Miss Simpson said that this tool was found at thirteen feet in depth in the master pit, Haynes said that it probably "fell into the excavation." Ironic in light of the 1970 conference, when all were commending Leakey for the meticulousness of the Calico excavation.

New evidence for the presence of ancient toolmakers at Calico

A stone tool from Louis Leakey's Calico Hills, California, site. The tool has steep flaking around its edges and a number of flakes have also been removed to shape a point at the end. This tool provides conclusive evidence that man was present at Calico in the distant past. *Daniel J. Griffin, San Bernardino County Museum*

Hills also comes from the detailed edge-wear studies recently begun by Clay Singer, a doctoral student at the University of California at Los Angeles.[12] In 1972, archaeologists at Harvard, adapting a Russian analytical technique, conducted carefully controlled experiments on stone tools. The test tools were used to shave wood, saw on bone, slice meat, and scrape hides. After each few minutes of use, the working edges of the tools were examined under powerful microscopes and changes in the tools' working edges were noted. The scientists identified several characteristic patterns of wear, each related to the type of stroke used and the type of material being worked on.[13] Following up on John Witthoft's ignored study, Singer applied this new sophisticated technique to some of the Calico Hills material and quickly found tool-use wear patterns just like those discovered at Harvard. On pieces of chert and chalcedony which "looked like" engravers, Singer found wear patterns characteristic of tools used on relatively resistant materials such as bone. Pieces of chert which "looked like" piercing and boring tools had distinctive rotational wear patterns, and on what Leakey called scrapers there were the distinctive wear patterns associated with tools used on wood, hides, and fiber. Based on this analytical technique, there is no question in Singer's mind that many of the flakes found at Calico were used as tools. "Given the nature of the raw lithic material," said Singer, "the tools reflect a simple but efficient knapping technology."[14]

Further endorsement for the validity of Calico Hills comes from one of the deans of early-man studies in the New World, Dr. Alex Krieger, a professor of anthropology at the University of Washington. After completing a new, detailed study of the materials, Krieger wrote in a 1978 paper that "at least several hundred objects do reveal consistent patterns of shaping into recognizable tools that can be compared with tools in many other places."[15] And Dr. Philip Tobias, head of the Department of Anatomy at the University of Witwatersrand, Johannesburg, South Africa, said, "I have no hesitation in saying that at least a proportion of pieces . . . show signs of human workmanship."[16]

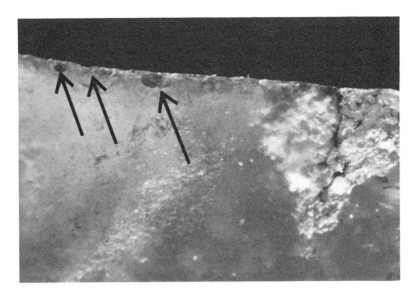

Characteristic alteration of the working edge of a stone tool by use wear. Recently developed techniques for wear study demonstrate that the specimens from Calico Hills, California, and Flagstaff, Arizona, were indeed made by man.

Tobias has been in on many of the major excavations of man's earliest ancestors in Africa and is quite familiar with the signs of toolmaking. In fact, it was reported in the Summer 1979 issue of *The San Bernardino County Museum Quarterly* that on a visit to Calico in November 1974, Tobias's experienced eye caught another key detail that had been missed at the 1970 conference. While examining the so-called questionable hearth, he noticed small pockmarks on the insides of the stones comprising the circle. Such pockmarks result from fire action and prove finally that the stones' magnetic properties came from a campfire instead of a lightning bolt. Excited about this added evidence, the usually conservative Tobias exclaimed, "It is beginning to look more and more as if the late Dr. L. S. B. Leakey was right in claiming that man was present on the American continent from an early period."[17] "It is indeed unfortunate," Alan Bryan wrote in 1978, "that Louis Leakey did not live to see validation of his last great flash of insight."[18]

As Leakey hoped, Calico was only the first of the truly early American archaeological sites dating back to 100,000 years and even earlier. There are now a total of ten additional sites (see chart, pages 95–96) in various stages of confirmation and recognition which indicate that modern man inhabited the Americas long before he appeared anywhere else in the world, supporting the theory of migration in reverse. Besides the Old Crow (ID. H on map and chart), Crown Point, San Diego, and Santa Barbara (ID. G), Sunnyvale (ID. I), and the ten sites greater than 38,000 years in age (ID. K) which were discussed in Chapter 6, there are:

Hueyatlaco and El Horno, Mexico (ID.'s B and C)

From the same Valsequillo basin near Puebla, Mexico, where artifacts had already been dated to 22,000 to 24,000 years in age (Tlapacoya Site #17, discovered in 1966) come dates ten times as old. In 1967, Dr. Cynthia Irwin-Williams, of the Paleo-Indian Institute at Eastern New Mexico University, dug in to deposits almost one hundred feet in depth. At two separate sites, Hueyatlaco and El Horno, she found very sophisticated artifacts in association with extinct fauna such as mammoths. For example, at Hueyatlaco there were leaf-shaped projectile points, wedges and scrapers made on "blades" (long thin flakes with parallel sides), and blade knives. The advent of making stone tools such as scrapers and knives on blades rather than on flakes marks the replacement of Neanderthal man by *Homo sapiens sapiens* in Europe. In the archaeological record to date, blade tools and projectile points are found only with fully modern men possessing an advanced technology. So, while no human bones were found, there was no question that the toolmaker at Hueyatlaco was fully modern. However, although there was consistency in the composition of the tool kit, problems arose when Dr. Williams brought in a team of geological experts to date the two sites. The geological team, working under a grant from the National Science Foundation, consisted of Dr. Harold Malde and Dr. Virginia Steen-McIntyre, both of the U.S. Geological Survey, and the late Dr. Roald Fryxel of Washington State University. After completing their work, which involved several independent dating techniques, this team announced their findings at the 1973 annual meeting of the Geological Society of America and a few months later at the Southwestern Anthropology Association's annual meeting. The problem was that they had dated the materials from Dr. Williams's excavation as being at least 250,000 to 300,000 years old!

"We're confronted with a dilemma," Dr. Fryxel said, "in which we have apparently sound geological data that lead to a head-on confrontation with . . . archaeological data."[19] This confrontation was not so much with archaeological data as it was with established academic beliefs about man's past in the New World and man's origins in general. For those archaeologists who couldn't believe in the 38,000+-year-old Clovis point from Lewisville, the idea of a quarter-million-year-old American projectile point was especially ridiculous. At the time of Williams's original report (1967) on the sites, she had no idea that the forty-one undisputed artifacts could be so incredibly old. In a later report (1969), she registered her shock over the new datings, writing that "These tools surely were not in use at Valsequillo (Hueyatlaco) more than 200,000 years *before* the date generally accepted for the development of analogous tools in the Old World" (emphasis added). And, she added, these tools couldn't have been in use hundreds of thousands of years *before* the appearance of *Homo sapiens sapiens.*[20] But Bada's early dating (1973) of Paleo-Indian skulls was still years away; she did not even consider the possibility that *Homo sapiens sapiens* was much older in the New World than in the Old World.

Since such outrageously old dates were involved, the geologists had gone to great lengths in their dating of these two sites. One team member, Barney Szabo of the U.S. Geological Survey, wrote that the team had recognized that their initial datings "conflicted

SITES IN VARIOUS STAGES OF CONFIRMATION AND RECOGNITION
WHICH CALL FOR THE REVISION OF MODELS FOR THE ORIGIN OF
MODERN MAN

Map ID. (see page 46)	Site and Location	Human Remains (H) or Artifacts (A)	Date (Years Ago)
A	Calico Hills, California	A	500,000(?)
B	Hueyatlaco, Mexico	A	250,000(?)
C	El Horno, Mexico	A	250,000(?)
D	Flagstaff, Arizona	A	100,000–170,000
E	Mission Valley, San Diego, California	A	100,000
F	Texas Street, San Diego, California	A	70,000–170,000
G	1. Crown Point, San Diego, and 2. Santa Barbara Beach Terraces, California	A	70,000–170,000
H	Old Crow (1977 discovery) Yukon, Canada	A	70,000–170,000
I	Sunnyvale, California	H	70,000
J	El Bosque, Nicaragua	A	70,000
K	The ten verified sites greater than 38,000 years in age from the previous chart (pages 95–96	H & A	38,000

with all prior archaeological evidence here and abroad," and quickly prepared to defend their datings "against an onslaught of archaeological thought."[21]

This explains why no less than six dating techniques were eventually used. According to the team, great geological age at Hueyatlaco was indirectly reflected by: (1) the great depth of burial, (2) correlation of the volcanic deposits found at the site with volcanic units of known ages, (3) the high degree of weathering of the minerals in the volcanic deposits, and (4) the amount of water that had accumulated in the closed bubble cavities of the volcanic glass—a measuring process known as

hydration dating (a similar technique has long been used by archaeologists to date obsidian). One member of the team, Dr. McIntyre, was awarded a Ph.D. for her research on this sophisticated technique and it has since been proven to be effective in dating deposits from around the world.

The geological team also obtained direct or absolute dates by:

1. Uranium-isotope decay dating. At Hueyatlaco, a camel pelvis associated with the tools yielded a radiometric-uranium/thorium date of 245,000 years; at El Horno, a tooth fragment from a butchered mastodon yielded a date of at least 280,000 years. As a control, this uranium dating technique was applied to two other deposits from the area and to two early-man sites from Colorado. These four other areas had previously been radiocarbon dated, and their uranium datings yielded results consistent with the radiocarbon datings.
2. Fission tract dating on the Hueyatlaco ash, which produced dates of 170,000 to 570,000 years with the most likely date at 370,000 (not a surprising range for archaeological dating). This is consistent with the uranium series datings.

Almost apologetically, Dr. Fryxel said, "We have no reason to suppose that over decades, actually hundreds of years, of research in archaeology in the Old and New World our understanding of human prehistory is so inaccurate that we suddenly discover that our past understanding is all wrong. . . . On the other hand, the more geological information we've accumulated, the more difficult it is to explain how multiple methods of dating which are independent of each other might be in error by the same magnitude."[22]

Even more unnerving, there are artifacts at Hueyatlaco which must be even more than 250,000 years old, since somewhat less sophisticated artifacts were found in beds underlying those which were dated by the team. A marked geological unconformity, representing a break in deposition, separates the two units; such unconformities usually involve great periods of time and drastic changes in climate. These lower artifacts could be as much as 500,000 years old or even older, bringing to mind the age of the Calico site. But archaeologists can't accept these early dates. They fairly question the stratigraphy and note how the incredibly early dates in the zone in question seem to be out of sequence with the dates of some zones above and below it. The geologists counter that the deposits do not represent a simple sequence of deposition; these river-lain (alluvial) deposits contain many intraformational (dissecting) channels which were subsequently filled in with younger deposits and occasional violent floods have removed huge sections of some deposits. Both circumstances explain why younger deposits are found adjacent to or even below much older deposits at the site.

In 1973, the geological dating team, before making their announcement, returned to the site area and dug several new trenches to illustrate this point, and to prove that the controversial deposits with the extremely early dates did pass beneath the younger deposits; they were successful on both counts. But as most archaeologists are neither conversant with the specialized techniques used to date Hueyatlaco and El Horno nor trained to deal with complex stratigraphic situations, it will take some time before the significance of the team's work will be felt and the dispute as to the true age of the site resolved.

Further, due to lack of funding, the geologists have not been able to return to the site to carry out additional research which they believe would hasten this resolution. Perhaps this is not surprising: even scientific disciplines are not likely to finance their detractors when they can barely drum up enough funds to keep the work of the faithful in progress. Unfortunately, however, professional gamesmanship has extended beyond the financial to the personal level. Several members of the geological dating team have encountered reactions of genuine hostility from archaeologists. Dr. McIntyre, for example, says that a leading archaeologist accused the team of "ruining the career" of Dr. Cynthia Irwin-Williams by connecting her excellent work with such fanciful dates.[23]

Flagstaff, Arizona (ID.D)

For the past several years, I have been excavating a deep shaft and tunnel into ancient deposits on a mountainside near Flagstaff, Arizona, with help from amateurs, graduate students, and professors Alan Bryan and Ruth Gruhn of the University of Alberta. A 25,000-year radiocarbon date was obtained at the fifteen-foot level of the shaft; and based on geological correlation, geologists at the U.S. Geological Survey believe that the twenty-seven-foot level of the shaft is at least 125,000 years in age. Crude stone tools have been found at the deepest levels, indicating man's presence in Flagstaff at least 125,000 years ago. In my work, I encountered resistance similar to that experienced by Leakey at Calico Hills, but in 1979 an engraved stone like those recovered at Cro-Magnon sites in Europe was found by graduate students in a zone believed to be approximately 100,000 years old. Now there is no doubt that modern man was present at the site—in effect, he left his autograph. The stone also indicates that man in the New World had the conceptual ability to engrave things purposefully some 70,000 years earlier than Old World man. (The history of this site and further details of this exciting discovery—which also supports Hopi mythology—will be discussed in Chapter 10.)

El Bosque, Nicaragua (ID.J)

Crudely flaked stones, tools, and hearthlike features were found with the bones of long-extinct mammals at El Bosque, Nicaragua. Jorge Espinosa dug the site in 1975 with the assistance of archaeologists from the University of Toronto and the University of Alberta. Animal bones from the deepest zones did not have enough carbon left in them for radiocarbon dating and thus are at least 40,000 years old. A very highly mineralized camel bone found at the site provoked Dr. Carl Gustafson of Washington State University, an expert in such matters, to guess its age at

150,000 years. In addition to the Canadian archaeologists who dug at the site, Richard MacNeish acknowledges the authenticity of El Bosque, and Alan Bryan gives it a date of 70,000 years in age. The main fossil bed at the site has yet to be excavated and promises many new finds.[24]

Texas Street, San Diego, California (ID. F)

Texas Street is the site Dr. George Carter found over thirty years ago, the site from which he argued that man was in North America during interglacial times, 70,000 to 170,000 years ago (see pages 81–83). At this site, Carter said, he found hearths and crude stone tools. His claims were scoffed at: His supposed tools, said to be the products of nature, were dubbed "Carterfacts." Although Carter's 1930s suspicions about the great age of the Del Mar and La Jolla skulls were proven correct in 1973 by Bada's racemization dating technique, some academics are still laughing at his Texas Street "Carterfacts." While the unusually long and narrow lithic materials from Texas Street looked very tool-like, they lacked "bulbs of percussion." (A bulb of percussion is the characteristic convex bulge appearing on the face of a flake at the point of impact when man strikes a flake from a core rock with a stone hammer. Flakes struck accidentally by natural forces rarely have such a bulb.) Thus, the Texas Street materials were rejected. But over the last few years, archaeologists have come to recognize another human flake-manufacturing technique, "bipolar flaking," which leaves no bulbs of percussion. In this technique, a fist-sized core of lithic material is placed on an anvil and an unusually long flake is detached by striking the core with a hammer. The addition of the third element, the anvil, sets up opposing forces and, depending on the material used, produces flakes without bulbs. This technique was experimented with and carefully described in 1972 by Donald Crabtree of the Idaho State Museum, one of the world's foremost experts on stone tool making.[25]

John Witthoft, virtually the father of lithic technology studies in America, and Alan Bryan have both recognized (in 1978) the "bi-polar" industry in the Texas Street material, thereby vindicating Carter.* Witthoft said that "the Texas Street Industry represents the most expert and sophisticated application of the bipolar technique which I have seen. Geographically, the nearest known occurrence of an industry in bipolar techniques is in the Lower Paleolithic of China, at Choukoutien. Here the quartz tools split from pebbles by Peking Man were amateurish things compared to the slivered cores of Texas Street."[26] The bi-polar flakes of the Texas Street site are more properly called "blades"†; blades of comparable quality, unique to fully modern man, don't appear in Europe until 35,000 years ago.‡

Mission Valley, San Diego, California (ID.E)

Supporting the early presence of man at Texas Street, another site was found just a few miles away in 1977. At the 1978 annual meeting of the Society for American Archaeologists in Tucson, Arizona, Dr. Brian Reeves, professor of archaeology at the University of Calgary, in Canada, reported that he found in Mission Valley human tools which he believes are at least 120,000 years old. Reeves found the simple stone tools—choppers, flakes, and scrapers—during a year-long sabbatical. Reeves was also asked to present his findings to one thousand archaeologists attending the formal program of the Southwestern Anthropological Association.

Reeves, one of the few archaeologists with extensive training in geology, said that proof of the age of the relics rests on a simple framework. Sands found in the valley atop marine terraces, called the Bay Point Formation, are known to be 120,000 years old

---

* Dr. Alex Krieger, professor of anthropology at the University of Washington, and Bryan note that this bi-polar technology is now also recognized at other very early California sites such as Calico Hills, China Lake, Yuha, and Buchanan Canyon. In 1970, H. L. Minshall found the Buchanan Canyon site just a few miles from the Texas Street site; it duplicates all the material at Texas Street, including the blades.

† A blade is a long, thin flake with parallel sides.

‡ In 1977, Bryan found a perfect example of a blade in the Calico Hills collection.[27]

because shells found within the sands have been paleontologically pinpointed to this age. Since Reeves's stone tools were found buried within these sands, they must be of the same age.

Many archaeologists—in a now familiar pattern—rejected the stones Reeves found as having been man-made, attributing their shape to nature. But, Reeves said, "there are certain ways nature breaks rocks and certain ways man breaks rocks"; these rocks, he argued, bore the imprint of human activity. IIe related how nature can mimic human influence on material, giving the example of a rock tumbled over the edge of a one-hundred-and-fifty-foot waterfall and shattered on boulders below. "But," he maintained, "most of these artifacts have been discovered on mesas here and there are no big waterfalls here." He hopes to protect the site areas from housing developments so major digs can be started. Reeves believes the stakes are high: As he told an Associated Press reporter, "I think it is even possible that skeletal remains may be found. Yes, possibly the remains of a 100,000-year-old man."[28]

Leakey said that "Calico will not long remain the oldest known site of its kind." At last the many truly early sites he predicted are coming to light. Taking up Leakey's boldness and imagination, today a growing number of archaeologists (including Drs. Bryan, Espinosa, Gruhn, Irving, Krieger, Lee, MacNeish, Morlan, Reeves, Simpson, Singer, Stephenson, and Witthoft) acknowledge man's presence in the Americas during relatively warm interglacial times 70,000 to 170,000 years ago. Even conservative archaeologists such as Gordon Willey of Harvard have made room for this possibility in their charts describing America's prehistory. Unfortunately, nonarchaeologists such as the U.S. Geological team from Hueyatlaco, Carter, and Childers (the discoverer of Yuha man), with their claims for early, early dates, have provoked a negative emotional response.

From the history of scientific discovery, we know that it is usually only a few threads of evidence, insight, and inspiration that signal the most important innovations. A new theory is seldom proved overnight; rather, supporting evidence is amassed gradually as the theory is explored. In fact, scientific texts and scientists are usually ten years behind the most recent discoveries in their field. Archaeology is no exception. Leakey pointed out that although the first Australopithecus skull was discovered by Dr. Raymond Dart as long ago as 1924, and although many subsequent finds were made by Dart and others in the years that followed, it was not until twenty-three years later that there was general acceptance that the Australopithecenes were hominids (on the lineage of man) and not pongids (on the lineage of apes). I hope it won't take the scientific community twenty-three years to acknowledge man's great antiquity in the New World. New dating techniques, the recognition of new prehistoric tool-manufacturing techniques, edge-wear analysis, and new discoveries in the field create great barriers for those who hope to disavow the Indians' long residence in the Americas.

My theory of an American genesis—of the Paleo-Indians being the first true *Homo sapiens sapiens* in the world, of their migrating to the Old World and participating in its evolution—is based on two factual pillars: the earlier dates for modern man's presence in the Americas than anywhere else, and the earlier dates for a technologically modern tool kit coming from the Americas. This tool kit includes projectile points, blades, sophisticated bone tools, grinding tools, basketry, and engraving clearly demonstrating fully wise or sapient behaviors. To prove this theory wrong, not only must earlier dates for *Homo sapiens sapiens* be found in a different part of the world, but they must be associated with a tool kit which demonstrates sapient knowledge.

Further support for my "America first" thesis comes from many individual bits and pieces of information in the archaeological record which, taken together, serve to fingerprint and document specific migrations in reverse. This trail of archaeological spoor will be presented in the next two chapters.

8

Migration in Reverse: The Artifacts

Diffusion from America to Japan would be just as possible
as diffusion in the opposite direction.
                    —Alan Bryan,
                        in *Early Man in America,*
                        1978

It was a gray, misty morning. Excitement was in the air. Today
was going to be the day of the first big hunt in the new land.
Kotori, the old chief shaman, himself was going to preside. As a
number of young braves emerged from their part of the cave,
they jokingly held their noses. The cave still smelled of the heaps
of animal bones the Indians had found strewn about when they
took the cave over from the previous occupants. Although these
Paleo-Indians had cleaned up the bones and the other refuse in
the cave, the stench still hung in the air. The day before, to make
things neater, they had laboriously hauled in gravel to lay down a
floor. Their backs were still sore from the work, and not having
the hides to cover the hard gravel didn't help. They were eager to
leave the caves and begin the big hunt.

They kidded about the rugged-looking Neanderthals who had
run from the cave several days before, grunting and squealing
like giant-sized hairy children. The cave had been filled with
smoke—because they didn't know how to ventilate their fires
properly. The Neanderthals were the first men the Indians had

seen since they began their migrating journey over four years ago. Ten tribes had traveled from their home in the central plains, west to the Pacific Coast, where they had joined with some tribes in southern California, then north over the Bering Straits through the barren tundra land of ice and snow, then south along the coast. Fish had been a staple for this part of the journey. But then the tribes split. Half of them took the skin boats and continued south into what today is Japan and China, some even eventually reached the Philippines, Borneo, and Australia. The other group decided to take their chances inland, and headed across the Russian steppes. They spent six months at Lake Baikal and again the tribes split. Some headed south, toward the Near East, and some continued on through eastern Europe and into southern France. In France, on the southern fringe of the glacier that choked off northern Europe, the tribes led by the shaman Kotori finally found what they were looking for: teeming herds of big game animals. As far as the eye could see there were camels, horses, reindeer, mammoth, and most important, their staple, buffalo. The buffalo supplied them with food, clothing, shelter, and the raw material for tools. But they had a reverence for the animal: For tens of thousands of years the clan that bound this group of tribes together had hunted the buffalo but had killed only what they needed.

The night before the hunt, in one of the far alcoves of the enormous cave, under flickering torchlight, the shaman priests drew magnificent multicolored pictures of the buffalo and offered their prayers for a good hunt. Small animal fetishes and spear points were coated in red ocher. They prayed that no one would be hurt under the thundering hooves of the herd they would stampede. Each of the hunt leaders left his handprint on the cave wall as a bond.

By mid-morning, all was set for the hunt. Kotori was clad in a buffalo-skin robe and buffalo-horn headdress just like those drawn the night before in the cave painting ceremony. With the dignity of his great age, he climbed to a perch high atop the stout medicine post that had been erected in a narrow ravine. The snow on the steep slopes had been packed hard and smooth by the hunters; the stream at the bottom was a ribbon of ice which ended in a small frozen pond. The Indians' careful preparations had created a natural slide.

Among the tribes, Kotori was believed to have the power to lure a herd of buffalo wherever he wished. He raised his staff adorned with duck feathers and blew his bone whistle. The hunt began. There was a long silence, then the swelling thunder of hooves. Soon the shouting voices of women and children could be heard as they wildly waved hides to drive the stampeding bison between a runway of sticks and brush down into the treacherous ravine. The animals slid about hopelessly, the surge of the stampeding herd driving the lead animals past the medicine post. Those who fell were quickly trampled to death. When the first buffalo reached the pond at the end of the ravine, they immediately fell through the ice and were set upon by the hunters who had been quietly lying in wait. The panic-stricken beasts floundered and thrashed in the slush. Spears whistled through the air, answered by the dying bellows of wounded animals.

Soon it was all over. The snow was stained red as ocher, and the bodies of over one hundred buffalo lay lifeless. Kotori climbed down from his perch and ritually killed a male wolf that had been trapped and bound. He prayed in thanks, proclaiming that man the predator was killing one of the buffalo's natural predators in exchange for the good hunt, to keep the balance. Then the butchering of the buffaloes began in earnest.

While the preceding is imagined, most of its elements are based on fact. I believe this scenario fits the data better and offers a better explanation for certain key but puzzling events of the past than other scenarios currently put forth. The appearance of Cro-Magnon man has often been spoken of as an "invasion." Across Europe and Asia, it was as if someone blew a whistle and all the Neanderthals disappeared—then blew again and conjured up *Homo sapiens sapiens*. The long, relatively warm interglacial period approximately 170,000 to 70,000 years ago would have been an ideal time for Paleo-Indians to have explored and "discovered" Eurasia; the next relatively warm period, 35,000 to 27,000 years ago, would have been an ideal time for them to return in force. Interestingly, it is only at these two periods that we get evidence of human occupation anywhere near the Bering Bridge; the Bridge indeed was passable at these times. From the Old Crow region comes an interglacial date, and from Old Crow/ Dawson City, Tanana Uplands in the Yukon (see appendix), and Lake Baikal in Siberia come dates from 35,000 to 28,000 years in age. Most likely, these Paleo-Indian migrants came from the central plains where the buffalo was their mainstay and joined with Indians from southern California, the most ancient of population pools.

The scene depicted could have taken place in the hill country of southern France, near a site called Grotte de Renne. Though a full report is still lacking, French archaeologist Leroi Gourhan excavated this cave site and found that the strata bore evidence of the sudden transition from a Neanderthal (Mousterian) culture to a *Homo sapiens sapiens* culture. The deeper layers of the cave, formed while Neanderthals were in residence, were strewn with rubbish and lithic debris. Then, approximately 35,000 years ago, gravel floors that were continuously swept clean suddenly appear in the strata, marking the entry of Cro-Magnon man with a new concept of hygiene and aesthetics. From nearby sites at Pech de l'Azi, Combe de l'Aze, and La Mouthe we have learned how these caves were made more comfortable with man-made rock walls and hide windbreaks at the cave mouths, and lit with oil lamps made of stone with rope wicks. The rope wick would take advantage of the same technical skill used in the making of baskets which appeared at Meadowcroft in Pennsylvania over 20,000 years ago.

At Grotte de Renne, the strata also document that tool types changed at the very same time as cave-keeping habits. In particular, tools made on stone "blades" and tools of bone make their first appearance with modern man. While the tool kit of the Neanderthals had approximately sixty-two different items, the tool kit of *Homo sapiens sapiens* boasted over one hundred items. These new tools document the greater innovative powers of fully modern man over the Neanderthals.

At about the same time (35,000 years ago) the formidable giant cave bear suddenly became extinct, most likely succumbing to the improved weapons of the invading Paleo-Indians. Like American Indians today, Cro-Magnon man had high regard for bears, using their skulls in rituals. In a number of excavated European caves, bear skulls have been found in significant arrangements. The most remarkable instance comes from Regourdou, in southern France, where a rectangular stone-lined pit contained the skulls of more than twenty cave bears and was covered by an enormous flat stone slab. Regourdou is believed to be a Neanderthal site, but I suspect that *Homo sapiens sapiens* was the real perpetrator. Many Cro-Magnon cave paintings depict "killed" bears bleeding from the mouth and nose. To kill a giant cave bear, which stood up to fifteen feet high and weighed up to three thousand pounds, had to be a great act of courage, even if the bears were hibernating. It seems likely, based on Indian traditions, that the hunter believed that he took on the strength and powers of the bear.

The idea of a magical transference of powers from animal to man is central to the shamanistic rituals described in the scenario. Today, shamanism is the religion of indigenous peoples of northern Asia and Europe. A shaman, someone much like the Indians' medicine man, has the power to make contact with and control the unseen world of gods, demons, and ancestral spirits. Cro-Magnon man most frequently depicted his shaman with a buffalo-horn headdress and a buffalo cape; virtually the same dress is worn by American Indian medicine men. The dancelike body and hand attitudes of the shaman in the Cro-Magnon paintings make clear the ceremonial aspects. In both instances, the concept of the

Cro-Magnon man engraved and painted this sorcerer or shaman in a cave in France. The buffalo robes and head-dress and dancelike attitudes bring to mind the buffalo medicine man tradition of the American Indians.

priest as half man and half buffalo is stressed, symbolizing his ability to control the spirit of the buffalo or the animal in question. To embody this control and ensure a good hunt, the shaman might use a small doll-like buffalo fetish in a ritual that led to the painting of the buffalo in a secret part of the cave and its subsequent ritual killing. Since the killing was successful in the spirit world, a good hunt would be ensured the next day in the physical world.

Many such scenes have been discovered in Cro-Magnon cave paintings, along with plentiful evidence for the lavish use of red ocher and the handprints mentioned in the scenario. At a Cro-Magnon site called Dolne Vestonice in Czechoslovakia, the small circular hut of such a medicine man has been found. Inside was a beehive-shaped oven or kiln, and the clay heads of two bears, a fox, and some unfinished statuettes. The excavators of the site believe this was the sacred den where the medicine man shaped and hardened the images of beasts and of women to be used in his hunting and fertility rites. Thus, the fetish concept common in American Indian religion was used by Cro-Magnon shamans as well.

What about the shaman in the scenario, personally directing the hunt, whistle in hand, astride a medicine post specially erected for this purpose? The scene is imaginary, but has some solid support from archaeology. In 1973, Dennis Stanford, the head Paleo-Indian archaeologist at the Smithsonian Institute, dug a Paleo-Indian bison-kill site along the Arikaree River in northeastern Colorado. The site, called the Jones-Miller Location, is believed to be 10,000 years old. The bones of extinct buffalo, many with spear points still imbedded in them, were everywhere, indicating a massive slaughter. Since there were no cliffs nearby for the buffalo to be driven over, and since the tooth eruption pattern of the young animals indicated that they had been killed in the winter, Stanford reasoned that they were driven down the icy river draw at the site and ambushed. But most important, Stanford found the earth cast of a large post from the time of the bison hunt. He believes it was a medicine post. Supporting this interpretation, near the foot of this post Stanford found a tiny spear point, a bone whistle, and the butchered remains of a wolf, all of which seem to be ritual offerings. (Recall the ceremonial burial with offerings from the Paleo-Indian burial at Gordon Creek, Colorado, pages 77–78.) Stanford's reconstruction matches the accounts from early frontiersmen of the buffalo hunts of the Cree and Assiniboin Indians on the wintry Canadian Plains.[1]

Ritual, ceremony, belief in an afterlife, and belief in the spirit world are the warp and woof of the lives of the first modern men. Evidence of Cro-Magnon activities and beliefs has been preserved for us by their art. Art stands alone as their key legacy. In addition to their concern for the esoteric, their art demonstrates that they had language, and even shows us what they looked like and how they dressed. This art, which was fully developed from the start, includes the painting of multicolored murals on cave walls, and the painting, engraving, and sculpting of small objects and tools. One bone shaft cylindrically engraved with reindeer showed perfect perspective and detail. But the superimposition of cave paintings, sometimes four or five paintings layered over each other, suggests that the artistic experience was more important than the artwork itself. In other words, the goal was most likely magical, rather than aesthetic. Most celebrated are the ivory carvings, called Venuses, depicting voluptuous women with big buttocks and breasts. These Venuses were probably used for fertility rites.

The Cro-Magnons also fashioned, probably for purely aesthetic reasons, many items for personal adornment, such as animal teeth, shells transported from hundreds of miles away, pendants, and bone hairpins. Some objects were decorated with simple geometric designs. Since one can't learn how to draw in dark caves, the achievement of precision and style in all this art makes it clear that the Cro-Magnons most often expressed their art outside of caves, but it has only survived inside, where constant temperature and humidity and protection from the destructive elements have preserved materials that would otherwise have perished thousands of years ago. Actually, the Cro-Magnons spent much more time in open camp sites than in cave sites, but the ravages of time have left us only the merest traces of these exterior sites.

These circumstances of preservation (cave versus open-air sites) explain why we have not found the equivalent of Cro-Magnon art in Paleo-Indian sites: virtually all the Paleo-Indian sites discovered to date are open-air sites. If Paleo-Indian art was mostly executed on hide and wood, we couldn't expect survival. We get a hint of the Paleo-Indian art from:

1. The three massive stone carvings representing human faces from Malakoff, Texas, which are estimated to be at least 30,000 years old (page 102).

2. The carving of an animal face on the backbone of a llama found under forty feet of deposits at Tequixquiac, near Mexico City, estimated to be at least 30,000 years in age (page 102).
3. The engraving I found at Flagstaff, Arizona, which is at least 100,000 years old (pages 212–16).
4. The rich lode of rock carvings on shelter walls, depicting animals, geometric designs, and sun worship, from the 12,000-year-old Abrigo do Sol (Shelter of the Sun) Site in the jungles of Brazil (pages 113–14).
5. An engraving on a piece of mastodon bone found in Mexico and estimated to be 22,000 years old. Directly comparable to the art of Cro-Magnon man, this engraving depicts a mastodon and a large cat.[2]

Possibly the now-destroyed drawings of big game animals from a sealed cave in La Crosse, Wisconsin, discovered in 1878 should also be included here.[3] And then again, we may not yet have found the American sites where abundant art has survived. Considering the startling discoveries of the last ten years, what will the next ten years of fieldwork bring to light?

There is evidence that the Cro-Magnons had a calendar and astronomy. Alexander Marshack of Harvard's Peabody Museum has shown that a three-inch-long piece of bone engraved with a seemingly simple geometric design was worked by a very complex process. The item is called the Blanchard bone and it was found in a Cro-Magnon cave in France. Its sixty-nine markings involved twenty-four tool point changes—which correlated with the phases of the moon. William Williams, a civil engineer and amateur astronomer from Dallas, Texas, seems to have broken the code behind these human notations and demonstrated that the Blanchard bone is actually a complete lunar calendar which even provides for self-correcting leap days. The invention of the lunar calendar is usually attributed to the Babylonians, 30,000 years later. Williams also convincingly demonstrates that similarly marked bones record the movements of other heavenly bodies such as Venus and Mars.

There is another Cro-Magnon mystery which may point to an American origin: the Cro-Magnons' sophisticated art and astronomy suddenly disappeared 12,000 years ago. There is no continuity between Upper Paleolithic art and post-Pleistocene art. After the Pleistocene era, prehistoric-European art is confined to meager scratchings on pebbles. Provocatively, the essence of the older Cro-Magnon art, astronomy, and shamanism is preserved in American Indian tradition. What does this sudden disappearance mean? Perhaps the Cro-Magnon shamans, seeing that the abundant game herds in France and Spain were disappearing as a result of climatic changes, decided to return to the land of their forefathers where the buffalo continued to roam up until historic times. Did the medicine men, in a Moses-like exodus, leave the ignorant masses behind, taking their closest followers on the treacherous journey back to North America to rejoin their kin after their people's long sojourn in Europe? Or had there been constant travel between both continents during this 25,000-year period, with the European shaman branch eventually dying out? In either case, the result was most likely interbreeding between the motherland, the North American Paleo-Indian gene pool, and what over the millennia became their distinct European cousins. This hybridization would explain the great genetic variations we see in modern-day American Indian peoples.

Paleo-Indian Migration to Europe:
American/European Tool Parallels

Direct support for the Paleo-Indians' migrating to Europe and becoming the Cro-Magnons comes from the many correlations between specific tool types. It is hard enough to get details of any prehistoric event, let alone one which occurred over 30,000 years ago, nevertheless, evidence for specific tools' moving from the Americas to Europe fortunately comes from:

The Solutrean Culture of the Upper Paleolithic and
Stone Projectile Points

The time period from 35,000 to 10,000 years ago, when Cro-Magnon man held sway in Europe, is called the Upper Paleolithic. Prehistorians have divided the Upper Paleolithic into a number of shorter time periods reflecting the development of different cultural groups in different European regions. These cultural groups are distinguished by the particular make-up of their tool kits. According to Francois Bordes, the "Solutrean" was "a short-lived but vigorous culture of the Upper Paleolithic in western Europe. It lasted from about 19,000 B.C. to 16,500 B.C. and is characterized by very finely worked flint projectile points and knives, usually leaf-shaped."[1] In a number of papers, Bordes has called the appearance of this Solutrean culture in Spain and France, the same areas where the cave paintings are found, "abrupt," an "intrusion," and its "origin a mystery." Bordes also notes that this culture "suddenly disappeared in somewhat mysterious circumstances."[5] Most startling of all, Bordes has found a direct analogy between Solutrean materials and Paleo-Indian materials: The "Paleo-Indians have multiple star-shaped borers like the early Magdalenian [the culture that succeeds the Solutrean], leaf-shaped points and knives like the French Solutrean, projectile points with a concave or convex base like the Spanish Solutrean."[6] In another report he went so far as to say that "the Spanish Solutrean points would be perfectly in place in the Clovis or Folsom industries," adding that "the internal balance of the stone industry—numerous end scrapers, numerous projectile points and bifacial knives, well-developed borers, infrequent burins, side-scrapers in the Middle Paleolithic style, and fairly rare bone industries" also support this analogy.[7]

But here Bordes draws the line: He says that we can't expect these correlations between Paleo-Indian tools and Western European tools to be more than "convergences." Bordes, Bryan, and others consider that Paleo-Indian Clovis points were the first American patent or invention, and that the similar projectile points found in Paleolithic France and Spain were independently invented. While Bordes and other prehistorians were quite ready to believe in hunters from Asia bringing modern tools into the New World, based on much less evidence, for some reason the possibility of a reverse connection between Western Europe and the New World is unthinkable.

While the ancestral forms of the European projectile points have *not* been found on the Eurasian plains as prehistorians believed would be the case, ancestral forms for the American projectile points *have* been found. The Clovis point from Lewisville, Texas, which has been dated to over 38,000 years, shows that these projectile points were first invented in the Americas. The projectile points from geographically diverse sites such as Meadowcroft, Pennsylvania; McGee's Point, Nevada; and Tlapocoya, Mexico, support the validity of the Lewisville point. In fact, by the end of the Pleistocene epoch, there were a number of different point types and cultural traditions extant in the Americas, demonstrating that a great range of technological diversity had already been developed. In addition to the thin, leaf-shaped Clovis and Folsom points of North America, there were the thick, bullet-shaped El Jobo points in Northern Venezuela associated with extinct animals (approximately 14,000 years ago) and fish-tailed points from the tip of South America.

The blade industries from the truly ancient sites of Texas Street and Calico Hills may be ancestral to these American point industries. Calico Hills is in the same basin area where, along shorelines of fossil lakes, as-yet-undated points known as Lake Mojave points are found. Many experts believe that Lake Mojave points may prove to have been an ancestral form to Clovis points. And if the dating of the Hueyatlaco, Mexico, site at 250,000 years ago is accurate, then leaf-shaped projectile points and blades seem to go hand in hand with the presence of modern man, no matter how early. The first modern men may have been much smarter than we give them credit for being. Fortuitous discovery accompanied by a long period of development may not have been the way these points came into being; *Homo sapiens sapiens,* with all his wisdom, *could* have immediately conceived of these advanced tool technologies.

Conceived in the Americas, the knowledge of how to make projectile points most likely traveled to the Old World with the first fully modern men, the Paleo-Indians. We find an exact matchup in the case of the abrupt appearance of the Solutrean points. And the "Solutrean-like" material found in Russia may mark the path one group of Paleo-Indians took as they traveled to the caves of Spain and France.

The great similarity of *several* different types of American projectile points with Cro-Magnon points was one of the prime factors in E. F. Greenman's 1963 theory of Cro-Magnon man's canoeing from Spain and France to the Americas. Although his theory is invalid, the discoveries Greenman made while formulating it are still valid. In the late 1950s, Greenman sent a graduate student of his, Arthur Jelinek, to Spain to examine closely the ancient points there. Jelinek, now a professor of archaeology at the University of Arizona, found some unnerving correspondences. Incredibly, the Clovis points of the American southwest and the Spanish points looked as though they had been made by the same hands. Not only were the American and Spanish points of the same exact shape and made by the same techniques, but both had a peculiar grinding at their bases. Jelinek said it would be virtually impossible to distinguish one from the other.

Greenman also found a unique resemblance between the rare American Sandia points and similarly unusual points from the French Solutrean. Sandia points were found in only two sites: at Sandia Cave in central New Mexico, below layers of soil containing Folsom and Clovis points, and at the nearby Lucy site. There is a great deal of confusion regarding the age of these points; guesses run from 10,000 to 25,000 years. Unlike the symmetrical Clovis points, Sandia points only have a single shoulder, and they lack the characteristic central fluting of Clovis points. The single

A comparison of replicas of projectile points. *Top row, left to right*: Clovis points from Naco, Arizona, and Dent, Colorado. *Second row, left to right*: Sandia I and Sandia II points from Sandia Cave, New Mexico. *Third row, left to right*: Folsom points from Folsom, New Mexico, and Lindenmeier, Colorado. *Bottom row, left to right*: stemmed point from Fell's Cave in Patagonia and Solutrean laurel leaf point from Laugerie-Haute, France.

The Clovis, Sandia, and stemmed points are exactly like points found in ice-age Europe, and the French laurel leaf point type was also used by Paleo-Indian hunters. All the Paleo-Indian points seem to have been in use long before their European (Cro-Magnon) counterparts.

shoulder of the Sandia points indicates a different type of hafting technique.

The uniqueness of the Sandia points makes them ideal for pinpointing contacts. When Greenman compared them with similar points from southwest France, he found that they both frequently had a special feature, a distinct small break in the curve of the blade which French archaeologists call an "aileron."[8]

Bordes was impressed enough by the similarity between the single-shouldered points of the French site of Laugerie-Haute and those of Sandia Cave to write a special paper on it. Bordes also believes that true Sandia points and associated tools also come from Alberta, Canada.[9] I believe an accurate dating of the New Mexican, Canadian, and French Sandia points could reveal the route north to the Bering Bridge and the Old World from New Mexico.

Bone Projectile Points

The Clovis sites at Blackwater Draw, New Mexico, Lindenmeier, Colorado, and the Sandia Cave, New Mexico, also yield polished projectile points made of animal bone in common with the Solutrean and other Upper Paleolithic cultures.

No doubt there have been several migrations from North America to Europe and back again. The bone projectile points and associated tools have been used to pinpoint a comparatively recent migration from North America to the Old World. Appreciating the fact that the ice-free corridor of 6,000 to 10,000 years ago had to gradually open from the south to the north, from its warmer latitudes to its cold northern margins, a number of archaeologists have recognized evidence that the traditional Clovis hunters migrated from the southwest northward to Alaska and then to Siberia at this time.[10]

Gordon Willey of Harvard has stated that "American-invented blade and point forms diffused . . . from North America to Asia in the early post-Pleistocene [approximately 10,000 years ago]."[11]

Bone projectile point of a type that is found in both ice-age North America and Europe.

For example, an antler pick just like those used at Old Crow in the Yukon was found in a Neolithic (approximately 8,000 years ago) burial from the Lake Baikal region of Siberia, and projectile points just like Paleo-Indian projectile points came from other Neolithic sites in this area.[12]

Bone Tools and Ivory Disks at Laugerie-Haute

The French site of Laugerie-Haute (dated to 19,000 years ago), which yielded the single-shouldered "Sandia" stone projectile points, has other features in common with Paleo-Indian sites. From Laugerie-Haute comes a wide range of bone implements such as bone awls, needles, and disks. Similar bone needles and awls are found at the Lindenmeier, Colorado, site, and an awl made from the wing bone of a loon was recently found at the Old Crow site, which now dates back to interglacial times (70,000–170,000 years ago). The Old Crow awl's much earlier date specifically demonstrates the primacy of the American sites for the origin of a sophisticated bone technology.

Most remarkable, though, is the discovery at Laugerie-Haute of a decorated ivory disk just like the three disks found at Lindenmeier which were incised with small lines around their edges (see page 165).

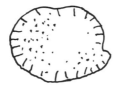

A bone disk found in a Paleo-Indian site at Lindenmeier, Colorado, which is exactly like bone disks found in ice-age France.

Batons de Commandement

A Baton de Commandement is a bone object consisting of a six to twenty-four inch shaft or handle with a large hole at the end. Batons served as ice-age wrenches; they were apparently used to straighten bone spear foreshafts, which were first made pliable by immersion in boiling water. Batons are found at many Cro-Magnon sites, and were often decorated with animal images or with the type of geometric markings shown by Alexander Marshack to be lunar notations. It is believed that the highly decorated batons, especially those that show no signs of wear, were actually used for ritual purposes.

At an open-air site at Murray Spring, Arizona, a Paleo-Indian shaft straightener, exactly like those found in Cro-Magnon Europe, has miraculously survived. In 1967, Vance Haynes found what today is the only known American shaft straightener at this Clovis mammoth kill site believed to be 12,000 years old. In view of the much earlier dates for Paleo-Indian projectile points, we might expect eventually to discover American shaft straighteners much older than the European examples.

Boats

E. F. Greenman, arguing for an ocean crossing from coastal France and Spain, said deep-water skin canoes called "Beothuk" were used to make the crossing.

Beothuk canoes are very different from the typical birchbark canoes of the American northeast. Beothuk canoes are actually useless in shallow waters because they have a V-shaped cross section, deeper than the birchbark canoe's U-shaped cross section. The top line of these large crescent-shaped canoes rose to a small peak amidships; skins could be stretched over this peak to provide a cabin for the occupants.

The Beothuk Indians of Newfoundland who used these canoes up until the eighteenth century can be traced back to similar late Pleistocene cultures in the far northeast (e.g., the Debert Site in Nova Scotia, 10,600 years ago), cultures not too unlike those of Cro-Magnon man in Europe. Greenman, recognizing the unique Beothuk canoe shape in a wall painting from the Cro-Magnon cave of Castillo on the Spanish Coast, went on to discover boatlike shapes on the walls of other Upper Paleolithic caves in coastal Spain. Critics, unimpressed, described these distinctive canoe-like shapes as "naviform." Greenman's interpretation of the cave paintings drew heavy fire; there was no clear-cut evidence that boats had been used at such early dates. No boat-building materials have been identified at sites, and there are no paintings showing men in boats. But today, almost twenty years after Greenman's presentation of his theory, it is believed that the first modern men had watercraft, based on the discovery of 20,000-to-30,000 year old *Homo sapiens sapiens* sites in Australia. (There are no evolutionary forms of man in Australia, so for modern man to appear there, he would have to boat across the great body of water between Asia and Australia.) Thomas Jacobsen, chairman of Indiana University's Classical Archaeological Program, reported in 1978 that new evidence from a Greek cave in the Mediterranean indicates that seafaring is at least 11,000 years old.[13] If the crescent-shaped drawing from the Castillo cave does represent a Beothuk canoe, we have yet another fingerprint the Paleo-Indians left with Cro-Magnon man.

A Paleo-Indian wrench made out of mammoth bone which was used for straightening spear foreshafts of bone while the shafts were still green and pliable. This "shaft straightener" is from Murray Spring, Arizona, and it is exactly like objects used by Cro-Magnon man in Europe which French archaeologists call Batons de Commandement. *The Arizona State Museum*

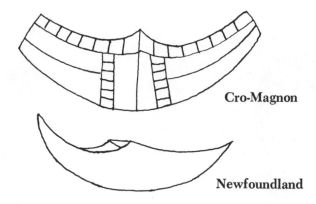

Cro-Magnon

Newfoundland

Drawings of a uniquely shaped, deep-water skin canoe used by the historic Beothuk Indians of Newfoundland compared to a cave painting of a similar canoe made by Cro-Magnon man in coastal Spain during the ice age. In 1963, anthropologist Dr. E. F. Greenman, formerly curator of the University of Michigan's museum, said that the use of such unique canoes on each continent provided additional evidence for direct contact between the Paleo-Indians and Cro-Magnon man. *Adapted from Greenman, 1963*

Migration from a Common Source: South American/European Tool Parallels

Indirect clues to the influence of the Paleo-Indians over the Cro-Magnons also come from similarities between the tools of South America and Europe. Engraving tools (burins) and strangled blades from South American sites such as El Inga in Ecuador look exactly like those of Cro-Magnon man's first cultures (Perigordian and Aurignacian). According to Bordes, the El Inga tools would "be absolutely in place in French Upper Perigordian."[14] The El Inga site also has fishtailed projectile points which are considered an unusual point type of the Spanish Solutrean. The catch is that El Inga and similar South American sites are only 11,000 to 16,000 years old, too recent to have fathered the cultures in Europe. Instead of evidence for direct contact between the two areas, I think these similarities provide evidence for something just as important. In my view, the reason for these South American/European correspondences is that both areas received their education in toolmaking from an intermediate source, from a school of flintknapping that began tens of thousands of years before either South America's or Europe's fully modern cultures. Given the early southern California dates, I think Paleo-Indian migrants from there moved both north across the Bering Bridge to Europe and south across the Isthmus of Panama to South America.

Picture a Garden of Eden-like atmosphere in southern California for the first *Homo sapiens sapiens* reaching as far back as 500,000 years. Eventually a fully human curiosity, and perhaps more practical impulses, sent some of these early men journeying in different directions. Remember that by 40,000 years ago these men had already learned to live in a number of different California environments, from the coast to the inland lakes. In addition to moving north and south, perhaps they went eastward—this would explain the early date for the recently discovered and surprisingly advanced eastern site of Meadowcroft (20,000 years ago) in Pennsylvania. I expect even earlier dates than the 35,000-year Cro-Magnon dates to turn up in the east coast and in South America in the years to come. If modern man radiated out from southern California, dates from South America and the east coast earlier than from Europe, would occur since they are both geographically closer and more accessible to southern California than Europe.*

Diffusion from America to Japan

Alan Bryan has noted that unique lanceolate-stemmed projectile points 11,000 years old are found in Alaska which owe their inspiration to older (14,000 years) projectile-point styles found

* Inspired by recent surprising discoveries in Brazil, Alan Bryan is planning a massive search there.

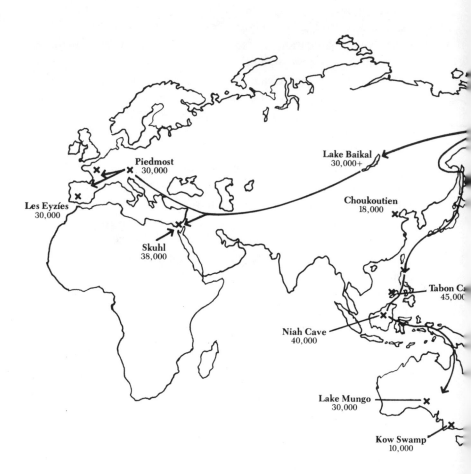

Possible paths of the Paleo-Indians. The first fully modern stock called
"proto-Caucasoid/Paleo-Indian" possibly moved out from its southern
California "Garden" and traveled south to South America, east to the
Atlantic Seaboard, and north across the Bering Bridge into Asia and
Europe.

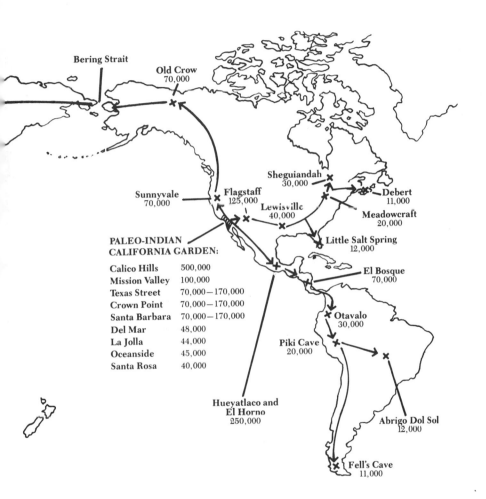

Bering Strait

Old Crow
70,000

Sunnyvale
70,000

Flagstaff
125,000

Sheguiandah
30,000

Lewisville
40,000

Debert
11,000

Meadowcraft
20,000

Little Salt Spring
12,000

**PALEO-INDIAN
CALIFORNIA GARDEN:**

Calico Hills	500,000
Mission Valley	100,000
Texas Street	70,000 – 170,000
Crown Point	70,000 – 170,000
Santa Barbara	70,000 – 170,000
Del Mar	48,000
La Jolla	44,000
Oceanside	45,000
Santa Rosa	40,000

El Bosque
70,000

Otavalo
30,000

Piki Cave
20,000

Hueyatlaco and
El Horno
250,000

Abrigo Dol Sol
12,000

Fell's Cave
11,000

far to the south. These Alaskan projectile points are very similar to Tachikawa points from Hokkaido, Japan, which date to about 10,000 years ago. Since these unique points are much older in the Americas than in Japan, Bryan was led to speculate that diffusion from America to Japan was "just as possible" as the traditional scenario of diffusion in the opposite direction.[15]

9

Migration in Reverse: The Skulls

. . . the [earliest] Paleo-Indians demonstrate population
affinities with Caucasian groups.
—Janice Austin,
Paper read at the Society for
California Archaeology, 1976

The appearance in the Old World of specific tools derived from
the advanced American tool complex indicates migration between
specific regions. Even more convincing evidence for reverse migration arises by pursuing the question of what these first families
of *Homo sapiens sapiens* looked like. Thanks to the new American datings and discoveries, the comparative Paleo-Indian sample
is no longer so fragmentary. New analytical techniques are also
helping us to learn the true message of Paleo-Indian remains.

Surprisingly to some, the Paleo-Indian skulls did not look Asian
at all. Instead, these oldest fully modern skulls looked like the
forefathers of *both* the present-day Indians and the Cro-Magnons.
In racial terms, the very earliest Indian skulls looked like
present-day Caucasians with an Indian cast, just as Cro-Magnon
man did. Over thousands of years' residence in the Americas,
this first Indian skull type, here called "proto-Caucasoid,"
developed into the characteristic Indian racial appearance we
now know, while in Europe, the Cro-Magnon descendants of
this founding American stock developed the appearance we now

associate with "Caucasians." After the first migrations from the southern California gene pool to the Old World, successive return migrations led to the hybridization and great physical variation among the American Indians, and possibly to three separate modern Indian racial pools. The main support for these observations and interpretations comes from a special study conducted by Janice Austin, a graduate student in physical anthropology at UCLA. Austin was the first researcher to have access to the newly-dated Del Mar and "Black Box" skulls for comparative purposes.

In the 1940s and 1950s, leading physical anthropologists such as Ernest Hooten of Harvard University, Carleton Coon of the University of Pennsylvania, and J. B. Birdsell of the University of California at Los Angeles broke with traditional views, suggesting that the first Paleo-Indians were not Mongolian but Caucasian. Birdsell, still following the traditional Old World to New World migration scenario, speculated that if this movement took place in the third interglacial period, the first Americans "could be expected to be purely Caucasoid and to show no Mongoloid characteristics."[1] I think Birdsell's conclusion about the first Paleo-Indians being purely Caucasoid is correct, but his reasoning is backward.

Birdsell's hypothesis led Austin to test for the racial affinities of the first Paleo-Indians using the newly-dated ancient California skulls. To determine the racial group of the first Paleo-Indians, she compared these skulls to a number of skulls of modern man from Europe, Asia, and the Americas, using some ancient *Homo sapiens sapiens* skulls from Asia as a control.

To make the comparison, Austin used a sophisticated computer-based statistical analytical technique called multivariate analysis. This entails analyzing the shape, or morphology, of the skull reflected by twenty-five different measurements (metric data). Cranial breadth, cranial length, orbital (eye socket) breadth, orbital height, biorbital breadth, nasal breadth, nasal height, cheek height, and facial height are among the most revealing measurements. These measurements are then statistically compared in different combinations in order to determine variations in three-dimensional shapes. Physical anthropologists believe that these measurements and shapes reflect genetic relationships. For example, one study using skeletal material from southwestern sites showed that facial morphology persisted over a one-thousand-year period. Another study, stressing cranial morphology, has shown a close relationship between the protohistoric (prior to the appearance of written records) Pawnee and two groups of descendant Arikara.[2]

While Austin used racial terms to describe her comparative groups, she was referring to their population affinities, i.e., the range of measurements and shapes characteristic of a large population. This overcomes the errors inherent in racial stereotypes. While the human eye may tend to see what it expects—or what it wants to see—detailed cranial measurement statistics do not bend to the bias of the observer. Austin tested only essentially complete skulls with established ages. These stringent conditions eliminated many of the Paleo-Indian skulls on which some researchers had based their traditional theories.

Austin was trying to compare the morphological modern populations dating from A.D. 800 to A.D. 1700 from different regions. She measured modern cranial populations (averaging sixty individuals each) from medieval Norway, medieval Hungary, Austria, the Ainu of Japan, Tibet, Burma, Buriat-Siberia, Eskimo Greenland, the Yauyos Indians of Peru, the Arikara Indians of South Dakota, and the Santa Rosa Island Indians. The control group of ancient Asian skulls consisted of a distinctly Mongolian skull from the Upper Cave at Choukoutien, China, radiocarbon-dated to 18,000 years in age, and an undated skull from Java believed to be of similar age. The Paleo-Indian skulls included the Del Mar skull, one skull from the "Black Box" site, the La Brea Woman skull from Los Angeles, and three skulls from the Tranquility site in central California.[3]

The Del Mar skull, an adult male which Bada dated to 48,000 years in age, was distinctly longheaded (dolichocephalic). The earliest fully modern populations in the Old World were long-headed. Physical anthropologists have documented a slow general transition in *Homo sapiens sapiens* from ancient longheadedness to modern roundheadedness in the populations of the world. Thus, the Del Mar skull's longheadedness adds confidence to its dating. The "Black Box" skull and the Tranquility skulls, also very old, are also longheaded. Following the general trend toward roundheadedness over the centuries, more recent Paleo-Indian skulls such as Gordon Creek man (10,000 years old), Texepan man (10,000 years old), and Marmes man (11,000 years old) all have skulls of intermediate length (mesocephalic), while modern Indians have shorter, roundheaded skulls (brachycephalic).

The most startling aspect of the Del Mar skull, though, was that its closest population affinities were with the Caucasoids. Statistically, its closest morphological kinship was with the Ainu people of northern Japan, a present-day group which is acknowledged to be a surviving ancient Caucasoid strain isolated in eastern Asia for many millennia. The probability of group membership was an amazing ninety-one percent. The Del Mar skull also had very close affinities with the Santa Rosa Island Indians and the medieval Norse.

The "Black Box" skull, which had been racemization-dated to at least 50,000 years, also had close population affinities with the Caucasoids. It matched most closely with the Yauyos Indians of Peru, but was also *extremely* close to the Norse and the Austrian comparative groups. The "Black Box" skull was even closer to the Caucasian groups than the Del Mar skull; this may be explained by its being somewhat older and closer to the original proto-Caucasoid form.

The three skulls (two adult females and one adult male) from the Tranquility site, which may be as much as 31,000 years old, showed similarities to the medieval Norse and medieval Hungarian groups; their closest affinity was with the Norse population.

The La Brea skull, that of a woman between twenty and thirty years old at the time of death, has a radiocarbon date of only 9,000 years; its closest population affinity was with modern American Indian groups such as the Yauyos Indians of Peru and the

Santa Rosa Islanders. Austin felt that the La Brea skull demonstrated "hybridization" or transition: Both the "Black Box" skull and the La Brea skulls classified closest with the Yauyos of Peru, the "Black Box" skull secondarily classified extremely closely with the European Caucasoids, while the La Brea skull secondarily classified with another American Indian group (Santa Rosans). The La Brea skull seems to illustrate the transition from the much older longheaded proto-Caucasoid Del Mar, "Black Box," and Tranquility Paleo-Indians to the roundheaded modern-day Indians. This transition seems to have taken 30,000 to 40,000 years, and distinct changes in skull shape would be expected.

Austin presented her findings in a paper at the 1976 Annual Meeting of the Society for California Archaeology. She concluded that the results of her analysis "indicated the 'Black Box,' Del Mar and Tranquility specimens had population affinities with Causasoid groups. The La Brea specimen had affinities with American Indian groups."[4] She believes that the first Paleo-Indians were a Caucasian group who in time developed uniquely Indian traits.

It appears from this statistical analysis that the traditional anthropological classification of the American Indians as a branch of the Asian Mongolians is all wrong. The traditional interpretation was highly subjective, based on the lumping together of physically diverse American Indian groups; it is supported by little metric data and no chronology. Based on the new datings and the new statistical data, the Paleo-Indians should be classified as proto-Caucasoids who evolved into various American Indian peoples, giving the modern-day American Indians their own racial grouping as separate from the Mongoloids as are the Caucasoids. On the other hand, the European Cro-Magnons should be classified as a branch of the proto-Caucasoid Paleo-Indians who evolved into what we now describe as modern Caucasoids. Similarly, based on the many analogies noted between ancient Mongolian skulls and some ancient American Indian skulls, the first Asians could also be classified as a branch of the proto-Caucasoid Paleo-Indians who became Asiatic Mongolians. Thus, from the parent proto-Caucasoid Paleo-Indian population, the first *Homo sapiens sapiens* to appear in the world, we get migration to the Old World and the gradual simultaneous development in relative geographic isolation of three now distinct racial stocks: the American Indians, the Caucasoids, and the Mongolians. During this time of relative isolation, minor travel back and forth across the Bering Bridge probably resulted in hybridization and the variations found among the historic American Indians. The only American Indian groups to show true affinities with Asian populations are the Athapascans (Navajo and Apache) and the Eskimos. Their distinctly Mongolian ancestors represent a recent return migration (5,000 to 6,000 years ago) from the Old World by distant descendants of the first Paleo-Indians who had by this time become fully Mongoloid. Their relatively recent intermixture and extremely rapid population growth probably is responsible for much of the variation among the historic Indians. These Mongoloid features often predominate and mask the proto-Caucasoid element.

Besides the skull measurements, other genetic traits reflect this relative isolation and the separateness of the American Indian from the modern Caucasians and the modern Mongoloids. While the absence of slanted eyes and conspicuously flat facial profiles, taken with the presence of aquiline noses and skin color ranging from white to mahogany brown, should make the Indians' significant differences from the Mongoloids obvious enough, unseen genetic traits mark the difference even more strongly. Genetically transmitted traits such as blood types, ear wax, fingerprint patterns, and PTC tasting clearly testify to the American Indians' uniqueness.

For all practical purposes, the gene is the simplest unit of heredity material. Genes carry sets of instructions for building the specific physical characteristics that are passed on from parent to child and from family to family over the generations. Interbreeding between groups changes their genetic makeup, i.e., their gene frequencies. The different races of the world are characterized by differences in gene frequencies.

A look at the genetically controlled blood types of man show that the American Indian is different. In serology, the study of blood groups, the basic blood group classification is the A-B-O system. Blood types A and B are the most common in the Old World,* with blood type O occurring only sporadically and in relatively low frequencies. On the other hand, the highest incidence of type O blood in the world occurs among the American Indians, while A and B are totally absent or extremely rare among pure-bloods. If the American Indians all came from Mongoloid stock, one would expect their characteristic blood group to be B or A. In the Native Americans, blood group B occurs only among the Eskimos, while blood group A occurs only among the Athapascans (Navajos and Apaches). This is consistent with their clearly Mongoloid appearance, linguistic affinities, and late entry into the New World.

More detailed serological data such as the MN blood grouping present the very same picture: The American Indians, with the exceptions of the Eskimos and Athapascans, have much lower frequencies for the N group than do Asiatics. In the Rh system, the "Rh negative" factor is totally absent from all the known Indian populations of North and South America.

Several physical anthropologists feel that these serological characteristics, along with other genetic peculiarities, justify one step beyond the "segregation" of the Eskimos and Athapascans— they also see a major subdivision within the remaining older American Indian groups. On the basis of rather considerable gene frequency differences, they see a separation between North and South American Indians which would give us a total of three different groups: (1) Eskimo and Athapascans, (2) North American Indians, and (3) South American Indians. Dr. Marshall Newman of the University of Washington writes in an article about geographic races in *Current Anthropology* that "Genes A,

---

* In particular, blood type A is dominant in most of Europe and Asia; the maximum frequency of type B is found in northern India and Central Asia. It is possible to visualize a geographical gradient showing that the frequency of type A increases and the frequency of type B decreases as one moves westward from the Pacific Coast of Asia to the Atlantic Coast of Europe.

M, P and Fya are definitely lower in frequency in the southern continent while R (C De) is higher."[5] Genetic information reflected by an ability to secrete certain substances in the urine and to taste certain chemical compounds (PTC) are also cited by Newman as supporting this division. This three-part division of the Native Americans based on blood typing and geographic concentration seems reasonable.

Fingerprint patterns, consisting of arches, loops, whorls, and ridges, are also useful in genetic studies, because they are formed in the eighteenth week of fetal life and are not influenced by the environment afterward. It has been found that differences between the fingerprints of closely related individuals quantitatively reflect the degree of kinship between them (dermatologlyphics). For example, the ridge count in identical twins is almost identical. The different races of the world are characterized by different fingerprint patterns, and here again the American Indians are unique. As compared to the Asiatic Mongoloids, the Indians tend to have more arches, loops, and whorls. In addition, Dr. Newman has noted fingerprint differences *between* the different American Indian groups.[6]

The wax that exudes from human ears comes in two forms, sticky and dry. These two forms of earwax are genetically controlled; different races have different gene frequencies for dry earwax. Dr. Carleton Coon notes that these frequency differences "drive a thick wedge between Asiatic Mongoloids and American Indians."[7] For example, the Northern Chinese have a ninety-eight percent occurrence of this trait, while the Maya Indians have only a two percent occurrence.

My theory that the Proto-Caucasoid Paleo-Indians fathered today's European Caucasoids and today's Asiatic Mongoloids can be illustrated if we go back and examine a simplification of the chart Austin used to summarize her findings (see chart, page 184). This chart represents a three-dimensional model reflecting the shape of various cranial components for the population distributions of the groups in her test analysis. On this chart the

Paleo-Indians as represented by the Del Mar, "Black Box," and Tranquility specimens occupy the top and center. Below the Paleo-Indian position on the chart and to the left is the La Brea specimen and slightly below this, the modern American Indians, represented by the Santa Rosa and Yauyos Indians of Peru. Directly below the Paleo-Indian position on the chart are the modern Caucasians represented by the Ainu, Norse, and Austrian groups. Finally, also below the Paleo-Indian position but to the right, are the ancient Asians represented by the two ancient Mongoloid specimens, one of which has been noted to have some affinities with modern American Indians. If we let the Paleo-Indians represent the proto-Caucasoids and add a time dimension with arrows to the simplified chart, we get a model of the theory I am proposing. From the 50,000-year-old Paleo-Indian/proto-Caucasoids, three main arrows reach out. One goes down and to the left to the 9,000-year-old La Brea specimen, then continues down just a bit to the modern American Indian groups. Another arrow would go straight down to the modern Caucasoids, and the third arrow down and to the right to the 18,000-year-old ancient Mongolians who in time became the modern Asiatic Mongolians.

The observations and impressions of many scholars over the last one hundred years support Austin's findings and suggest my theoretical interpretation or model of modern man's worldwide spread. In regard to the Paleo-Indian/European Caucasoid connection, several French archaeologists—Cottevieille-Giraudet, for one—have at least noted similarities in skull shape between Europe's Cro-Magnon men and modern Indian groups such as the Sioux, Huron, Delaware, Cherokee, and Iroquois.[8] George Carter says that it is "probably no accident that some of our northeastern Indians have repeatedly been described as European in appearance."[9] In view of the close resemblance of the modern Caucasoid Ainu skulls with those of Cro-Magnon man, Birdsell pointed to the Ainu as the living model of the first fully modern men.[10] Since the Del Mar skull most closely resembles the Ainu (ninety-one percent probability of identical group membership, according to Austin's study), Del Mar man thus must closely resemble the

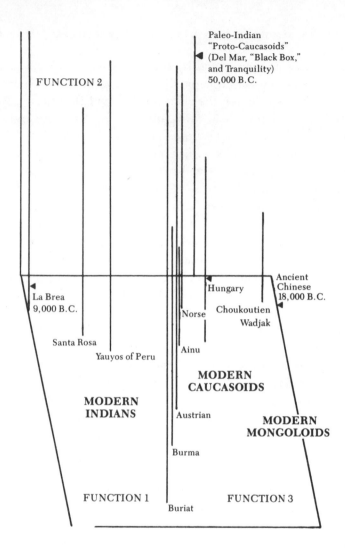

The Paleo-Indians as Father of Modern Man. An interpretation of a three-dimensional population study conducted by UCLA which included the newest American datings. The modern-day Indian, Caucasoid, and Mongoloid races seem to have sprung from the "proto-Caucasoid/Paleo-Indian" stock, the first fully modern stock. This stock appeared in southern California at least 50,000 years ago. By 18,000 years ago, types intermediate in racial characteristics developed in the Americas, Europe, and Asia. By 10,000 years ago, the modern-day racial types were fully established. *Adapted from Austin, 1976*

Cro-Magnons. Further, Spencer Rogers of the San Diego Museum notes that the ancient La Jollan Indian population, of which the Del Mar skull is considered a very early member, showed a marked divergence in stature between males and females. Of thirty-one worldwide populations studied for this relationship, Rogers says, "the only ones as high as the La Jollan are European."[11]

As for the distinctive Asian races also stemming from older Paleo-Indian ancestry, Carleton Coon, like Birdsell, believes that the generalized physical traits that distinguish the Mongolian peoples of East Asia didn't come into being until 10,000 to 20,000 years ago. Birdsell and Coon believe that the Mongolians developed from a primitive Caucasoid stock then present in China in response to extreme rigors of climate and isolation. François Bordes believes that man did not even enter Japan until just 25,000 years ago.

Coon has said that "the old man of the Upper Cave [Choukoutien, China] . . . resembled the large faced tribes of American Indians, like those still living in the Plains."[12] Dr. Erik Reed, a physical anthropologist from the University of New Mexico, echoes this view: "I have examined a cast of the Upper Cave [Choukoutien, China] male and can find only very slight differences in minor details from what I am accustomed to seeing in western North American Indian crania."[13] The old man of the Upper Cave from Choukoutien is the very same ancient Mongolian specimen Austin used in her study. When Coon and Reed made the above statements, the Indians were believed to be only 12,000 years old, and the Choukoutien skull, though undated, was believed to be considerably older. Today, we know of Indian skulls more than 70,000 years in age and the Choukoutien skull has been radiocarbon dated to just 18,000 years. As the 9,000-year-old La Brea specimen marks the transition of the Paleo-Indians to modern Indian form in the Americas, the 18,000-year-old Choukoutien specimen could be marking the start of the transition of the migrant Paleo-Indians to modern Mongolian form in East Asia.

Flesh reconstruction of the skull from the Upper Cave at Choukoutien, China. This skull has been noted to bear a resemblance to the American Indians'. It has recently been dated as 18,000 years old as compared to Paleo-Indian skulls recently dated to 70,000 years ago. Migration from the Americas to Europe is indicated—migration in a *reverse* direction from traditional theory.   *American Museum of Natural History, Maurice Putnam Coon*

Physical anthropologist Spencer Rogers, Director of the Museum of Man in San Diego, has studied the skull of a young adult male from the Yuha, California, burial dated to 22,000 years ago. On the basis of its skull shape, narrow face, and quadrangular rather than round eye socket, he finds that Yuha man mainly aligns with the Caucasoids. Rogers sees a resemblance between Yuha man's skull and early skulls from the San Diego area, including the Del Mar skull. (He believes that the first southern California desert populations as represented by Yuha man were biologically related to the first southern California coastal populations.) Rogers has also found similarities in some skull measurements between the 44,000-year-old La Jolla skull and a prehistoric population of only 8,000 years ago from the Island of Kyusha in southern Japan, along with resemblances between the Del Mar skull and more recent skulls of Mongolians from Ancient East Asia.[14] T. D. Stewart, the head physical anthropologist at the Smithsonian, has also noted a generalized American Indian-Mongoloid type in late Pleistocene (8,000 to 10,000 years ago) crania (Tzeyang and Liukiang) from western and southern China.[15]

Further support for this concept of transition from a Paleo-Indian base comes from Lawrence Angel, another physical anthropologist at the Smithsonian. In 1966, Angel recognized that proto-Mongoloid, late Pleistocene skulls from East Asia had similarities to the same Tranquility specimens which Austin later used in her study, and to modern groups in the southern San Joaquin Valley, where the ancient Tranquility skulls were found.[16] While Angel suspected great age for the highly mineralized Tranquility bones, representing a population of over thirty individuals, he didn't suspect anything like the 31,000-year date recently obtained. Based on the much earlier date for the Tranquility specimens than that for the East Asian specimens, it seems that over the years the Asians became more Mongolian in their traits, while the San Joaquin populations, stay-at-homes in the land of the parent proto-Caucasoid population, remained much the same. Angel provided even more evidence for the Paleo-Indians being the proto-Caucasoids who in China became the proto-Mongoloids in a 1963 paper where he also pointed out resemblances between the Tranquility remains and Upper Paleolithic Cro-Magnon skulls.[17]

The American Indians, the Mongolians, some northern European Caucasoids, and the Ainu are the only people in the world to have distinctively curved incisors characterized by anthropologists as "shovel-shaped." In dental shoveling, the inner surfaces of the front teeth are concave as though scooped out. Anthropologists believe that shoveling is a very specialized genetic trait. The American Indians have a much greater incidence of shoveled incisors—and a more intense degree of shoveling—than any other people. In the ancient La Jollan population Rogers studied, all the incisors in good enough condition to be observed showed shoveling. The incisors of the 30,000-year-old skull from Otavalo, Ecuador, too, were all shovel-shaped. Thus, the trait seems to have been present among the first Paleo-Indians, while it doesn't appear in East Asia until a much later time. With this trait appearing much earlier, in purer form, and with higher incidence among the American Indians, we see yet another genetic footprint where the Indian progenitors touched East Asia, resulting in the first appearance of fully modern man there.

Taking things one step further, Birdsell and other physical anthropologists believe that proto-Caucasoids (stemming, as I have demonstrated, from the Paleo-Indians) pushed south through East Asia (China and Japan) to Southeast Asia, where their descendants are today's Australian aborigines.[18] Moving south from Japan they would have first encountered the Philippines, then Indonesia, and finally Australia. Traditional theory holds that man could not cross large bodies of water to reach these island regions until just 10,000 years ago. But recent discoveries show that *Homo sapiens sapiens* entered each of these three areas over 30,000 years ago. Tools from Tabon Cave in the Philippines may reach the 40,000-to-45,000-year range, a fully modern skeleton skull found at Niah Cave in Borneo (in the Indonesian Islands) has been dated to 40,000 years ago, and the remains of a perfectly modern man have been found in a geological context datable to 30,000 years ago at Lake Mungo, Australia.[19]* Physical anthropologist Santiago Genoves of the Mexico National University reports that the Niah Cave specimen and other Southeast Asian specimens "bear a close physical resemblance to some American Indians." Frank Howells of the University of California at Berkeley has also noted these resemblances.[20] And Rogers has noted distinct similarities between the crown diameters (a genetic racial marker) of Yuha man's teeth and those of the Australian aborigines.[21] Besides these resemblances in the skeletal record, resemblances between the American Indian and Southeast Asian artifacts have also been noted in the archaeological record.[22]

A circum-Pacific concept of the distribution of early man around the Pacific rim, with a focus on early man in America, was the subject of a special symposium at the Thirteenth Pacific Science Congress which met in Vancouver in 1975.[23] Scientists from sixteen countries attended and presented papers. At this symposium, George Carter noted that the La Jollan Paleo-Indian culture (which included 48,000-year-old Del Mar man and 44,000-year-old La Jolla man) had parallels with very early Australian cultures: Beyond their common use of practical tools such as millingstones and identical stone cores, Carter noted, both cultures also used curved throwing sticks, bull roarers in initiation ceremonies, and ceremonial stone alignments and circles.[24]

In fact, one unmistakable cultural practice in itself may chart the long migration of the Paleo-Indians to Europe and Asia—the bear cult. Bear cults are well known among American Indian groups and, as already noted, Europe's Cro-Magnon man had them also. Evidence has also been found for the presence of a bear cult in Asia among the modern-day Ainu of the most northerly of Japan's islands, Hokkaido, and the neighboring Russian island to the north, Sahkalin. A people migrating from Alaska and

---

* Ironically, origins dates have been pushed steadily backward in Australia over the last decade much as they have in the Americas.

across Siberia could easily have struck the Pacific coast across from the isle of Sahkalin. Recall Austin's finding that the Del Mar skull most closely grouped with the Caucasian Ainu, and Birdsell's identification of the Ainu with the first ancient European Caucasoids.

The Ainu have light skin with ruddy tones as do Europeans; unlike their Mongoloid neighbors, they have a great profusion of beard and body hair. The Ainu eye folds are shaped as in Europeans and American Indians, rather than with the characteristic epicanthic fold which "slants" the eyes of Mongoloid peoples. Like the Europeans and the Indians, the Ainu have noses standing out in high relief: Evidently their resemblance to these racial groups has persisted since the days of Cro-Magnon man and Del Mar man.[25]

Some archaeologists are wary about taking the occurrence of parallel cultural traits such as buffalo shaman and bear cults to indicate direct cultural contact or even inspiration from a common source. But these cultural patterns are backed up by many specific parallels between cultural materials such as stone projectile points and associated tools, bone projectile points, ivory disks, batons, and boat styles. And these cultural parallels are in turn backed up by skeletal or genetic parallels. I believe that these constitute powerful and persuasive evidence for the Paleo-Indians' having migrated to Europe and Asia. One may ask why the Indian cultures didn't take better hold in the Old World. Perhaps the harsher climates of Europe and Asia were the downfall of a culture native to mild California; the last ice age may have been their *coup de grace*. Maybe, as I have said, after a while the shamans, seeing the game herds disappearing and the climate changing, decided to take their most dedicated followers and return home. Maybe it was because the Indian migrants were too susceptible to the common Eurasiatic diseases such as measles, the common cold, and tuberculosis. These diseases are known to have decimated Indian populations when the European came to the Americas after Columbus's time. The question remains unanswered.

Del Mar man, buried over 48,000 years ago, had a cranial capacity of 1,672 cubic centimeters,[26] almost twenty percent greater than twentieth century man's. In coastal southern California, Del Mar man chose one of the most idyllic year-round climates and environments in the world for his home, and he had a full tool kit. Since it appears that modern man may have lived in southern California for upward of 500,000 years, the question now is not where the Paleo-Indians traveled to, but where they came from. With the Old World eliminated as a source, Indian myth provides a satisfying answer.*

* We must look for either a lost continent or evolution in America as an answer. Alan Bryan believes that the incomplete mineralized remains of a beetle-browed skull he photographed in a Brazilian museum in 1970 was a few rungs down the evolutionary ladder from modern man; it may have been a vital clue to the possibility of evolution in the New World, but the skull has since been lost. Based on this sole such specimen of uncertain provenance, as archaeologists say, Bryan believes that ". . . biological evolution probably occurred within America from a paleoanthropic ancestor to explain at least some of the highly diverse populations of Modern American Indians."[27]

10

A Myth Comes to Life—
The Flagstaff Dig

The legend of the fall of man, possibly may be all that
has survived of such a time before, for some unknown
reason, the whole world was plunged back again under the
undisputed sway of nature, to begin once more its upward
toilsome journey through the ages.

—Frederick Soddy,
Nobel Laureate, 1921

At the beginning of the First World, there was only endless space
with no beginning and no end. Then Taiwa, the Great Creator,
made Sotuknang, the first person, to carry out his plan for life.

Sotuknang, following Taiwa's instructions, created the universe. On the earth, air, water, and mountains were brought into
being. Then Sotuknang created Kokyanwuti, Spider Woman,
who was to remain on earth as his helper. Spider Woman in
turn took some *tuchvala* (saliva) and molded it into two twin
beings. She covered these twins with a cape made of creative
wisdom itself, and sang the Creation Song over them. When
Spider Woman removed the cape, the two beings came to life.
The twins traveled far and wide, setting all the earth's vibratory,
or spiritual, centers in motion, and the universe quivered in tune.
Thus the earth was made an instrument of sound, vibration, and
spirit for carrying praise to the Creator. After this, one of the
twins was sent to the North Pole and the other to the South Pole.

The twins were placed in charge of the earth's vibratory centers to keep the earth stable and rotating properly.

In the same manner as she created the twins, with earth and *tuchvala,* Spider Woman created the birds, the animals, and finally many human beings in the image of Sotuknang. Each human being was given vibratory centers within his body, in resonance with those of the earth and the universe. One center was the heart that pulsed with the spirit of life itself. Sotuknang gave each group of human beings speech and the power to reproduce and multiply. The People of the First World understood the mystery of their parenthood and the nature of man.

The first people went out in different directions and multiplied in number. They knew no sickness; not until evil entered the world did people get sick in body or spirit. Those who permitted evil feelings to enter their hearts were said to be of two hearts. Only the wise medicine men, who knew how man was constructed, could tell what was wrong with a person and how to correct it. A medicine man would use small crystals to look at the body's vibratory centers and make his diagnosis.

Eventually, evil in the form of jealousy and suspicions ran rampant in the world. People began to wage war against each other. Only a few in every group lived by the laws of Creation. Sotuknang, displeased, decided to destroy the world and create another one so the good people could start over again. The good people were gathered up and led to a big mound where the Ant People lived. When they were all safe, Taiwa commanded Sotuknang to destroy the world by fire because the Fire Clan had been its leader. All the volcanoes of the world opened up and the skies rained fire.

To cool the world off, Sotuknang had the land and the waters change places. Then the good people emerged from their ant hill into the Second World. The people quickly multiplied in numbers. They built homes and villages. From the Ant People they had learned to store food. They made things with their hands and began to trade and barter with one another; this is where the trouble started. Everything they needed was in the Second

World, but they began to want more. They traded for things they didn't need. Once again the people drew away from the ways of the Creator. The people began to fight and wars began between villages. Again the good people who sang the song of the Creator were gathered up and put in the care of the Ant People underground. Then Sotuknang told the twins to abandon their stations at the poles. The earth teetered off balance, tumbled over, and froze into solid ice, and the wicked people died.

After Sotuknang made the Third World ready for occupancy, the good people emerged again. This time, big cities and entire countries were built up. There were mighty civilizations with many advancements, but eventually the creative powers were' used in destructive and evil ways. Some people made a *patuwvota*, a shield made of elephant hide, and made it fly through the air with their creative power. On this shield these people flew to big cities and attacked them. Corruption and war doomed the Third World like the other worlds.

Sotuknang instructed Spider Woman to save the worthy, those with the song still in their hearts, by sealing them up in hollow reeds with some cornmeal and water. Then Sotuknang destroyed the Third World by loosing the waters upon the earth. Waves higher than mountains rolled upon the land, and the rains never stopped. Continents broke up and sank beneath the sea. Cities and worldly treasures were left at the bottom of the sea. When all was over the people in the reeds floated about in the waters of the new world, the present Fourth World.

As the people floated about, they passed by steep mountains and came to rest on one peak jutting above the waters. Here Spider Woman showed them how to make boats out of the hollow reeds they came in. Then the people set off to find a place where they could make their new home in the Fourth World. They drifted with the wind toward the rising sun and reached a rocky island, but it was not big enough.

They drifted east, sometimes paddling, stopping at island after island. Finally, they came to a big land stretching north and south as far as they could see. In places, mountains rose from the shores. This land had grass, and trees, and an abundance of seeds and nuts for food. The people were content to stay there year after year. But Spider Woman said that they would have to leave: Life was too easy and pleasant here, and the people would soon fall into evil ways again. Then Sotuknang appeared before them. Looking across the water to the west the people could see the islands they had left behind. Sotuknang sank one island after another, washing away the footprints of their Emergence. He told them that if they preserved the memory and the meaning of their Emergence, these steppingstones would someday emerge again to testify to the truth of their origins.

The people separated and traveled in different directions to claim all the new land for the Creator. They were told that to the north they would find cold and ice. This was the Back Door to this land; those who would later come through this Back Door, they were told, would enter this new land without their consent.

The Hopi tribe, after traveling far and wide, came to settle in their present home, Oraibi in northern Arizona. The Bear Clan was the first to arrive; they were appointed the leading clan on this Fourth World. The Oraibi area was poor in resources. There was no running water to irrigate their crops; the Hopi people depended on the scanty rainfall which they had to evoke with their prayers. To survive in this desolate land, they had always to remember and have faith in the supremacy of their Creator, who had brought them to this Fourth World.[1]

The preceding account is from Hopi Indian myth. The Hopi are Puebloan Indians whose residence on the dry, desolate northern Arizona plateau can be traced back at least 3,000 years. Their key village of Oraibi is the oldest continuously occupied settlement in North America, dating back to at least the third century after Christ. The Hopi are genetically and linguistically very different from all their Indian neighbors. Their world view is deeply religious in nature; its esoteric meanings have been kept inviolate among the traditionalists. In this day of airplanes and televisions, they faithfully practice and preserve their beliefs in a year-long mytho-religious system of ceremonies and rituals. These activities are punctuated by dances, songs, recitations, meditations, fastings, and prayers as complex and esoteric as any in the world. In one ceremony, they pray over their seeds and water to effect faster growth; in another, they dance with live poisonous rattlesnakes in their mouths to symbolize the uplifting of the serpent, or sexual force. Of all North American Indian groups, they have maintained the purest and most direct connections with their roots and origins. The Hopi Indian world is the least anglicized of all North American tribes. More than any other Indian group, the Hopi's occult world preserves the shamanistic tradition of the Paleo-Indians and the Cro-Magnons.

The Hopi are secretive about their culture and myths, and what they do reveal is often intentionally distorted. As Ruth Beebe Hill, author of *Hanta Yo*, has said, "As soon as you take out a pencil and paper with the Indians, you're one thing to them—an anthropologist—and what they tell anthropologists is always distorted." As a result, Hopi and other Indian beliefs are generally dismissed as crude folklore with little relationship to "enlightened science." But on occasion, scientists have become close with Indian wise men and made key discoveries by interpreting what little they were told of the Indians' oral history and myths. For example, the recent discovery of the Paleo-Indian Abrigo do Sol site in Brazil's Amazon basin (see page 113) resulted from following up on Indian oral history. In 1971, South American Indians, the wild Wasusu Indians of Brazil, were moved from their home in the jungle to a reservation on the savannah. The land they had been living on was needed for its valuable lumber and then for farms. The government charged that the Wasusu, like other local groups, were really a savannah tribe who had no claim to the jungle lands. In a desperate search for friends in order to end their exile, the Indians turned to a photographer they trusted, Jesco von Puttkamer. One Indian spokesman told Puttkamer, "If you will help us, I will show you secret things we would never show to any other *civilizado*. These things will prove to the big people of the government that our land in the jungle has belonged to the Indians since long before any *civilizados* came, and thus it is our home now. If the big people know this, then they will let us move back."[2]

The Indians took Puttkamer deep into the jungle to a large stone cave. Subsequent archaeological excavation has shown that this unsuspected Paleo-Indian site has been continuously inhabited for 12,000 years, though no evidence of Paleo-Indians had previously been found anywhere in this region. The carvings on the walls of the cave showed that many of the Wasusu ceremonial traditions went back to the days of the cave's first inhabitants. There were depictions of masks worn by medicine men, sun worship, and the widespread Amazon custom of men playing sacred bamboo flutes—the Brotherhood of the Flute. (Legend has it that women once possessed the flutes and power over men.) The usually cooperative Indians fell silent when questioned about a certain ceremonial stone found in the cave and the rituals performed there, these being too sacred to tell white men about.

The valuable information that came to light in the cave about South American Paleo-Indians produced heartwarming results: The Wasusus were permitted to leave the savannah reservation and return to the jungle. The government acted to restore their homeland under a law which said that any land on which Indians have lived and are now living cannot be taken away from them. The land titles the government had given the big agricultural and industrial combines to work in the valley were rescinded, and the territory was made the property of the Wasusu people forever.

In the earliest period of southwestern archaeology, between 1880 and 1910, the living Pueblo Indian tribes were seen as surviving examples of a culture of great antiquity. Their myths and migration legends were intensively collected. For example, F. H. Cushing* studied among the Zuni Indians of New Mexico, and

---

* Cushing was sent out by the Smithsonian Institution. He spent four and a half years with the Zuni and became one of their war chiefs.

Jesse Walter Fewkes did so with the Hopi Indians of Arizona in an effort to reconstruct a reasonable history of the Pueblos. Both men found this information basic for interpreting the prehistoric ruins of the southwest. When Fewkes checked on the stopping points of various migrations and the architecture used at the time as described in myth, he was often successful in locating new prehistoric sites. Fewkes also spent time deciphering symbols on pottery, trying to trace these migrations more effectively. On this basis, Fewkes surveyed the archaeological sites of northern Arizona. Despite Fewkes's successes, this productive line of inquiry was abandoned by later archaeologists, who complained about the inconsistencies and vagueness in the oral accounts and ignored the truths the legends contained.

I have taken the abbreviated version of the Hopi origin myth presented in the beginning of this chapter from what I believe to be the best version available, one with a great deal of truth, and many verifiable aspects regarding Indian origins. While it is basically like other Hopi origin myths, this version clarifies many important elements for the first time. This version was essentially presented in the *Book of the Hopi* by Frank Waters. Waters was able to get close to the Hopi through a Hopi artist who lived in Old Oraibi, Oswald White Bear Fredericks, a nephew of the last village chief of Oraibi. White Bear gathered the source material for Waters from some thirty Hopi elders over the course of several years. Many of these elders, who spoke no English, were relatives and/or clan brothers of White Bear. Much of the information could only be given under certain conditions because of its sacred character. Each Hopi spokesman gave only the information he was qualified to impart by reason of his clan affiliations and ceremonial duties. No informant fees were paid. The elders cooperated because they regarded the compilation of Waters' book as an important task which would give their children's children a written expression of the traditional viewpoint.

This origin myth describes the Hopi ancestors' coming to the Americas from a now-sunken land in the Pacific, and their three previous worlds representing cultural rises and falls. The San

Francisco Peaks, lofty mountains outside of Flagstaff, Arizona, can clearly be seen from the Hopi mesas seventy miles to the east. The Hopi refer to these mountains as their traditional home. They have a number of shrines in these peaks; it is there that the Kachina people live, the spiritual beings who the Hopi say have helped them over the ages. In their ceremonies, the Hopi dress up in the costumes of the various Kachinas. Interestingly, these peaks contain geologic evidence for the destruction of the three previous worlds as described in myth. The destruction of the last, or third, world by water could correspond to the flooding that occurred in the San Francisco range approximately 25,000 years ago. The destruction of the second world by ice could represent the glacial activity that took place in the peaks approximately 100,000 years ago. And the destruction of the first world by fire could represent the violent volcanic activity that erupted in the mountains approximately 250,000 years ago. Thus, as with the account of creation and the flood in the Bible, the basic elements and sequence of Hopi myth could be correct.

There is even some evidence for the now-sunken Pacific homeland. In June 1977, Drs. Amos Nur of Stanford University and Zvi Ben Abraham of the Wiseman Institute in Israel reported to the Annual Meeting of the American Geophysical Association that they had discovered evidence of the existence of what was once an eighth continent, which they have named "Pacifica." According to Science News, Nur and Abraham said that Pacifica broke into various pieces which "collided with and rumpled the western coastline of North America. . . . other fragments in the meantime were bumping into South America, Alaska, Kamchatka, Japan and East Asia. . . . Pacifica may have left behind little remnants of itself which sank for unknown reasons in the Pacific Ocean."[3] The main physical elements of the origin legend are entirely plausible; the problem with Hopi myth, however, is that no matter how it is interpreted, it places sophisticated and fully modern men in North America at an incredibly early date.

Since 1973, I have been conducting a deep excavation in the San Francisco Peaks, on a slope the Hopi say figures in their mythology. (In July 1975, when I went to re-open the excavation, I was surprised to see many Hopi Indians gathering blue spruce bows for their key summer ceremony, Niman Kachina. In this ceremony, the Hopi bid goodbye to the Kachinas, who have lived with them on their mesas for the first part of the year and are now returning to their home in the San Francisco Peaks. In effect, my excavation constituted a direct confrontation with Hopi myth and origins.) In 1971, I had dug two shallow test pits on this wooded slope to see if the Hopi myth could be supported by archaeology as it was by geology.* I found one small, creamy-colored stone tool that had unmistakably been made by man. The tool was a hide scraper; when its edge became dull, the user had resharpened it by removing a series of slivers from this edge, producing a new sharp but now scalloped edge. Archaeologists call this process "retouch." Considering the fact that chunks of chert (called nodules) were scattered all over the slope, this single piece was all I needed for support. These chert nodules, if found at depth, would have provided Paleo-Indians with an ideal source material from which to make their tools. Chert sources, rare in northern Arizona, would likely have attracted early man.

My excavation goal was to dig a ten-foot square shaft to a depth of thirty-five feet to determine if there was any evidence of human occupation in the very deep and very old deposits of the slope. I chose a relatively level spot next to a dry creek wash for the exploratory shaft. If I found something convincing, then large-scale excavation would be warranted.

In 1973, I dug for almost six months, from June until November, when cold weather and snow forced me to shut down. The shaft reached a depth of twenty feet in one quadrant. Only one-quarter to one-half of the material to twenty feet was actually removed, since the shaft was dug down in staircase fashion with a series of landings. The material left in place would also give

---

* The detailed story of how I came to select this particular slope and location has been told in a paper I presented at the American Anthropological Association's Annual Meeting in 1974 in Mexico City and in my first book, Psychic Archaeology.

independent investigators a chance to later verify my findings. To prevent the sides from caving in, the shaft was braced with heavy wooden timbers and lined entirely with wooden boards. Shovels and small hand tools were used to move the material from the shaft into a large bucket. When the bucket was filled, it was winched up to the surface and then swung on a boom over to the screening area.

In the first seven feet, digging was made almost impossible because of the big boulders which had to be circumvented. Dynamite, air hammers, sledge hammers, and chisels were used to break them up.

All the deposits we dug through were colluvial in nature, the result of rocks and soil being moved downslope by the force of gravity and sometimes water. Only a few zones had the distinctive horizontal bedding which results from water deposition. In the first four feet of excavation we found nothing. Then, from four feet to fifteen feet, flakes and crude stone tools made of chert started to appear. At six feet, a piece of an ancient wooden house post was found. From fifteen to seventeen feet came what I considered to be "classic" stone tools: a chopper and two large scrapers. From the small area excavated at twenty feet came a single scraper just like those found by Richard MacNeish at his site in Ayacucho, Peru. As Leakey had noted at Calico Hills, the stones that looked most like man-made tools instead of "naturefacts" were of the best quality chert.

While I was closing up the site, I received a radiocarbon date from one of the intermediate levels. The bouldery jumble we were digging through at fifteen to sixteen feet was interrupted by a fine-grained water-lain deposit which had bands of charcoal in it. For a full week, with tweezers and dental picks, we laboriously collected bits of charcoal to submit for dating. Teledyne Isotopes (one of the top radiocarbon dating laboratories) determined a date of approximately 25,000 years ago! U.S. Geological Survey geologists who had been periodically visiting the excavation since the start felt that this was an accurate date on the basis of comparative deposits. This was astounding; few truly early Paleo-

A "chopper tool," an artifact from the Flagstaff, Arizona, site. The serrated edge resulting from use wear has been experimentally reproduced on test specimens by "sawing" on dried bone. This artifact was found sixteen feet down, one foot below a zone radiocarbon dated to 25,000 years.

Indian sites had been reported by 1973. Despite the prevalence of the "late entrant" model at that time, it seemed that early man had been at Flagstaff and that this aspect of Hopi myth was right.

In 1974, I showed the artifacts I had collected to Dr. Dennis Stanford, the head paleoanthropologist at the Smithsonian Insti-

A photo of Dr. Thor Karlstrom, a senior geologist at the U.S. Geological Survey, in the shaft at Flagstaff, Arizona. Karlstrom believes that the deeper levels of the shaft are at least 125,000 years old.

tution, who felt that my key problem was to work out thoroughly the geology at the site, thereby forestalling any arguments to the effect that the artifacts might have somehow gotten mixed in with the wrong deposits and been faultily dated. I resumed excavation at Flagstaff in the summer of 1975, digging for only six weeks. In a new section of the shaft, we reached a depth of twenty-eight feet, and in the last week of our digging we turned up several

A "blade" artifact from the Flagstaff, Arizona, site. This artifact was found twenty-seven to twenty-eight feet down in a zone geologists believe to be at least 125,000 years old.

surprises. (Those who think archaeology is exciting ought to try an early-man site. Up until the last week, nothing was found. It was clear that, as at Calico Hills, the tool candidates were in discrete zones, instead of the random pattern one would expect if natural forces were doing the shaping—and we had not found any of the artifact-bearing zones.) The bouldery deposits we were digging in suddenly gave way to a "paleosol," a fossil topsoil where the rich organic ground surface is buried and preserved just as it was ages ago. A paleosol represents a long period of stability with no erosion. If man once inhabited the area, it is upon this thin veneer that he would actually have trod, so this is the best place to look for the relics of primitive man. Our digging in this zone was quickly rewarded. We found flake debris, the waste material from the manufacture of stone tools, and a blade. While geological processes often produce flakes, many experts believe that only a very definite and well-placed blow carefully struck by a human hand can produce a stone blade. This thin and fragile blade came from a depth of twenty-seven to twenty-eight feet. Dr. Thor Karlstrom, a senior geologist with the U.S. Geological Survey, and several of his associates believed the deposits at this depth dated to at least 125,000 years. Based on the dates for the North American glacial sequence and correlating from the 25,000-year date from the fine-grained deposit at the fifteen-foot level, the fine-grained paleosol beginning at twenty-two to twenty-three feet was taken to represent the start of the last interglacial period (70,000 years ago), a relatively warm and stable period.

An added clue for man's presence at the time the blade was struck came from a pollen study conducted for me by Dr. Richard Heavely of Northern Arizona University. Heavely's study showed that the paleosol was dominated by pollen from herbaceous, weedy types of plants. Even though the site was in the middle of an enormous forest, at times in the past weeds had grown in the immediate area. Heavely pointed out that this pattern typically occurs in areas which have been highly disturbed. The question is, who did the disturbing: nature (via a fire) or man (via camping and cutting)?

As another hint of man's presence, we found an "Apache tear" at the sixteen-foot level. Apache tears, round drops of volcanic glass, were collected as ornaments by early man in the southwest. There are no Apache tear deposits in the San Francisco Peaks, and the closest source was probably more than seventy miles away.[5] The Apache tear we found had apparently been carried in and left at the site by an ancient collector over 25,000 years ago.

As was the case with Leakey at Calico Hills, some archaeologists agreed with me that I had found bona-fide artifacts while others were noncommittal or disagreed. Like Drs. Arthur Jelinek and Vance Haynes of the University of Arizona, Dennis Stanford agreed that many of the materials from above fifteen feet were tools, but he felt that nature could somehow have struck the blows required to produce the stone flakes from the deeper zones (greater than 25,000 years old) during violent downhill tumbling. This interpretation dismisses the fact that most of these flakes came from fine-grained deposits representing episodes of gentle deposition. Further, the markings on these flakes were unlike those noted by several archaeologists who have carried out research concerning the exact nature of alterations to rocks resulting from stream or downhill movement. Dr. Francois Bordes, as he held the blade found at twenty-seven to twenty-eight feet, rejected the "downhill Mother Nature theory," pointing out that the delicate blade couldn't have been moved very far from where it was struck or it would have been broken; its edges, at least, would show signs of abrasion. Dr. George Carter unequivocally declared the blade man-made and similar to one from Calico Hills and those found at the very early San Diego sites. Dr. Richard MacNeish, the highly regarded director of the Peabody Archaeological Foundation, wrote, "It is highly probable that many of the objects were made by man—particularly the three lowest 'choppers' and the lower flakes have possibilities that should be further investigated."[6]

On the other hand, Dr. Paul Martin of the University of Arizona*, a staunch supporter of the 12,000-years-ago "late-entrant model" and the prime devil's advocate against earlier Paleo-Indian dates, wrote after visiting the site, "At Flagstaff, I was impressed with Jeff's field technique, willing to believe his geological-age interpretation, and dubious about his supposed artifacts. Were they indeed man-made and not the result of weathering? . . . if those who diagnose tools all agree that Jeff has the real thing, then I must yield."[7]

Dr. Martin's requirement that I find artifacts at Flagstaff that would be acceptable to all diagnosticians may have been overly stringent; as Professor Alex Krieger of the University of Washing-

---

* Dr. Martin is Professor and Chief Scientist, Laboratory of Paleoenvironmental Studies, Department of Geosciences.

ton has said, "Nothing in archaeology that I have ever heard of, or seen, has been entirely satisfactory in every way!"[8] In the summer of 1977, I returned to Flagstaff for six more weeks of excavation, little daunted, but fervently wishing I had Leakey's Calico Hills budget so I could stop such piecemeal excavation seasons and finish the shaft. I was eager to resolve the controversy once and for all, and to vindicate the Hopi origins myth, since the question of the age of early man in the Americas and Indian origins was still an open one in 1977.

At Harvard in 1976, I consulted Mark Roberts, who had worked closely with Ruth Tringham, who had done the seminal studies on edge wear. Looking at the Flagstaff materials in regard to edge wear, he said that even without a microscope he could see distinctive edge-wear patterns on several of the items. Roberts recommended that I do some controlled experiments of my own using the chert from the site.

Excavating in 1977, I had in my crew two graduate students from Northern Arizona University experienced in flintknapping. These students chipped chert from the site to the same shapes and edge angles as my tool candidates and we conducted wear tests. In these preliminary experiments, we quickly learned how to reproduce the two distinct edge-wear patterns observed in the collection. One wear pattern was reproduced by "shaving" on green ponderosa pine in the same way as a carpenter uses a plane. After ten minutes of "shaving," small straight-sided micro flakes snapped off parallel to the edge on the side of the edge making contact with the wood, and on the opposite side parallel rounded (scaler) micro-flakes with ridges between them came off. "Shaving" leather—as if to scrape a hide clean—did not produce these features; "shaving" on bone and antler was found to be inimical to the production of any kind of edge features at all. The second distinctive wear pattern was reproduced by "sawing" on dry bone. After fifteen to twenty minutes of sawing, alternating micro-flakes came off both edge surfaces in a pattern reminiscent of a "serrated" knife edge. Sawing on ponderosa pine did not produce these edge features.

That summer, I decided to follow the more productive soil zone which seemed to be developing more strongly toward the creek side of the shaft. To do this, we had to tunnel into the shaft wall. After six weeks we had tunneled back nine feet, shoring up the sides and roof as we went along. We found more waste flakes, another blade, and several items with edge wear.

It was now clear that the tools in the paleosol were in two discrete zones: one from twenty-two to twenty-three feet and one from twenty-seven to twenty-eight feet in depth. One distinctive tool motif for the entire collection was now emerging. We had recovered a total of seven tool candidates with the same triangular carpenter's-plane-like design, which are called end scrapers. Five of these tools were made of chert and two of basalt. Even more reassuring, all seven showed edge wear in the same distinctive position and pattern. These items looked like "shavers" and all showed the edge wear "shaving" characteristically produced. An additional prize came from sixteen feet, where, while trying to dislodge a large boulder, one student found a chert core. Along one edge of this core someone had removed as many as eight flakes in a row. By the end of 1977 field season, we had flaking debris, flakes, blades, and cores, as well as tools which showed distinctive wear patterns. While we hadn't found any material suitable for radiocarbon dating in the deeper zones, the U.S. Geological Survey geologists (including Dr. Thor Karlstrom, a senior geologist) we consulted with were still sure we were at least 125,000 years back in time. In fact, they thought we were far enough back in time that the deposits could possibly reflect evidence for a magnetic reversal—i.e., a change in the polarity (positive and negative) of the earth's magnetic poles, which occurs every several hundred thousand years—and they collected appropriate samples.

In 1978 the Society for American Archaeology held its annual meeting in Tucson, and a number of archaeologists from different institutions looked at my Flagstaff materials. Dr. Alan Bryan, the early-man specialist from the University of Alberta, was very impressed by what he saw. He picked out twenty-one bona-fide flakes, noting that several had been retouched or showed edge wear. Brian Reeves from the University of Calgary, in Canada, said he liked most of the material and, like Bryan, thought the deepest materials were the best. Emma Lou Davis of the Los Angeles Museum and R. Esmee Webb of London University were also convinced by the materials. Most important was the opinion of Robson Bonnichsen of the University of Maine. Bonnichsen, a skilled flintknapper, is familiar with many of the techniques the Paleo-Indians used to make their tools. Usually the severest of critics, Bonnichsen said that he had no problem accepting some of the materials as man-made. He especially liked the chert core from which many parallel flakes had been removed, agreeing with Bryan that it seemed as though the ancient toolmaker had also tried to sharpen the nose of the core by removing two large flakes in opposite directions.

At the end of the week, Bryan accompanied me to Flagstaff to visit the site. In addition to his archaeological training, Bryan has had postdoctoral training in geology, and after walking the slopes with me and picking through naturally broken chert piles, he agreed with me that Mother Nature had nothing to do with what I called artifacts, and felt that further work at the Flagstaff site had the potential to make *all* archaeologists finally acknowledge the presence of truly early man in the Americas. He agreed to help me during the next dig season.

In the summer of 1979, Bryan, his wife Dr. Ruth Gruhn who is also an archaeologist at the University of Alberta, and two of their graduate students came to Flagstaff to excavate for three weeks. They hoped to find one "super" artifact that would serve to clinch the case for the earliest of Paleo-Indians' having been at Flagstaff. Instead of having to rely on the unexciting fine points of microscopic lithic analysis, we all hoped for one artifact that even "the man on the street" could see was unquestionably made by man. I agreed to let Bryan do whatever he wanted during this time, purposefully keeping away from the day-to-day excavation activity so that Bryan's effort could serve as independent verification of my earlier work.

I felt I was in good hands. Bryan has conducted more early-man excavations than any other archaeologist; Gruhn excavated the 14,500-year-old Wilson Butte cave site, and they have both visited virtually every known early-man site.

Before excavation began, both Gruhn and Bryan agreed that a good percentage of what I had found at the site showed the work of human hands; they were full of good spirits and optimism. But day after day they dug with nothing to show for it. Bryan even tried going deeper, and took part of the shaft down to thirty-five feet. After two weeks, with just one week of digging left, Gruhn began to think that since they weren't excavating near a clear-cut cultural feature such as a campsite, a hearth, or a "kill," they weren't going to find anything very conclusive.

Finally they found several items that fit the edge-wear pattern at twenty-eight feet in depth. But just as things were starting to look up, Bryan's father passed away and he and Ruth left immediately.

When I arrived to close the site, everything was being wrapped up. Samples were packed and ready to go, some to the University of Alberta for pollen analysis and others to the Smithsonian for radiocarbon dating. There was some excitement because one of the graduate students, Doug Schnurrenberger, had found a medium-sized ear bone in the tunnel at twenty-eight feet. (Subsequent analysis has shown that the ear bone is not that of a man or any common animal such as a deer or camel; the bone is presently at the Smithsonian for typing. I suspect it may belong to a marine mammal which would, of course, have great implications concerning the presence of man.)

Following my usual pattern, I began going over the other materials found during the week. There were the usual oddly shaped fragments of chert, but there was also a flat stone, a piece of hard volcanic ash approximately four inches by six inches in size which had a number of straight lines on both of its sides. It looked like

The broken side of "The Flagstaff Stone"—an engraved stone found twenty-three feet below the surface in the side of a mountain in northern Arizona. The stone is believed to be approximately 100,000 years old and shows that fully modern, technologically sophisticated Paleo-Indians lived in the Americas two or three times earlier than fully modern Cro-Magnon man appeared in Europe. Note the grooves radiating from a common intersection near the center bottom edge of the stone and how this pattern is repeated at the edge of the stone.

an engraving; it had to be an engraving! There was no way nature could score such a small stone with so many absolutely straight lines at such angles—on one side, three lines crossed at a single point in a kind of asterisk near the center of the stone and this pattern was repeated near the edge of the stone (see illustration, page 212). Here, finally, was the conclusive piece we had all hoped for. It was as if a Paleo-Indian had left his irrefutable signature for us.

The unbroken side of "The Flagstaff Stone." Note the long, straight line which goes across the stone from bottom right to top left. This "double" line gives the impression that the engraving tool jumped out of its initial groove and superimposed a second line over the first line.

This engraved stone had come from the productive twenty-three-foot zone in the last foot dug in the tunnel about fifteen feet into the mountainside. Ironically, it had been tossed on the table the day before and almost gone unrecognized. Now a Paleo-Indian site had an engraving to rival the Old World sites; in fact, this engraving had to be two to three times as old as the earliest Cro-Magnon engraving. Despite what I'm sure will come to be increasing dissent, I believe that here in one artifact alone there is evidence of fully modern man's earlier presence and earlier so-phistication in the New World than in the Old World.

While engravings of reindeer and bison catch the eye, geometric engravings usually have a much greater significance. As noted earlier, Alexander Marshack of Harvard's Peabody Museum has shown correlations between geometric markings and the phases of the moon. The Australian aborigines have developed a highly abstract art wherein a piece of bark painted with geometric signs may represent a map to a sacred area. The interpretation of these geometric symbols is passed on from one generation to another in a ceremonially prescribed way. The making of such art is a highly restricted privilege, and the designs are meaningful only to initiates. The aborigines' social structure is heavily dependent on this hierarchical right to knowledge.[9] One can only wonder about the Paleo-Indian social world that led to the production of the "Flagstaff Engraving," and what specific information it preserves.

In March 1980, just before this book went to press, Marshack examined the engraved stone from the Flagstaff site and concluded that the Flagstaff stone "looked" intentionally engraved.[10] He agreed with me that the very straight long doubled lines* were the best examples of engraving. He said that the lines on the stone looked just like those he has seen on many stones engraved by Cro-Magnon man in Europe. But Marshack's analysis also turned up some problems which distressed him. The highly weathered and now very soft surface of the stone was apparently damaged in cleaning and thus many of the lines had been stripped of bits of information which would have let Marshack make a more conclusive determination. Marshack said that if we could resolve these problems then the "Flagstaff stone" would be one of the most important artifacts ever found in the entire world.[11]

In an effort to get answers to Marshack's questions, I took the stone to a petrographer, a geologist who specializes in the microscopic description and study of rocks. I selected a petrographer

---

* Doubled or "twinned" lines which consist of two lines side by side in a fashion remindful of the parallel grooves on a record, most likely made when the sharp engraving tool skipped out of its track and made a line adjacent to the first line.

who specialized in rocks of the same volcanic type as the stone was made of. Dr. Arend Meijer, a geology professor at the University of Arizona, studied the stone in relation to Marshack's report for several days. It turned out that Meijer could reconstruct some of the damage done to the stone. Most important, Meijer, with the aid of a powerful microscope, was able to see that the very straight long doubled line on the more complex face did not suffer any damage during cleaning and was indeed a very "old groove." Meijer said that this line retained its original contour (shape) and even contained a clearly undisturbed coating of the soil in which the stone was originally buried.[12]

Meijer also put to rest the question of possible natural origin. Meijer said that: "The geometric arrangement of the grooves, especially the fact that some of the grooves radiate from a common intersection, makes it highly unlikely that the grooves were formed naturally in a streambed or similar environment. The consistent depth of the grooves also argues against a natural origin."[13]

When I went to pick up the stone, Meijer's parting words to me were, "I am convinced it [the stone] is a man-made effect."[14] In May of 1980, I will be presenting a research report on the stone at the Society for American Archaeology's annual meeting in Philadelphia. On April 30, 1980, just before leaving for this meeting, in order to get further clarification on the stone and the general age of the grooves, I sought the opinion of a second petrographer. Dr. John Ferry of Arizona State University's Geology Department was able to make some critical added observations. Ferry concludes that the clay in most of the grooves on both sides of the stone was original (preexcavation) material which was *not* introduced during the cleaning process. To Ferry, this means that *all* the grooves with clay in them were old.

Ferry, like Meijer, is also impressed by the geometric pattern and the generally consistent depth and width of the grooves and is able to show that the lines did not downcut at the edges of the stone and were once part of much longer lines. He believes the stone was once part of a much larger stone which had lines on it.

Ferry projects the following history for the stone: The engraving of a much larger stone and subsequent fracture resulted in the stone we now have. As evidence for this, he cites the truncation of the lines at the stone's edges, especially the partial starlike pattern at the edge of the stone which is immediately below the complete starlike pattern. The double or V lines which occur near the edges also seem significant. Ancient handling of this stone resulted in its well-rounded and worn edges. Breakage of the tip off one side of the stone followed by burial soon thereafter resulted in the entire stone being coated with clay. This accounts for the still relatively rough edge of the broken portion of the stone.

The stone is still under study in an effort to extract more details about its manufacture and history. We want to determine how much the stone weathered before it was engraved, how much it weathered after it was engraved, and how much time elapsed between engraving and burial. I would also like to find out what the Hopis have to say about the "Flagstaff Engraving."

Alan Bryan and I plan to resume excavation at the Flagstaff site in 1981 or 1982. Our prospects have continually improved as we have tunneled back toward and under the dry creekbed which would have acted as a natural trap in times past. What new surprises lie directly under the creek?

11

Gifts From the "Before People"— Life in the Garden

On ancient so-called fables: Can we not read into them some justification for the belief that some former forgotten race of men attained not only to the knowledge that we have so recently won, but also to the power that is not yet ours?

—Frederick Soddy,
Nobel Laureate, 1921

If we give imagination free rein and try to flesh out the world of the physically modern Paleo-Indians who we already know possessed sophisticated tools, some very provocative speculations arise. These 40,000-to-100,000-year-old Paleo-Indians may have possessed virtually every key ingredient of civilization, including skills not believed to have been developed until just 7,000 to 9,000 years ago in Egypt and Mesopotamia. The birth of these civilizations may have been based on the application of technologies learned from Paleo-Indians who invented and mastered these skills tens of thousands of years earlier. Going one bold step further, these Paleo-Indians may even have possessed many of the technological innovations credited to nineteenth-century man and some of those we are just now discovering in our day.

Our debt to the Paleo-Indians could include the first domestication of plants, the first domestication of animals, the first practice of freeze-drying food, pottery, the calendar, astronomy, and the applied understanding of the physics behind electro-magnetics and Einstein's gravity waves. In the field of medicine, the debt seems to include the use of aspirin, quinine for malaria, insulin for diabetes, the predecessor to digitalis (a heart stimulant), anesthetics, powerful narcotics and hallucinatory drugs, and even birth-control pills. Admittedly, it seems unlikely that many of these items were invented twice; crediting the Paleo-Indians with such crucial and fantastic discoveries may seem like reaching for straws in the wind. Nevertheless, there are definite threads of evidence leading to every one of these speculations.

Cultivation of Plants

The American Indians developed crops that now provide over half of the world's food. The Indians, first-rate farmers, harvested more varieties of plants than were used or even known in any other region of the world. These included corn, beans, squash, pumpkins, amaranth, potatoes, tomatoes, peanuts, pineapples, papayas, manioc, chives, chilies, cashews, sarsaparilla, vanilla beans, and cocoa. The Indians also cultivated rubber, chicle (chewing gum), tobacco, and cotton.

In addition to this cornucopia, it seems that the Indians were the first to make the miraculous jump from the gathering of wild plants to the development and sowing of domesticated plants. Domesticated wheat and rye first appeared in the Near East 9,000 years ago. Summer squash and pumpkins appeared in the Americas by 8,000 years ago, and corn cobs have been found in Tehuacan, Mexico, dating to 9,000 years ago. But the grinding tools found in the Americas dating to interglacial times (70,000 to 170,000 years ago) indicate a much longer incubation period for the manipulation of plants in the New World than in the Old World. In fact, we have evidence that the Indians had a domesticated plant during interglacial times—corn, or as Indians called it, maize. No wild form of corn has ever been found. In 1954, Dr. Elsa Barghoorn, a botanist at Harvard University, conclusively identified fossil pollen grains from a drill core as being those of corn. These fossil pollen grains came from a depth of two hundred feet below Mexico City and were given an interglacial date of approximately 80,000 years in age.[1] Since this period antedated the accepted appearance of man on the North American continent, the pollen was thought to be that of a wild corn which has since become extinct, even though these pollen grains were indistinguishable from those of modern cultivated corn. With the new interglacial datings for man and grinding tools in the Americas, this fossil corn pollen could easily have come from domesticated corn. Hopi legend maintains that they had cultivated corn from the start.

Domestication of Animals

The domestication of animals, like the cultivation of plants, is generally believed to have begun in the Near East 7,000 to 9,000 years ago, when goats, pigs, sheep, cattle, and dogs were domesticated in the Old World. The domestication of animals in the New World is believed to be a late event—5,000 years ago— limited to the dog and turkey in North America and the dog, guinea pig, duck, llama, and alpaca in South America. To explain this markedly later date, scientists point out that in the richer environment of the New World men would have had no need of such an (artificially) guaranteed food source.

Dogs were the first animals to be domesticated in the Old World and in northwestern Europe the date may reach as far back as 11,000 years ago. But once again a new discovery in the Americas sinks traditional beliefs, showing that the Paleo-Indians led the way. At the Old Crow excavations in the Yukon, paleontologist Brenda Beebe said, "Our most surprising discovery is the jaws of several domesticated dogs, some of which appear to be at least 30,000 years old. This is almost 20,000 years older than any other known domesticated animals anywhere in the world."[2]

Even more tantalizing is the possibility that the Paleo-Indians had domesticated horses. The horse evolved in the Americas and eventually migrated to the Old World across the Bering Bridge hundreds of thousands of years ago. Then, around 10,000 years ago, the horse apparently became extinct in the Americas. The Spanish Conquistadores reintroduced the horse to the New World in the fifteenth century. Yet many Indian legends, including those of the Hopis, talk about how their ancestors rode animals.

The horse is the most frequently encountered animal in Cro-Magnon cave art. Archaeologists generally consider that the horse was only a source of food for Old World and New World ice age hunters. But why did the cave artists draw so many horses when reindeer and buffalo were a more easily available and important food supply? Why did Cro-Magnon man frequently depict his horses in a state of pregnancy? Perhaps the depiction of pregnant mares signified the best time to follow mares in order to capture foals, which are helpless for at least four hours after birth. Once a foal was captured, the devoted mother would likely follow to supply milk to the infant; such a "tamed" horse would be easy to break for riding. During hard times, or after injury or death, the animal could always be eaten. With scholars believing that the horse wasn't domesticated until about 5,000 to 7,000 years ago, the main objection to Paleo-man's domestication of the horse has been that the date would be "too early," but with the 30,000+-year-old domestication date from Old Crow, this all changes.

One may ask for some direct evidence of Paleo-man having ridden the horse, but after such a long time, rope or leather halters, bridles and saddle pads could not be expected to survive. Instead, possible direct evidence comes from a Cro-Magnon engraving. The "Arudy horse head," from France, is carved on a piece of horn and shows in remarkable detail a piece of rope around the horse's muzzle and knotted under the chin. Other sections of rope run diagonally up along the cheekbone, probably crossing behind the ears, but this area is obliterated. This pattern is exactly like that of a modern-day rope halter. Rope halters of this sort are believed to be forerunners of the modern bridle.

Horse remains are also found at many Paleo-Indian sites. The horse bones from Old Crow show a provocatively high incidence of fracture of the splint bones. "In modern horses," reports Dr.

William Irving, the leader of the Old Crow excavations, "this accident occurs when animals are forced to run at top speed over hard ground. Such fractures are extremely rare in wild populations."[3]

Freeze-Drying

The freeze-drying of food to preserve it, a boon to backpackers, is generally believed to be a modern invention (1940s). But Indians in the high Andes Mountains of Peru and Bolivia have been using a primitive freeze-drying process to preserve their potatoes for at least 8,000 years. *

According to Peruvian Indian legend, the potato is a gift of the gods and apparently so was the freeze-drying process, though Europeans didn't catch on to this second gift until only recently. Professor Norman R. Thompson of Michigan State University, in a *Los Angeles Times* News Service story which appeared in the *Tucson Citizen* on December 19, 1979, described this Indian freeze-drying process: "They spread the potatoes on rock ledges 10,000-14,000 feet above sea level, where heavy night frosts freeze them solidly. Intense solar radiation thaws them the next day. Alternate freezing and thawing breaks the cell structure, and moisture begins to leave, helped by tramping on them with bare feet. The result is a freeze-dried product that keeps indefinitely."

Pottery

In the complex of ancient technological breakthroughs leading to settlement and civilization in the Near East, the making of pottery vessels joins with plant and animal domestication. The

---

* Today the potato of the American Indian is a staple in virtually every country of the world. In the United States and Europe it is the most important home-grown food. According to many experts, the potato has even helped change the history of the world. For example, studies attribute the European population explosion of the 18th century to the introduction of the potato. Some experts say that the salable food surpluses it provided made the Industrial Revolution possible.

discovery of how to treat clay, to temper it, form it, and then fire it to obtain a product with qualities vastly different from what one started with, is considered to be one of man's major achievements; undoubtedly, pottery vessels for cooking and storage made life much more pleasant.

The 8,000-to-9,000-year-old Near East pottery date has recently been superseded by 13,000-year dates from Fukui cave and Senfukuji rock shelter in Kyushu, Japan. While this indicates that ice age man (greater than 12,000 years in age) eventually developed pottery, the idea of the Paleo-Indians making pottery is considered ridiculous: the earliest known pottery in the New World comes from Ecuador and the Caribbean and is only 6,000 years old. But the new perspectives on the Paleo-Indians suggest that a re-analysis of a forgotten paper by Max Uhle, the father of Peruvian archaeology, is in order. Given (in German) in 1928 at the Twenty-Third International Congress of the Americas, Uhle's paper reported on the finding of an extinct mastodon associated with pottery.[4] The skeleton was found buried near Quito, Ecuador, by Professor Franz Spellman of the University of Quito. Uhle, who helped Spellman, said that the mastodon showed wound marks and evidence of butchering and burning. Obsidian flakes, a bone point, and about one hundred and fifty potsherds were found around the bones. In 1928, the idea that man and elephants co-existed in the Americas conflicted with the accepted theories of the time, and the paper was greeted with skepticism, to say the least. Now it provides confirmation of both man's early presence in the New World and his use of pottery during the ice age.

Medicine

One of the most celebrated areas of the American Indians' contribution to knowledge is in the field of medicine. Indian medicine men, or shamans, traceable to Paleo-Indian times, became acquainted with the physiological effects of a large number of drugs found in plants and other natural substances. Many Indian remedies have been proven worthless, as have many European folk remedies, but today there are over two hundred Indian drugs in the Official Pharmacopoeia of the United States and the National Formulary—one hundred and seventy from North America and fifty from Central and South America.[5]* The Indians had effective remedies for healing nervous disorders, astringents for wounds and surgery, antiseptics, cathartics such as cascara, febrifuges for fevers, and vermifuges for intestinal worms.[6] Was this extensive knowledge the fruit of trial and error over tens of thousands of years, or was it directly inherited from the omniscient ancestors referred to in Indian myth, the sages whose genius has been distorted and often misinterpreted by later generations?

Not only did Indian shamans have a full kit of drugs, but prior to contact with the Europeans they wielded bulbed syringes for cleaning wounds and injecting medicine into them, rubber enema bulbs, and dental inlays of gold and jade. They performed successful amputations, open-skull surgery called trephination, and Caesarian sections. For paralysis, some South American Indians used the mild shock of the electric eel. There were preventatives and remedies for indigestion: for example, before eating potatoes the Quechuas of Lake Titicaca dip them into an aqueous suspension of clay to prevent "souring of the stomach." Upon examination, the clay was found to consist mainly of kaolin. Not until the 1950s was kaolin introduced into modern medicine as a protective agent and remedy for bacterial infection of the stomach—check the ingredients on a package of your favorite antacid. And the Indians' obstetrical practices, notably the method of expelling the placenta (anticipating the Crede procedure developed centuries later), were far more advanced than those of the invading Europeans.[7]

The Indians' influence on American medicine and pharmacology is not only measured by the enumeration of officially recog-

---

* Dr. Virgil Vogel of Truman College in Chicago has carefully summarized these drugs in his book, *American Indian Medicine*.

nized drugs borrowed from them. Millions of pioneer Americans never saw a doctor, yet their ailments were often effectively cared for. Anyone born in rural America up until World War I can recount the use of a variety of home remedies (sometimes listed in *Farmer's Almanac*), most of which were borrowed from the Indians and handed down over the generations. In short, American folk medicine was heavily influenced by Indian herbal lore.

During the nineteenth century, trained physicians were scarce on the frontier. Even when present, they were not always wanted: There was a revulsion against some of their harsh drugs and objectionable practices, such as bleeding. A group of white lay healers sprang up who based their healing arts on those of the Indians. This folk medicine acted as an intermediary on the road toward official acceptance of many native remedies. The esteem in which Indian cures were held by whites in pioneer days is illustrated by the success of traveling "Indian" medicine shows, which proffered miraculous cure-alls allegedly composed of the red man's most secret *materia medica*. Such potions, of course, were usually just mixtures of alcohol and flavoring with little therapeutic value, aimed solely at taking advantage of the Indian's reputation as healer. Though often exaggerated, it is difficult to believe that such a reputation among the early settlers was founded solely on myth.

One of the Europeans' first encounters with Indian medicine occurred in the bitter-cold winter of 1535–1536. The three ships of Jacques Cartier were locked in the ice of the St. Lawrence River near Montreal. Four feet of snow lay on the ground. By mid-March, scurvy was so rampant that 25 of 110 men had died; the others were desperately ill. The local Indian chief, Domagaia, hearing of the white man's troubles, had the Indian women gather branches of a "certain tree and boil the bark and leaves for a decoction."[8] Drinking this brew, the crew members rapidly recovered their health.

These Indians had never heard of Vitamin C, but they had somehow discovered an effective internal remedy for scurvy, which comes from a deficiency of Vitamin C: the "juice and sappe" of the "certain tree" (hemlock spruce) contained this vitamin. Most Europeans believed that scurvy was caused by bad air. Not until 1776 did James Lind, a British naval surgeon who had read of the Cartier incident, conduct experiments which proved the dietary basis of scurvy. Indians in the Yukon at such ancient sites as Old Crow most likely prevented scurvy as their modern counterparts do, by first eating the adrenal glands of big game animals, making sure that each family member got an equal share. Modern science has very recently discovered that the adrenal glands are the richest source of Vitamin C in all animal or plant tissues.[9]

Long-standing ethnic arrogance held back many researchers, but others studied some of the Indian drugs and when they found them to be effective, had the active agents in these plants chemically synthesized. For example, Dr. Frederick Banting, the discoverer of insulin, credited Indian healers with the "pharmaceutical spadework" which led to the development of this elixir for diabetics.[10] The Indians of British Columbia are reported to have combatted diabetes with an infusion of the root of a spiny, prickly shrub called devil's club. Experiments on rabbits showed that devil's club reduced the blood sugar substantially without toxic effects, proving it effective in the prevention and treatment of diabetes.[11]

Dr. Harlow Brooks has praised the Indians for correctly using the American variety of foxglove for its properties as a cardiac stimulant hundreds of years before the extract digitalis was discovered.[12] Sometimes the natural Indian drugs have qualities the synthetic substitutes cannot duplicate. Cinchona bark was used by South American Indians to treat malarial fevers. After quinine, an extract of cinchona, was synthesized, the cinchona-bark industry was abandoned in South America, but in the Viet Nam war it was found that certain strains of malaria found there were resistant to the laboratory products but responsive to genuine cinchona-bark quinine.[13]

We also owe credit to the Indians for our most useful wonder drug—aspirin. The colonists quickly learned to use the Indian substance salicin, which we call aspirin, to reduce the pain from rheumatism. The Indians obtained salicin from the willow tree; today, a number of synthetic substitutes are available. There is also solid evidence that the Indians inadvertently used the working principle of modern antibiotics long before Dr. Alexander Fleming discovered penicillin in 1928. Fleming, working in a London hospital, made his discovery accidentally when he found that a species of mold secreted a substance that killed staphylococcus bacteria. The event has been hailed as a medical milestone, the first antibiotic, the first of the so-called "miracle drugs" which have saved millions of lives from infections and pneumonia. But the course of medicine might have changed much earlier had researchers purposefully studied certain Indian substances. For example, from wild ginger root doctors have isolated two antibiotic substances, one of which is "very active against Gram-positive pus forming bacteria."[14] Western Indians applied powdered ginger root to wounds, and the Meskwakis used it for throat trouble and earache. The Kwakiutls drew out boils by applying a soft, slimy fungus called "rotten on the ground." The Chickasaws had a similar practice. And there is an historic report of an Indian curing a North Carolina planter's ulcerated leg in the 1700s with "rotten, doated [decayed] grains of Indian corn."[15] Corn smut, a fungus, was also used by the Pueblo Indians.[16]

The chewing of coca leaves as a stimulant by the Incas is well known. The Incas also used coca as an anesthetic in operations, especially skull surgery. Cocaine, a narcotic, is made from the coca leaf; during the nineteenth century it was legally and widely used as a medicine. Sigmund Freud recommended it for fatigue, social timidity, "neuroasthenia," asthma, and nervous stomach disorders. Concoctions of wine and coca extract were very popular in the late 1800s: Thomas Edison used the brew for insomnia, Pope Leo XIII always carried a flask of it, and Ulysses S. Grant relied on it to relieve the pain of his last illness so he could complete his memoirs. A nonalcoholic version combining coca with the African kola nut was developed by an Atlanta pharmacist in 1886; it was the original formula of the now immensely popular soft drink, Coca-Cola. The government has since persuaded the proprietors to omit coca from their mixture.

Today, the medical profession uses cocaine only as a local anesthetic for eye surgery. Coca leaves are only 0.5 percent cocaine; they also contain fourteen other alkaloids and a number of vitamins and minerals. According to Dr. Andrew Weil, a fellow of Harvard Medical School, the effect of these other components as they are used by South American Indians is entirely different from that of cocaine. Weil told a session of the American Association for the Advancement of Science that the coca leaf may be a better medicine than those we now use for stomach disorders, depression, and fatigue. Users experience a pleasant taste followed by warmth in the stomach, an elevation of mood, and feelings of energy.[17] In 1979, another South American stimulant, this one quite legal, caught on in California—guarana, five times higher in caffeine than an equivalent amount of coffee.

The Indians' use of narcotics and hallucinogenic drugs is well known if not widely understood. These narcotics were usually taken in religious rites. Shamans gained great "magical" strength from these drugs and experienced meaningful visions. Recent research by the Russians indicates that subjects under the influence of such drugs demonstrated a variety of psychic abilities. Anthropologist Carlos Castaneda, in his books *The Teachings of Don Juan* and *Flight to Ixtlan*, has told of the "powers" he gained by taking peyote, a variety of cactus, under the guidance of a Yaqui shaman. Mexican Indians used a cereal fungus that is now synthesized as LSD; the early Spanish invaders also recorded their use of Teonanacatl, a "sacred mushroom" which produced visions. The Aztecs and the Mayas took ololiuhqui, which is derived from the seeds of the wild morning glory. The morning glory motif was a dominant theme in their art. And the Olmec of Mexico, the first recognized civilization in the Americas, were fond of a toad, *Bufo marinus*, that produced hallucinations when eaten. Abundant petrified remains of the toad are found at Olmec sites, and the Indians now living in the area still practice the custom.

Most amazing is the chemical insight the South American Indians demonstrated in their use of certain hallucinogenic drugs. Somehow they learned a way to extract complex chemicals from plants and then precisely combine and recombine these chemicals to produce new substances with remarkably different properties. One such chemical process is detailed by Dr. Richard Schultes of Harvard in an article entitled, "The Ethnotoxicological Significance of Additives to New World Hallucinogens."[18] Schultes reports that in the Amazon, the leaves of the woody vine ayahuasca, which contains B-carboline alkaloids, are used with another plant that possesses dimethytryptamine in its leaves. Dimethytryptamine is a hallucinogenic substance which, taken orally, becomes active only in the presence of an amine oxidase inhibitor; the alkaloids of the first plant do the trick. The powerful family of tryptamine drugs is known to Western science only as the result of Indian plant-use studies.

Dr. Marlene Dobkin de Rios of the Department of Psychiatry at the University of California at Irvine believes this chemical knowledge results not from trial and error, but is instead owing to the intelligence of primitive man, the first *Homo sapiens sapiens*. She pictures the native shamans, innocent of any laboratory training, acquiring their complex knowledge intuitively through the use of the right hemisphere of the brain.[19]

The left hemisphere of the brain (which controls the right side of the body) is predominantly involved with analytic, sequential-logical thinking, while the right hemisphere (which controls the left side of the body) is predominantly involved with holistic thought where many inputs are integrated simultaneously instead of sequentially. This right hemisphere has been associated with the intuitive processes of the artist, the musician, and the psychic.[20] Interestingly, the mystical, psychical world of Indians such as the Hopi, shunned by anthropologists, may hold the explanation for the much earlier appearance of sophisticated technologies in the New World than in the Old World. Did the Indians come to use drugs in an attempt to activate the right hemisphere, a hemisphere the first fully modern men readily used, one of the godlike powers Indian myth says man has lost?

We even owe a debt to the Indians for the birth control pill. In his book *American Indian Medicine* Dr. Vogel writes that "Indian fertility drugs helped to call attention to the possibilities and played a role in the research leading to recent discoveries in the field."[21] At the beginning of the nineteenth century, the great naturalist Alexander von Humboldt said that the leading cause of the depopulation of mission Indians on the Orinoco was "the guilty practice of preventing pregnancy by the use of deleterious herbs."[22] Many Indian groups believed that sterility could be artificially induced by taking certain substances. Most of these substances have proven worthless, but not all. One Indian oral contraceptive, stoneseed (Lithospermum ruderale), taken by the Nevada Shoshones, proved surprising when clinically tested. Experimental work showed that mice fed with an extract of this plant had their normal estrous cycle abolished, and the number of estrous smears decreased. Subsequent work with rabbits showed that stoneseed apparently inhibits the actions of gonadotrophins in the ovary. In 1965, researchers at Indiana University tested chickens and mice with this substance finding that it had "powerful inhibitory effects."[23]

Most recently, as reported in the scientific journal *Research in Reproduction*, May 1979, the Chinese are testing an extract of cottonseed as a male contraceptive. The more than four thousand healthy men who were given the extract became infertile after a two-month period. When the treatment was stopped, the men regained fertility in about three months.

Unlike Western medicine, Indian medicine is holistic. The medicine man treated the entire patient, not just the disease or wound. Indians regularly visited the medicine man in an effort to prevent disease. Aleut medicine men developed adaptive muscle surgery to prepare hunters better for their life's work of sitting upright in a kayak all day and drawing the arm far back to throw a harpoon. In treating illness, medicine men used chanting, dancing, prayer, meditation, smoke, incense, steam baths, massage, and talismans. It was believed that one of the main causes of disease lay in the mind of the patient himself, with unfulfilled desires and annoyances vexing the body. Anticipating the work of Sigmund Freud and Carl Jung, shamans often analyzed the patient's dreams in an effort to discover the inner cause of the trouble.

The very presence of the medicine man, who was impressively costumed with skins, necklaces, rattle, bear teeth, and face paint, could instill awe and fear in the patient. The medicine man was often believed to possess supernatural powers; here lay the heart of his effectiveness. What up until recently was considered mere suggestion resulting from faith in superstitious rites is now called the "placebo effect" by the medical fraternity. The dramaturgical structure within which drugs were given and taken clearly had a positive effect on the mind of the sick person; we now know that such influence has physiological consequences.

In 1979, at the University of California, San Francisco, experiments were conducted involving dental patients who were having molars extracted. They were given either a placebo or a pain-killing drug. In the experiments, the patients who received the placebos experienced less pain than those in the drug group. This led the researchers to conclude that placebos can activate a natural pain-relieving system within the body that relies on the secretion of endorphins. (Endorphins are recently discovered morphine-like pain relievers produced by the brain itself.) In another experiment, seventy percent of a group of patients with bleeding peptic ulcers improved after receiving injections of distilled water which their doctors told them was a new medicine. A control group given the same injection but told that it was only an experimental medicine of uncertain effectiveness showed a cure rate of only twenty-five percent. Confidence in one's physician clearly is a factor here, a detail Indian healers did not overlook.[24] Actually, the placebo effect seems also to be essential to the efficacy of many modern drugs.

Dr. Marshall Newman of the University of Washington believes that "only a small portion of native American Indian medical knowledge has come down to us, and all we have is an iceberg's tip."[25] The quantity and the quality of Indian drugs and herbal lore we know of is just a fraction of the prehistoric total. The medical documents of the Aztec and Maya Indian empires were purposefully destroyed by the Spanish Conquistadores and missionaries. Up north, the hostility of the Christian missionaries toward Indian society was particularly brought to bear against the medicine men.

Scientific Knowledge

The range of Indian scientific knowledge is bigger than one would expect. Some ancient Indian groups gained knowledge of the zero, a concept necessary for higher mathematics which the Romans failed to discover. The calendar of the Aztecs, accurate to within a second per year, predicted eclipses of the sun and moon as much as 850 years ahead. The Plains Indians were also diligent observers of the skies and built medicine wheels, circles of stones to enshrine their complex knowledge of the planets and astronomy. The Pawnee drew star charts on leather hides, while the Mayas built observatories just to study the planet Venus, which played a key role in their religion and mythology. Petroglyphs of the Pueblo Indians recorded the supernova of A.D. 1054.

While many are familiar with the Indians' skill with gold, silver, and copper, Dr. John Alden Mason, curator emeritus of the Pennsylvania Museum, notes that "The discovery of ornaments of platinum . . . has astounded modern metallurgists for its melting point (about 1770°C or 3218°F) is beyond the capabilities of primitive furnaces and it was unknown in Europe until quite late [1810]."[26]

Recently, scientists have learned that the Indians experimented with magnetism at least 4,000 years ago, over 2,000 years before the first evidence of Chinese experiments. Big, roly-poly stone

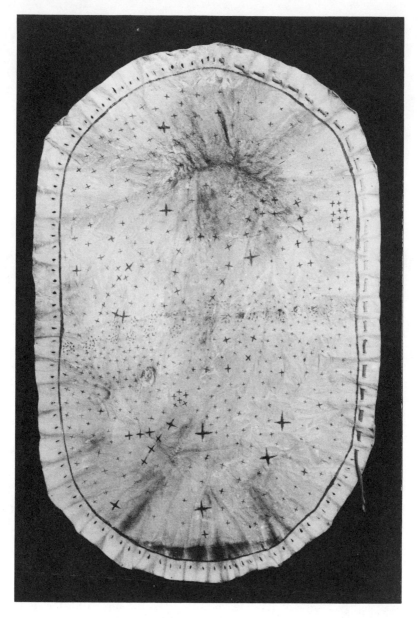

Pawnee star chart on leather hide. The Pawnee were careful sky observers. *Field Museum of Natural History, Chicago*

heads and torsos from ancient Guatemala, called "Fat Boys," were found to sharply attract the needle of a compass held to the navel of some statues or the right temple of others (right brain hemisphere symbolism?). The ancient artisans did not insert magnetic rocks into the figures, but rather carved them around natural magnetic poles in the original basaltic boulders. The "Fat Boy" sculptors apparently knew the physics of the lodestone, a primitive compass for locating direction and other magnetic rocks, some 3,000 years before the Europeans first began using magnetized needles in navigation. The Olmec, who built Mexico's first civilization, sculpted a 3,500-year-old figure of a turtle with a magnetic snout. Dr. Vincent Malmstrom of Dartmouth speculates that the Olmecs may have considered magnetism to be the magical power by which sea turtles found their way across great expanses of ocean.[27] (Another scientific mystery exists in the Olmec's small, polished circular crystals of hematite and magnetite. These concave crystals are polished to such precision and with such precise progressive radii of curvature near the edges that Dr. Ignacio Bernal of Mexico's Natural Institute of Anthropology and History has wondered if they were camera lenses.[28])

Dr. James Beal, a research engineer with the World Institute Council, has noted how in remote times the "holy" places singled out by tribal shamans may have indeed been special. Beal believes that such places could have been situated in the center of a dipole—a node in the earth's magnetic field: The paths of subterranean streams could have formed "a pattern generating changes in the earth's local magnetic field, and associated improvement in positive (+) electrostatic field strength and negative (−) ion concentration."[29] Beal notes that laboratory tests conducted for space exploration show that a locale with a surplus of negative ions in its electro-magnetic field has beneficial physiological effects such as improved performance, equilibrium, burn recovery and healing, and relief from pain and allergic disorders. Such a concern for electro-magnetic fields seems to have influenced the location and spacing of Mayan ceremonial sites. Albert Einstein was eager to see gravity waves harnessed as an unlimited power supply. He felt that these gravity waves could be tapped at certain locations along the earth's surface; perhaps the Indian holy places were also associated with these locations.

Recently, scientists were surprised to learn that a Brazilian tree pours pure diesel fuel. In September 1979, Nobel prize-winning chemist Melvin Calvin reported to the American Chemical Society that, intrigued by Amazon Indian tales of such a tree, he traveled to the Brazilian jungle and was introduced to the copaiba tree. A relative of the rubber tree, the copaiba tree literally pours a golden oil sap when tapped. The sap has been used as a healing ointment, but Calvin said "nobody realized it was diesel fuel 'til I got there this year." Calvin added that the Brazilians have already "put the sap in a car directly out of the tree, and it ran fine . . . what's more you don't even need an oil company."[30] A single drain hole cut in a mature tree (ninety feet high and one hundred years old) yields approximately 5.2 gallons within two hours, and the tree can be retapped at six-month intervals. Calvin and his team at the University of California have begun experimentation with the tree in what may be a novel solution to future gas shortages.

How different a world would we have had today if all the knowledge and practices of the American Indian, instead of being destroyed and suppressed, had been systematically collected without prejudice and preserved as a legacy of creative insight for future study and research. This lost potential is demonstrated by the fact that with all our advances in agriculture, botanists now see drought-resistant, high-yielding amaranth, once the major crop of the Aztecs, as the first of a new breed of supercrop whose cultivation may stamp out malnutrition in the world. Amaranth's seeds and leaves contain a balance of proteins of unusually high quality. In particular, they provide a high concentration of lysine, an essential amino acid lacking in modern cereals, which do not supply all the body's protein needs. Amaranth leaves can be eaten as green vegetables, and the tiny seeds can be ground into a high-quality flour for bread and pastries. The seeds can also be popped like corn. These qualities were well known to the ancient Indians of Central and South America, where amaranth has been cultivated for at least 8,000 years. Amaranth kept the Aztec empire's large population quite healthy, but when the Spanish Conquistadores learned that amaranth played an important part in "heathen" religious rites, they banned its cultivation. Overnight, one of the most important food crops of the Americas fell into disuse, a crop which is now viewed as the best possible answer to starvation in underdeveloped countries.[31] The world's debt to the Indians seems to increase more each year.

Afterword

The Only Good Indian
Is a Dead Indian—
Genocide and Misinformation

> . . . burning them up in the fire of His wrath, and dunging
> the ground with their flesh: It was the Lord's doings, and
> it is marvelous in our eyes!
> —Captain John Mason, leader of the
> Puritan attack on the Pequot Tribe in 1634,
> who set the fire that killed hundreds
> of them in their sleep[1]

Since the arrival of the Europeans, the native American Indians have been second-class citizens in their own land, seen as "savages," less than human, and a hindrance to growth and progress. This view of the Indian as being less-than-human was extremely convenient in economic terms to the European newcomers, for it permitted ill treatment and unscrupulous exploitation of the Indians. The survivors of the Puritan massacre-by-fire, for example, were taken to the Caribbean and traded off as slaves. Economic interest clearly influenced religious convictions and general beliefs about the Indians.

During the sixteenth and seventeenth centuries, the Portuguese and Spanish quickly put the Indians into forced labor on sugar plantations and in gold mines. Millions of Indians died from this slavery as well as from warfare, famine, European diseases, and the lack of will to live under foreign rulers. Entire cities were deserted and temples were left to crumble. (Only recently have the countries of Mexico and Peru regained the population and prosperity that they enjoyed at the start of the sixteenth century.) With Indians dying in large numbers, the Portuguese and Spanish had no compunction about importing blacks to replace them as slaves. When France, the Netherlands, and England began colonizing the Americas, they followed the pattern set by Portugal and Spain. The British ship that carried the Pequot Indians off to slavery in 1634 returned seven months later carrying cotton, tobacco, salt, and Negroes.

With the early explorers, adventurers, and conquistadores came priests in search of souls to be saved. But converting "heathens" did little to save them from forced labor and slavery. Political and economic control over the bountiful new land was steadily wrested from them. During the westward expansion of the eighteenth and nineteenth centuries, Indian tribes were displaced from their ancestral lands and herded onto reservations.

It was not until 1924, when there was little left to wrest away, "that the white man's Congress in Washington declared that Indians were citizens of the United States, with all attendant rights and obligations."[2]

Their new status didn't stop the government from breaking the many treaties made with the Indians. But there are some encouraging signs. In 1973, a federal judge upheld two nineteenth-century treaties, ruling that the state of Michigan had no right to impose fishing restrictions on Indians who historically have depended on fishing the Great Lakes for their livelihood. Treaties have also been upheld in the Pacific Northwest. On the east coast, tribes are suing for the return of vast tracts of land. In 1979, the U.S. Court of Claims awarded the Sioux an estimated $132.5 million settlement for seven million acres of land in the Black Hills of South Dakota taken from them 102 years ago. In 1971, Congress awarded $962.5 million to Native Americans of Alaska.

Ironically, the federal government, which as the self-appointed "trustee" for many tribes frequently acted against their best interests and against their will, is now often siding with the Indians in hundreds of new law suits. The economic stakes are in the billions of dollars, but the Indians see it more as a matter of their survival as a people. Even usually reticent—and usually feuding—Navajo medicine men and Hopi elders have banded together in an effort to guard the sanctity of their holy places in the San Francisco Peaks of Flagstaff, Arizona. "The Peaks are our flesh," explains Hopi elder Vet Lomahaftewa. "We cannot allow them to be disturbed."[3]

In 1978, a joint resolution of Congress passed the American Indian Religious Freedom Act. This act marked a major turning point in government attitudes toward Indian religion, which in the past has faced severe obstacles. Under this act the right to possess peyote for religious ceremonies has been supported in the courts, and U.S. Customs have allowed Blackfoot, Cree, and Mohawk Indians to cross the border from Canada into the United States without submitting their sacred medicine bundles to a search. The Indians' belief in the sacred nature of the land has long earned the respect and enthusiasm of many non-Indians, despite the atrocious image portrayed by Hollywood.

While the Indians' economic and religious rights are now beginning to be recognized, the contributions they have made to mankind still go unsung. As late as 1947, Colonel P. M. Ashburn of the U.S. Army Medical Corps declared that "the savage Indians . . . contributed little or nothing of value to any branch of medicine."[4] Today, in the teeth of the facts, many archaeologists still believe that every prehistoric invention of consequence was made in the Old World instead of the New World. In general, archaeologists have been very conservative in their speculations about the prehistory and the accomplishments of the Indians. Archaeological theories, arguing that the Indians themselves were relative newcomers to the Americas, seemed made to order for non-Indian economic interests with designs on America's rich resources.

Digging for their own roots, Caucasian archaeologists in Europe have had little trouble in funding the search for and excavation of Cro-Magnon sites, while American archaeologists have had a difficult time financing Paleo-Indian research. But now, with the exciting new American discoveries and datings, the Americas take center stage in the drama of modern man's evolution and development. Far from having been a continent of lost immigrants with few significant ties to the mainstream of mankind, the New World turns out to have been the launching pad for modern man's thrust toward civilization. This is a heritage all Americans can take pride in. We have reason to hope that a key chapter in all of mankind's past won't vanish with the "vanishing American," the Indian.

Appendix

Additional Early Sites*

American Falls (*Site #7 on chart of early sites, pages 94–95*)

In 1961, numerous bones of an extinct variety of bison were found at the American Falls dam near Pocatello, Idaho. No stone tools were found, but the former presence of man was clearly indicated by the human workmanship on one of the bones. A symmetrical notch had been cut into the bone, which also featured a circular perforation. The layer of peat stratigraphically above the layer containing the fossils gave a radiocarbon date of 43,000 years.[1]

Lewisville-Frieshenhahn Cave (*Site #9*)

Often mentioned along with Lewisville, and supportive of its early date, is another Texas site called Frieshenhahn Cave, which

---

* The sites listed in the Appendix have provided data which, for the most part, duplicates material discussed in the text. They are nonetheless important sites which should be noted.

was excavated in 1935. The remains of at least thirty different varieties of now extinct fauna have been identified in this central Texas cave, indicating a rich and flourishing animal population during glacial times. While no radiocarbon dating has been done, according to Dr. Richard MacNeish of the Peabody Foundation the fauna indicate a mid-Wisconsin (middle of the last glacial period) age of approximately 30,000 years. (The stone and bone tools found at the site lay immediately under the skeleton of a large saber-toothed tiger.)[2]

Dawson City (Site #10)

Dawson City lies in the northern Yukon, in Canada, far to the east of the Bering Bridge/ice-free corridor. At the Dawson City site, once a gold claim, a tool made of caribou antler, used to remove flakes in the manufacture of stone tools, and a buffalo horn showing signs of human modification were dated at more than 38,000 years old.[3]

Tanana Uplands (Site #13)

In May 1979, University of Washington geologist Lee Porter reported that she had found evidence for ancient man in the Yukon-Tanana Uplands of Canada. Porter found fossilized animal bones with chop marks, burn marks, and spiral fractures indicating that they were slaughtered by man. The bones, which include those of extinct lions, bison, musk oxen, "little wild horses," and woolly mammoths, have been radiocarbon dated to 29,000 years ago. The bones came from the bottom of a thirty-foot gold mine. Excited about the archaeological treasures of the area, Porter says that "it may be possible within the next ten years to uncover fossils of early man which date back as far as 60,000 years ago."[4]

McGee's Point (Site #20)

In 1892, W. J. McGee, a member of an exploratory party going to ancient Lake Lahontan, discovered a large obsidian laurel-leaf-shaped projectile point protruding from Pleistocene fossils beds in Walker River Canyon, Nevada. In 1969, Vance Haynes of the University of Arizona and Richard MacNeish argued that these beds are approximately 22,000 years old. Along with the points found at Tlapacoya and Hueyatlaco, Mexico, this point supports the great age of the Lewisville point (38,000) and thus bolsters the proposition that the projectile points appeared in the Americas well before they appeared in the Old World.[5]

Pikimachay Cave (Site #21)

From 1967 to 1969, Dr. Richard MacNeish led a multidisciplinary team of scientists in the excavation of Pikimachay Cave near Ayacucho, Peru. Various levels of human occupancy were uncovered. The deepest level consisted of animal bones associated with crude choppers and scrapers and was radiocarbon dated to 20,000 years ago. The next highest level, dated to 14,000 years ago, yielded more stone tools and a child's jawbone.[6] These revelations brought MacNeish into the growing camp of archaeologists who support earlier dates than those generally accepted.

Muaco (Site #23)

Split and burned bones of Pleistocene animals were found in a spring near Falcon, Venezuela, along with stone tools made of material foreign to the area. A radiocarbon date of 16,000 years ago was obtained.[7]

Wilson Butte (Site #25)

A soil layer from Wilson Butte Cave in Idaho was dated to 14,500 years ago. In 1965, Dr. Ruth Gruhn of the University of

Alberta excavated a blade, a projectile point, and a stone engraving tool from this layer. Gruhn believes that the idea of a 12,000-year-old entry date for man in the New World, as held by mainstream traditional archaeologists and as recently exhumed in a September 1979 *National Geographic* article, is definitely wrong.[8]

Taima-Taima (Site #26)

Stone tools including a projectile point were found in association with long-extinct animals at Taima-Taima, Venezuela. Dr. Alan Bryan excavated this site in 1973 and obtained a radiocarbon date of 14,400 years.[9]

Notes

Chapter 2

1. Kelly, D. H. "Culture Diffusion in Asia and America," in *The Alphabet and the Ancient Calendar Signs*, eds. H. A. Moran and D. H. Kelly, 1969.
   Meggers, B. J. "The Transpacific Origin of Mesoamerican Civilization," *American Anthropologist*, March 1975, pp. 1–28.
2. "Mormon Mystery." *Time* Magazine, July 11, 1977, p. 69.
3. Based on the oxygen isotope technique, where foraminiferal shells from deep-sea cores are studied. *Sea Frontiers*, September–October 1975, pp. 259–270.
4. "Sunken Continent Found, Soviet Feels." *Arizona Republic*, April 3, 1979.
5. Churchward, J. *The Lost Continent of Mu*, 1969 (Paperback Library).
6. Steiner, R. *Cosmic Memory: Atlantis and Lemuria*, 1959.
7. Waters, F. *Book of the Hopi*, 1963, pp. 22–28.
   Courlander, H. *The Fourth World of the Hopis*, 1971, pp. 21–40.
8. Lynd, Major James. *History of the Dakotas*. Major Lynd lived among the Dakota Indians from 1853 to 1862.
9. Bancroft, Hubert Howe. *Native Races of the Pacific States* (New York, 1874), p. 149.

10. Waters, op. cit., pp. 22–28.
    Courlander, op. cit., pp. 21–40.
    Personal interviews with Oswald "White Bear" Fredericks, a Hopi.

Chapter 3

1. Jennings, J. D. *Prehistory of North America*, 1974, p. 39.
2. Ceram, C. W. *The First American*, 1972, p. 292.
3. Ceram, op. cit., p. 306.
4. Kroeber, A. L., *Anthropology*, 1948, p. 777.
5. Haynes, V. "The Earliest Americans," 1969, p. 711.
6. Martin, P. "The Discovery of America," 1973, pp. 969–974.
7. Haynes, V. "Elephant-hunting in North America," 1966, p. 111.
8. Willey, G. R. *An Introduction to American Archaeology*, 1966, p. 29.
9. Haynes, op. cit., p. 709.

Chapter 4

1. Rainey, F. "The Significance of Present Archaeological Discoveries in Inland Alaska," in *Asia and North America: Transpacific Contracts*, ed. Marian W. Smith, 1953, p. 46.
2. Lorenzo, J. L. "Early Man Research in the American Hemisphere," in *Early Man in America*, ed. A. L. Bryan, 1978, p. 4.
3. Fladmark, K. R. "Routes: Alternate Migration Corridors for Early Man in North America." *American Antiquity*, January 1979, p. 60.
4. Bryson, R. "Radiocarbon Isochrones of the Retreat of the Laurentide Ice Sheet." *Technical Report #35*, Department of Meteorology, University of Wisconsin, 1967, p. 8.
5. Bryan, A. L. "Early Man in America and the Late Pleistocene Chronology of Western Canada and Alaska." *Current Anthropology*, October 1969, p. 341.
6. Fladmark, op. cit., p. 57.
7. Greenman, E. F. "The Upper Paleolithic and the New World." *Current Anthropology*, February 1963, pp. 41–91.
8. Bryan, op. cit., p. 339.
9. Fladmark, op. cit., p. 64.
10. Personal communication from Dr. Richard S. MacNeish, Peabody Archaeological Foundation, Andover, Massachusetts, 1977.
11. Willey, G. R. *An Introduction to American Archaeology—North and Middle America*, 1966, pp. 29 and 33.

12. Jennings, J. D. *Prehistory of North America*, 1974, p. 76.

Chapter 5

1. "Early Man Confirmed in America 40,000 Years Ago." *Science News*, March 26, 1977, p. 196.
2. Ibid. "America Born Much Earlier?" *Tucson Daily Citizen*, January 3, 1976.
3. Breternitz, D. A., and others. "An Early Burial From Gordon Creek, Colorado." *American Antiquity*, April 1971, p. 178.
4. "Florida Burial Site: Brains to Boomerangs." *Science News*, August 6, 1977, p. 90.
5. Holton, F. "One of the Most Important Archaeological Digs in America." *The New York Times*, July 15, 1973.
6. Haynes, V. C. "The Earliest Americans." *Science*, November 7, 1969, p. 713.
7. "Fossil Study Surprise—Man's New World Age Put at 50,000 Years." *Arizona Daily Star*, March 15, 1974.
8. Bada, J. L. and others. "New Evidence for the Antiquity of Man in North America Deduced From Aspartic Acid Racemization." *Science*, May 17, 1974, p. 791.
   Smith, C. "New Test Shatters Theory on Age of American Man." *San Diego Union*, May 15, 1974.
9. Rensberger, B. "Coast Dig Focuses on Man's Move to New World." *The New York Times*, August 16, 1976.
10. Bada, loc. cit.
11. Rensberger, loc. cit.
12. Ibid.
13. Ibid.
14. Bada, J. L., and Hilfman, P. M. "Amino Acid Racemization Dating of Fossil Bones." *World Archaeology*, 1975, p. 168.

Chapter 6

1. MacNeish, R. S. "Early Man in the New World." *American Scientist*, May–June 1976, p. 317.
2. Stalker, A. "Geology and Age of the Early Man Site at Taber, Alberta." *American Antiquity*, 1969, pp. 425–428.
   MacNeish, op. cit., p. 320.
   Lorenzo, J. L. "Early Man Research in the American Hemisphere," in *Early Man in America*, ed. A. L. Bryan, 1978, p. 6.
   Gruhn, R. "Earliest Man in the Northeast: A Hemisphere-Wide

Perspective." *Annals of the New York Academy of Sciences,* February 28, 1977, p. 163.

3. Davies, D. "Some Observations on the Otavalo Skeleton From Imbabara Province, Ecuador," in *Early Man in America,* ed. A. L. Bryan, 1978, p. 273.

"Fred's Skull May Alter Man's Past—Found in Ecuador." *Chicago Tribune,* March 16, 1973.

Bryan, A. L. "An Overview of Paleo-American Prehistory From a Circum-Pacific Perspective," in *Early Man in America,* ed. A. L. Bryan, 1978, p. 318.

4. Berger, R. "Advances and Results in Radiocarbon Dating: Early Man in America." *World Archaeology,* 1975, p. 180.

Lorenzo, loc. cit.

Gruhn, loc. cit.

Wormington, H. M. *Ancient Man in North America,* 1957, p. 231.

5. Childers, W. M. "Preliminary Report on the Yuha Burial, California." *Anthropological Journal of Canada,* 1974, pp. 2–9.

Rogers, S. L. "An Early Human Fossil From the Yuha Desert of Southern California—Physical Characteristics." *San Diego Museum Papers,* 1977.

Bryan, op. cit., p. 314.

Evans, T. "Yuha Man Pushes Back Frontier of Knowledge." *Our Public Lands,* Fall 1972, pp. 4–5.

6. Berger, op. cit., p. 178.

Gruhn, loc. cit.

Lorenzo, loc. cit.

Ceram, C. W. *The First American.* 1972, pp. 339–342.

7. Heizer, R. F. "Observations on Early Man in California." *Reports of the University of California Archaeological Survey,* 1950, pp. 8–9.

Austin, J. "A Test of Birdsell's Hypothesis on New World Migrations" (Paper presented at the annual meeting for the Society for California, Archaeology, April 1976), p. 8.

Wormington, loc. cit.

8. Wormington, op. cit., p. 58.

MacNeish, loc. cit.

Krieger, A. P. "Early Man in the New World," in *Prehistoric Man in the New World,* eds. J. D. Jennings and E. Norbeck, 1964, p. 45.

Willey, G. R. *An Introduction to American Archaeology—North and Middle America,* 1966, p. 30.

9. Alexander, H. L. "The Legalistic Approach to Early Man Studies," in *Early Man in America*, ed. A. L. Bryan, 1978, p. 20.
10. Wormington, op. cit., p. 58.
11. Alexander, loc. cit.
   MacNeish, loc. cit.
   Krieger, loc. cit.
12. Alexander, loc. cit.
   Wormington, op. cit., pp. 154–155.
13. Krieger, op. cit., p. 47.
   Wormington, op. cit., pp. 199–201.
14. Lee, T. E. "Sheguiandah: Workshop or Habitation?" *Anthropological Journal of Canada*, 1964, pp. 16–24.
   Lorenzo, op. cit., p. 4.
15. Lee, T. E. "Editorial Comments on the Antiquity of Man in America." *Anthropological Journal of Canada*, 1977, pp. 3–4.
16. Lee, T. E. "Editorial Comments on Pebble Tools and Their Relatives in North America." *Anthropological Journal of Canada*, 1966, pp. 18–19.
17. Morlan, R. E. "Early Man in Northern Yukon Territory: Perspective as of 1977," in *Early Man in America*, ed. A. L. Bryan, 1978, p. 87.
18. Irving, W. M. "Upper Pleistocene Radiocarbon-Dater Artifacts From the Northern Yukon." *Science*, January 26, 1973, p. 337.
19. Bonnichsen, R. "Critical Arguments for Pleistocene Artifacts From the Old Crow Basin, Yukon," in *Early Man in America*, ed. A. L. Bryan, 1978, pp. 102 and 115.
   Morlan, op. cit., pp. 82 and 84.
20. Morlan, op. cit., p. 90.
21. Morlan, op. cit., p. 87.
22. Mirambell, L. "Tlapacoya: A Late Pleistocene Site in Central Mexico," in *Early Man in America*, ed. A. L. Bryan, 1978, pp. 221–230.
   Lorenzo, op. cit., p. 4.
   MacNeish, op. cit., p. 319.
   Gruhn, op. cit., p. 163.
   Haynes, V. C. "The Earliest Americans." *Science*, November 7, 1969, p. 714.
23. Krieger, op. cit., p. 33.
24. Krieger, op. cit., p. 47.
   Wormington, op. cit., p. 222.
   Carter, G. F. "On Pebble Tools and Their Relatives in North America." *Anthropological Journal of Canada*, 1966, pp. 13–14.
25. Rogers, S. L. "The Physical Characteristics of the Aboriginal La

Jollan Population of Southern California." *San Diego Museum Papers*, 1963, p. 5.

Rensberger, B. "Coast Dig Focuses on Man's Move to New World." *The New York Times*, August 16, 1976.

26. Carter, loc. cit.

Carter, G. F. "The American Paleolithic," in *Early Man in America*, ed. A. L. Bryan, 1978, p. 11.

27. Adovasio, J. M., and others. "Meadowcroft Rockshelter," in *Early Man in America*, ed. A. L. Bryan, 1978, p. 156.

Bryan, A. L. "The Problem of Finding Early Man in the Northeast." *Annals of the New York Academy of Sciences*, February 28, 1977, p. 160.

28. Gruhn, op. cit., p. 164.

MacNeish, op. cit., pp. 318 and 323.

Bombin, M. "New Perspectives on Early Man in Southwestern Rio Grande Do Su Brazil," in *Early Man in America*, ed. A. L. Bryan, 1978, p. 301.

Bryan, A. L. "An Early Stratified Sequence Near Rio Claro, East Central Sao Paulo State Brazil," in *Early Man in America*, ed. A. L. Bryan, 1978, p. 303.

29. Puttkamer, W. J. von. "Man in the Amazon: Stone Age Present Meets Stone Age Past." *National Geographic*, January 1979, pp. 60–82.

Chapter 7

1. Birdsell, J. B. *Human Evolution*, 1972, p. 325.

2. "Modern Man: Mid-East Origins?" *Science News*, March 3, 1979, p. 132.

3. Birdsell, op. cit., p. 333.

4. Bordes, F. Preface to *Early Man in America*, ed. A. L. Bryan, 1978, p. vi.

5. Leakey, L., and others. *Pleistocene Man at Calico*, 1972, pp. 65 and 68.

6. Cole, S. *Leakey's Luck*, 1975, p. 355.

7. Cole, op. cit., p. 359.

8. Haynes, V. C. "The Calico Site: Artifacts or Geofacts?" *Science*, July 27, 1973, p. 307.

9. Jennings, J. D. *Prehistory of North America*, 1974, p. 79.

10. Leakey, and others, op. cit., p. 47.

11. Cole, op. cit., p. 351.

12. Singer, C. A. "A Preliminary Report on the Analysis of Calico

Lithics." *Quarterly of the San Bernardino County Museum*, Summer 1979, pp. 55–64.

Personal communications from Clay Singer.

Simpson, R. D. "The Calico Mountains Archaeological Site," in *Early Man in America*, ed. A. L. Bryan, 1978, p. 218.

Bryan, A. L. "An Overview of Paleo-American Prehistory From a Circum-Pacific Perspective," in *Early Man in America*, ed. A. L. Bryan, 1978, p. 312.

13. Tringham, R., and others. "Experimentation in the Formation of Edge Damage: A New Approach to Lithic Analysis." *Journal of Field Archaeology*, 1974, pp. 171–196.

Odell, G. H. "Micro-Wear in Perspective." *World Archaeology*, 1975, pp. 226–240.

Keeley, L. H. "The Functions of Paleolithic Flint Tools." *Scientific American*, November 1977, pp. 108–126.

14. Singer, op. cit., p. 59.

15. Krieger, A. P. "The Calico Site and Old World Paleolithic Industries." *Quarterly of San Bernardino County Museum*, Summer 1979, p. 71.

16. Tobias, P. V. "Calico Mountains and Early Man in North America." *Quarterly of the San Bernardino County Museum*, Summer 1979, p. 97.

17. Tobias, op. cit., p. 98.

18. Bryan, op. cit., p. 313.

19. "Date of Man's U.S. Debut Disputed—12,000 or 250,000 Years Ago?" *Tucson Daily Citizen*, November 14, 1973.

20. Szabo, B. J., and others. "Dilemma Posed by Uranium Series Dates on Archaeologically Significant Bones From Valsequillo, Puebla, Mexico." *Earth and Planetary Science Letters*, July 1969, p. 241.

21. Szabo, op. cit., p. 237.

22. "Artifacts Place Man in New World 250,000 Years Ago—Conventional View Contradicted." *Denver Post*, November 13, 1973.

23. Personal communication from Dr. Virginia Steen-McIntyre.

24. Page, W. D. "The Geology of the El Bosque Archaeological Site, Nicaragua," in *Early Man in America*, ed. A. L. Bryan, 1978, p. 254.

Bryan, op. cit., p. 314.

Gruhn, R. "A Note on Excavations at El Bosque in Nicaragua, 1975," in *Early Man in America*, ed. A. L. Bryan, 1978, p. 261.

MacNeish, R. "Early Man in the New World." *American Scientist*, May–June 1976, p. 319.

25. Crabtree, D. E. "An Introduction to Flintworking." *Idaho State University Museum Occasional Papers* #28, 1972, pp. 4 and 9.

Carter, G. F. "The American Paleolithic," in *Early Man in America*, ed. A. L. Bryan, 1978, pp. 10–19.

26. Carter, op. cit., p. 15.
27. Bryan, op. cit., p. 312.
28. "Stone Tools Estimated at 100,000 Years Old." *Arizona Republic*, April 3, 1977.

"Man Got to America Earlier Than Believed." *Tucson Daily Citizen*, May 11, 1977.

Reeves, B. O. (Paper presented at the Society for American Archaeology meetings, Tucson, Ariz., May 1978).

Personal communication from Dr. Brian Reeves.

Chapter 8

1. Stanford, D. "Bison Kill by Ice Age Hunters." *National Geographic*, January 1979, p. 119.
2. Canby, T. Y. "The Search for the First Americans." *National Geographic*, September 1979, p. 350.
3. Greenman, E. "The Upper Paleolithic and the New World." *Current Anthropology*, February 1963, pp. 44 and 81.
4. Bordes, F. *A Tale of Two Caves*, 1972, p. 160.
5. Bordes, F. *The Old Stone Age*, 1968, pp. 158–159.

Bryan, A. L. "An Overview of Paleo-American Prehistory From a Circum-Pacific Perspective," in *Early Man in America*, ed. A. L. Bryan, 1978, p. 324.
6. Bordes, F. Preface to *Early Man in America*, ed. A. L. Bryan, 1978, p. vi.
7. Bordes, 1968, op. cit., p. 217.
8. Greenman, op. cit., p. 60.
9. Greenman, op. cit., p. 88.

Bordes, 1968, op. cit., p. 214.
10. Bryan, op. cit., pp. 308–310, 316.

Bryan, A. L. "Early Man in America and the Late Pleistocene Chronology of Western Canada and Alaska." *Current Anthropology*, October 1969, p. 342.

Fladmark, K. R. "Routes: Alternate Migration Corridors for Early Man in North America." *American Antiquity*, January 1979, p. 57.
11. Willey, G. R. *An Introduction to American Archaeology—North and Middle America*, 1966, p. 34.
12. Bryan, 1978, op. cit., p. 310.
13. "Seafaring 11,000 Years Old." *Tucson Daily Citizen*, October 28, 1978.
14. Bordes, 1968, op. cit., p. 217.

15. Bryan, 1978, op. cit., pp. 309–310.

Chapter 9

1. Birdsell, J. B. "The Problem of the Early Peopling of the Americas as Viewed From Asia," in *Physical Anthropology of American Indian*, eds. W. S. Laughlin and S. L. Washburn, 1951, p. 20.

   Jennings, J. D. *Prehistory of North America*, 1974, p. 54.

   Wormington, H. M. *Ancient Man in North America*, 1957, p. 256.

   Willey, G. R. *An Introduction to American Archaeology—North and Middle America*, 1966, p. 13.

2. Jennings, op. cit., p. 57.

3. Austin, J. "A Test of Birdsell's Hypothesis on New World Migrations." (Paper presented at the annual meeting of the Society for California Archaeology, April 1976) pp. 3–5.

4. Austin, op. cit., abstract.

5. Newman, M. T. "Geographic and Microgeographic Races." *Current Anthropology*, 1963, p. 191.

   Genoves, S. T. "Some Problems in the Physical Anthropological Study of the Peopling of America." *Current Anthropology*, October 1967, p. 301.

6. Genoves, op. cit., p. 305.

   Coon, C. S. *The Living Races of Man*, 1960, p. 259.

7. Coon, op. cit., p. 255.

8. Genoves, op. cit., p. 309.

9. Carter, G. F. "On the Antiquity of Man in America." *Anthropological Journal of Canada*, 1977, p. 19.

10. Birdsell, J. B. *Human Evolution*, 1972, p. 499.

11. Rogers, S. L. "The Physical Characteristics of the Aboriginal La Jollan Population of Southern California." *San Diego Museum Papers*, 1963, p. 28.

12. Coon, C. S. *The Origin of Races*, 1969, p. 474.

    Jennings, op. cit., p. 54.

13. Genoves, op. cit., p. 306.

14. Rogers, op. cit., pp. 20 and 27.

    Rogers, S. L. "An Early Human Fossil From the Yuha Desert of South California—Physical Characteristics." *San Diego Museum Papers*, 1977, pp. 5–6.

    Smith, C. "New Test Shatters Theory on Age of American Man." *San Diego Union*, May 15, 1974.

15. Willey, op. cit., pp. 13–14.

16. Jennings, op. cit., p. 62.
17. Genoves, op. cit., p. 298.
18. Jennings, op. cit., p. 55.
    Bryan, A. L. "An Overview of Paleo-American Prehistory From a Circum-Pacific Perspective," in *Early Man in America*, ed. A. L. Bryan, 1978, p. 321.
    Aigner, J. "The Paleolithic of China," in *Early Man in America*, ed. A. L. Bryan, 1978, p. 40.
19. Bryan, op. cit., p. 318.
20. Genoves, op. cit., p. 297.
21. Rogers, 1977, op. cit., p. 5.
22. Morlan, R. E. "Early Man in Northern Yukon Territory: Perspective as of 1977," in *Early Man in America*, ed. A. L. Bryan, 1978, p. 94.
23. Bryan, A. L., ed. *Early Man in America From a Circum-Pacific Perspective*, 1978.
24. Carter, G. F. "The American Paleolithic," in *Early Man in America*, ed. A. L. Bryan, 1978, p. 11.
25. Birdsell, 1972, op. cit., p. 499.
    Willey, op. cit., p. 13.
26. Rogers, S. L. "An Ancient Human Skeleton Found at Del Mar, California." *San Diego Museum Papers*, July 1974, p. 5.
27. Bryan, 1978, op. cit., p. 323.
    Canby, T. Y. "The Search for the First Americans." *National Geographic*, September 1979, p. 351.

Chapter 10

1. Adapted from Waters, F. *Book of the Hopi*, 1963. (Personal communications from Oswald "White Bear" and Naomi Fredericks. White Bear provided the source material for *Book of the Hopi*.)
2. Puttkamer, W. J. von "Man in the Amazon: Stone Age Present Meets Stone Age Past." *National Geographic*, January 1979, p. 68.
3. "Extra Continent May Have Existed." *Science News*, June 18, 1977, p. 389.
4. Kuhn, T. S. *The Structure of Scientific Revolutions*, 1970, p. 101.
5. Personal interview and letter from Phillip Schaeffer of the U.S. Geological Survey dated June 29, 1978.
6. Written note from Dr. Richard MacNeish to me, May 22, 1977.
7. Goodman, J. *Psychic Archaeology: Time Machine to the Past*, 1977, p. x.
8. Krieger, A. P. "The Calico Site and Old World Paleolithic In-

dustries." *Quarterly of the San Bernardino County Museum*, Summer 1979, p. 72.
 9. Douglas, J. M. "The Origins of Culture." *Science News*, April 14, 1979, p. 254.
10. Letter report from Alexander Marshack, March 17, 1980.
11. Personal communication from Alexander Marshack, March 21, 1980.
12. Letter report from Arend Meijer, March 31, 1980.
13. Ibid.
14. Personal communication from Arend Meijer, April 1, 1980.

Chapter 11

 1. Mangelsdorf, P., and others. "Domestication of Corn," in *Prehistoric Agriculture*, ed. S. Struever, 1971, p. 474.
    Galinat, W. C. "The Evolution of Corn and Culture in North America," in *Prehistoric Agriculture*, ed. S. Struever, 1971, p. 534.
 2. Canby, T. "The Search for the First Americans." *National Geographic*, September 1979, p. 348.
    Reed, C. "Animal Domestication in the Prehistoric Near East," in *Prehistoric Agriculture*, ed. S. Struever, 1971, p. 436.
 3. Irving, W. N. "Pleistocene Archaeology in Eastern Beringia," in *Early Man in America*, ed. A. L. Bryan, 1978, p. 99.
 4. Carter, G. F. "Uhle's Mastodon." *Anthropological Journal*, 1968, p. 21. (Uhle's paper at the Twenty-Third International Congress of America was published in German by the Science Press, Lancaster, Pa., in 1928.)
 5. Vogel, V. J. *American Indian Medicine*, 1977, p. 267.
 6. Newman, M. T. "Aboriginal New World Epidemiology and Medical Care." *American Journal of Physical Anthropology*, November 1976, p. 670.
 7. Vogel, op. cit., pp. 19, 160, 193, 203, 232, 246, and 250.
 8. Vogel, op. cit., pp. 3–4.
 9. Vogel, op. cit., p. 250.
10. Vogel, op. cit., p. 4.
11. Vogel, op. cit., p. 198.
12. Vogel, op. cit., pp. 10 and 388.
13. Vogel, op. cit., p. 146.
14. Vogel, op. cit., pp. 392, 393, and 5.
    Newman, op. cit., p. 670.
15. Vogel, op. cit., pp. 198, 293, and 294.
16. Vogel, op. cit., p. 294.

17. "Coca Leaf Medicinal Value Cited—Effects Differ From Cocaine." *Tucson Daily Citizen*, February 20, 1978. Vogel, op. cit., pp. 163 and 168.
18. Schultes, R. "The Ethnotoxicological Significance of Additives to New World Hallucinogens." *Plant Science Bulletin*, 1972, pp. 34–40. Vogel, op. cit., pp. 163–168.
19. Dobkin de Rios, M. "Is Science Catching Up With Magic? A Look at the Content and NOT the Structure of Belief Systems" (Paper presented at the American Anthropological Association meetings, November 1974) pp. 4–5.
20. Ornstein, R. *The Psychology of Consciousness*, 1972.
21. Vogel, op. cit., p. 244.
22. Vogel, op. cit., p. 240.
23. Vogel, op. cit., p. 245.
24. "Are Placebos Magical or Real?" *Time*, July 30, 1979, p. 70.
25. Tiger, L. *Optimism: The Biology of Hope*, 1979.
26. Mason, J. A. *The Ancient Civilizations of Peru*, 1968, p. 268.
27. Nelson, I. "Temples, Turtles and Fat Boys—On the Origins of the Mesoamerican Mother Culture." *Dartmouth Alumni Magazine*, September 1979.
    "A Pre-Columbian Mystery—The Fat Boys." *Time*, September 3, 1979, p. 63.
28. Bernal, I. *The Olmec World*, 1969, p. 78.
29. Beal, J. B. "Electrostatic Fields and Brain/Body/Environment Interrelationships" (Paper presented at American Anthropological Association meetings, November 1974) pp. 5 and 9.
    Beal, J. B. "Field Effects, Known and Unknown, Associated With Living Systems" (Paper presented at the Institute of Electrical and Electronics Engineers Convention and Exposition, March 26, 1974) p. 3.
30. "Brazilian Tree Pours Pure Diesel Fuel." *Science News*, September 15, 1979, p. 182.
31. Hindley, K. "Reviving the Food of the Aztecs." *Science News*, September 8, 1979, p. 168.

Afterword

1. Sanders, R. *Lost Tribes and Promised Lands*, 1978, p. 338.
2. Ceram, C. W. *The First American*, 1972, p. 249.
3. Weathers, D., and Huck, J. "A Fight for Rites." *Newsweek*, April 9, 1979, p. 98.

4. Vogel, V. J. *American Indian Medicine*, 1977, p. 6.

Appendix

1. Lorenzo, J. L. "Early Man Research in the American Hemisphere," in *Early Man in America*, ed. A. L. Bryan, 1978, p. 4.
2. Krieger, A. P. "Early Man in the New World," in *Prehistoric Man in the New World*, eds. J. D. Jennings and E. Norbeck, 1964, p. 45.

   Wormington, H. M. *Ancient Man in North America*, 1957, p. 219.

   Alexander, H. L. "The Legalistic Approach to Early Man Studies," in *Early Man in America*, ed. A. L. Bryan, 1978, p. 20.
3. MacNeish, R. S. "Early Man in the New World." *American Scientist*, May–June 1976, p. 320.
4. "Golden Discovery: Oldest Bering Man?" *Science News*, May 12, 1979, p. 311.
5. MacNeish, op. cit., p. 318.

   Haynes, V. C. "The Earliest Americans." *Science*, November 7, 1969, p. 714.
6. MacNeish, op. cit., p. 317.

   MacNeish, R. S. "Early Man in the Andes." *Scientific American*, April 1971, pp. 36–46.

   Lorenzo, op. cit., pp. 4 and 6.
7. Lorenzo, op. cit., p. 5.
8. MacNeish, 1976, op. cit., pp. 318 and 322.

   Personal communication from Dr. Gruhn, August 1979.
9. Lorenzo, op. cit., p. 5.

   MacNeish, 1976, pp. 318 and 322.

Bibliography

Books

Adavasio, J. M., and others. "Meadowcroft Rockshelter," in *Early Man in America*, ed. A. L. Bryan, Edmonton, Alta., Canada: Archaeological Researches International, 1978, pp. 140–180.

Aigner, Jean. "The Paleolithic of China," in *Early Man in America*, ed. A. L. Bryan, Edmonton, Alta., Canada: Archaeological Researches International, 1978, pp. 25–41.

Alexander, Herbert L. "The Association of Aurignacoid Elements With Fluted Point Complexes in North America," in *Pleistocene Extinctions: The Search for a Cause*, eds. P. S. Martin and H. E. Wright, Jr., New Haven: Yale University Press, 1967, pp. 21–32.

———. "The Legalistic Approach to Early Man Studies," in *Early Man in America*, ed. A. L. Bryan, Edmonton, Alta., Canada: Archaeological Researches International, 1978, pp. 20–22.

Berlitz, Charles. *The Mystery of Atlantis*. New York: Grosset & Dunlap, 1969.

Bernal, Ignacio. *The Olmec World*. Los Angeles: University of California Press (Berkeley), 1969.

Berger, Rainer. "Thoughts on the First Peopling of America and Australia," in *Early Man in America*, ed. A. L. Bryan, Edmonton, Alta., Canada: Archaeological Researches International, 1978, pp. 23–24.

Birdsell, J. B. *Human Evolution*. Chicago: Rand McNally, 1972.

———. "The Problem of the Early Peopling of the Americas as Viewed From Asia," in *Physical Anthropology of the American Indian*, ed. W. S. Laughlin and S. L. Washburn, New York: Viking Fund, 1951, pp. 1–68.

Bombin, M. "New Perspectives in Early Man in Southwestern Rio Grande Do Sul Brazil," in *Early Man in America*, ed. A. L. Bryan, Edmonton, Alta., Canada: Archaeological Researches International, 1978, p. 301.

Bonnichsen, Robson. "Critical Arguments for Pleistocene Artifacts From the Old Crow Basin, Yukon," in *Early Man in America*, ed. A. L. Bryan, Edmonton, Alta., Canada: Archaeological Researches International, 1978, pp. 102–117.

Book of Mormon. Salt Lake City, Utah: The Church of Jesus Christ of Latter Day Saints, 1961.

Bordes, Francois. *The Old Stone Age*. New York: McGraw-Hill, 1968.

———. *A Tale of Two Caves*. New York: Harper & Row, 1972.

———. Preface to *Early Man in America*, ed. A. L. Bryan, Edmonton, Alta., Canada: Archaeological Researches International, 1978, pp. v–vi.

Brace, Loring O., Nelson, H., and Korn, H. *Atlas of Fossil Man*, New York: Holt, Rinehart & Winston, 1971.

Bryan, Alan Lyle. "An Early Stratified Sequence Near Rio Claro, East Central Sao Paulo State Brazil," in *Early Man in America*, ed. A. L. Bryan, Edmonton, Alta., Canada: Archaeological Researches International, 1978, pp. 303–305.

———. "An Overview of Paleo-American Prehistory From a Circum-Pacific Perspective," in *Early Man in America*, ed. A. L. Bryan, Edmonton, Alta., Canada: Archaeological Researches International, 1978, pp. 306–327.

Bryan, Alan Lyle, ed. *Early Man in America From a Circum-Pacific Perspective*, Edmonton, Alta., Canada: Archaeological Researches International, 1978.

Buettner-Janasch, John. *Origins of Man*. New York: John Wiley & Sons, 1967.

Carter, George F. "The American Paleolithic," in *Early Man in America*, ed. A. L. Bryan, Edmonton, Alta., Canada: Archaeological Researches International, 1978, pp. 10–19.

Cayce, Edgar Evans. *Edgar Cayce on Atlantis*. New York: Paperback Library, 1968.

Ceram, C. W. *The First American.* New York: Mentor Books, 1972.

Cervc, Wishar S. *Lemmuria—The Lost Continent of the Pacific,* San Jose, Calif.: The Rosicrucian Press, 1954.

Churchward, James. *The Lost Continent of Mu,* New York: Paperback Library, 1969.

Claiborne, Robert. *The First Americans.* New York: Time-Life Books, 1973.

Clark, LeGros W. E. *The First Evidence for Human Evolution,* 2nd ed. Chicago: University of Chicago Press, 1969.

Cole, Sonia. *Leakey's Luck.* New York: Harcourt Brace Jovanovich, 1975.

Coon, Carleton S. *The Living Races of Man.* New York: Alfred A. Knopf, 1960.

————. *The Origin of Races.* New York: Alfred A. Knopf, 1969.

Courlander, Harold. *The Fourth World of the Hopis.* Greenwich, Fawcett, 1971.

Davies, David M. "Some Observations on the Otavalo Skeleton From Imbabara Province, Ecuador," in *Early Man in America,* ed. A. L. Bryan, Edmonton, Alta., Canada: Archaeological Researches International, 1978, p. 273.

Davis, Emma Lou. "Associations of People and a Rancholabrean Fauna at China Lake, California," in *Early Man in America,* ed. A. L. Bryan, Edmonton, Alta., Canada: Archaeological Researches International, 1978, pp. 183–217.

Donnelly, Ignatius. *Atlantis—The Antidiluvian World,* ed. Edgarton Sykes, New York: Harper & Row, 1949.

Eggan, Fred. *Social Organization of the Western Pueblos.* Chicago: University of Chicago Press, 1969.

Galinat, Walton C. "The Evolution of Corn and Culture in North America," in *Prehistoric Agriculture,* ed. Stuart Struever, New York: American Museum of Natural History, 1971, pp. 534–543.

Gladwin, Harold S. *Men Out of Asia.* New York: McGraw-Hill, 1947.

Goodman, Jeffrey. "Psychic Archaeology: Methodology and Empirical Evidence from Flagstaff, Arizona," in *Extrasensory Ecology— Parapsychology and Anthropology,* ed. Joseph K. Long, Metuchen, N.J.: Scarecrow Press, 1977, pp. 313–329.

————. *Psychic Archaeology: Time Machine to the Past.* New York: Berkeley, 1977.

Gruhn, Ruth. "A Note on Excavations at El Bosque, Nicaragua in 1975," in *Early Man in America,* ed. A. L. Bryan, Edmonton, Archaeological Researches International, 1978, pp. 261–262.

Hall, Manly Palmer. *The Secret Teachings of All Ages,* 17th ed. Los Angeles: Philosophical Research Society, 1971.

Hayden, Brian, ed. *Lithic Use-Wear Analysis.* New York: Academic Press, 1979.

Hooten, Earnest A. *Up From the Ape,* rev. ed. New York: Macmillan, 1946.

Hopkins, David M., ed. *The Bering Land Bridge.* Stanford, Calif.: Stanford University Press, 1967.

Irving, W. N. "Pleistocene Archaeology in Eastern Beringia," in *Early Man in America,* ed. A. L. Bryan, Edmonton, Alta., Canada: Archaeological Researches International, 1978, pp. 96–101.

Irwin-Williams, Cynthia. "Associations of Early Man With Horse, Camel, and Mastodon at Hueyatlaco Valsequillo-Puebla Mexico," in *Proceedings of the International Conference on the Prehistory and Paleo-ecology of the Western North American Arctic and Sub-Arctic,* ed. S. Raymond and P. Schlederman, Calgary, Alta., Canada: University of Calgary Archaeological Association, 1974, pp. 21–32.

Jennings, Jesse D. *Prehistory of North America,* 2nd ed. New York: McGraw-Hill, 1974.

Kelly, David H. "Culture Diffusion in Asia and America," in *The Alphabet and the Ancient Calendar Signs,* ed. H. A. Moran and D. H. Kelly, Palo Alto, Calif.: Daily Press, 1969.

Kreiger, Alex P. "Early Man in the New World," in *Prehistoric Man in the New World,* ed. J. D. Jennings and E. Norbeck, Chicago: University of Chicago Press, 1964.

Kroeber, A. L. *Anthropology.* New York: Harcourt Brace, 1948.

Krupp, E. C., ed. *In Search of Ancient Astronomies,* New York: Doubleday, 1977.

Kuhn, Thomas S. *The Structure of Scientific Revolutions,* 2nd ed. Chicago: University of Chicago Press, 1970.

Leakey, Louis S. B., Simpson, R. D., and Clements, Thomas. "Man in America: The Calico Mountains Excavations," in *1970 Britannica Yearbook of Science and the Future.* Chicago: Encyclopaedia Britannica, 1970, pp. 64–79.

Leakey, Louis S. B., Simpson, R. D., Clements, T., Berger, R., Witthoft, J., and others. *Pleistocene Man at Calico.* San Bernardino, Calif.: San Bernardino Museum Association, 1972.

Leonard, J. *Ancient America,* New York: Time-Life Books, 1967.

Lorenzo, Jose L. "Early Man Research in the American Hemisphere," in *Early Man in America,* ed. A. L. Bryan, Edmonton, Alta., Canada: Archaeological Researches International, 1978, pp. 1–9.

Mangelsdorf, P., MacNeish, R., and Galinat, W. "Domestication of Corn," in *Prehistoric Agriculture,* ed. S. Struever, New York: American Museum of Natural History, 1971, pp. 471–486.

Marriott, Alice, and Rachlin, C. K. *American Indian Mythology.* New York: Mentor Books, 1972.

Marshack, Alexander. *The Roots of Civilization.* New York: McGraw-Hill, 1972.

Martin, Paul S., and Wright, H. E. "Pleistocene Extinctions: The Search for a Cause," in *Proceedings of the Seventh Congress of the International Association for Quaternary Research.* New Haven: Yale University Press, 1967.

Mason, J. Alden. *The Ancient Civilizations of Peru.* Baltimore, Md.: Penguin, 1968.

Minshall, H. L. *The Broken Stones.* San Diego, Calif.: Copley Press, 1976.

Mirambell, Lorena. "Tlapacoya: A Late Pleistocene Site in Central Mexico," in *Early Man in America,* ed. A. L. Bryan, Edmonton, Alta., Canada: Archaeological Researches International, 1978, pp. 221–230.

Mochanov, J. A. "The Paleolithic of Northeast Asia and the Problem of the First Peopling of America," in *Early Man in America,* ed. A. L. Bryan, Edmonton, Alta., Canada: Archaeological Researches International, 1978, pp. 54–67.

Morlan, Richard E. "Early Man in Northern Yukon Territory: Perspective as of 1977," in *Early Man in America,* ed. A. L. Bryan, Edmonton, Alta., Canada: Archaeological Researches International, 1978, pp. 78–95.

Muck, Otto. *The Secret of Atlantis.* New York: Pocket Books, 1979.

Neumann, G. K. "Archaeology and Race in the American Indians," in *Archaeology of the Eastern United States,* edited by J. B. Griffen, Chicago: University of Chicago Press, 1952, pp. 13–34.

Ornstein, Robert. *The Nature of Human Consciousness—A Book of Readings.* San Francisco: W. H. Freeman, 1972.

———. *The Psychology of Consciousness.* San Francisco: W. H. Freeman, 1972.

Page, William D. "The Geology of the El Bosque Archaeological Site, Nicaragua," in *Early Man in America,* ed. A. L. Bryan, Edmonton, Alta., Canada: Archaeological Researches International, 1978, pp. 231–260.

Pilbeam, David. *The Ascent of Man.* New York: Macmillan, 1972.

Reed, Charles. "Ancient Domestication in the Prehistoric Near East," in *Prehistoric Agriculture,* ed. S. Streuver, New York: American Museum of Natural History, 1979, pp. 426–450.

Rogers, D. B. *Prehistoric Man of the Santa Barbara Coast.* Santa Barbara, Calif.: Santa Barbara Museum of Natural History, 1929.

Sanders, Ronald. *Lost Tribes and Promised Lands.* Boston: Little, Brown & Co., 1978.

Simpson, Ruth Dee. "The Calico Mountains Archaeological Site," in *Early Man in America,* ed. A. L. Bryan, Edmonton, Alta., Canada: Archaeological Researches International, 1978, pp. 218–220.

Steiner, Rudolf. *Cosmic Memory: Atlantis and Lemuria.* Blaunett, N.Y., Rudolf Steiner Publications, 1959.

Stokes, William L. *Essentials of Earth History.* Englewood Cliffs, N.J.: Prentice-Hall, 1961.

Tiger, Lionel. *Optimism: The Biology of Hope.* New York: Simon & Schuster, 1979.

Vogel, Virgil J. *American Indian Medicine.* Norman, Okla.: University of Oklahoma Press, 1977.

Waters, Frank. *Book of the Hopi.* New York: Viking Press, 1963.

Wauchope, Robert. *Lost Tribes and Sunken Continents.* Chicago: University of Chicago Press, 1970.

Wheeler, Sir Mortimer. *Archaeology From the Earth.* New York: G. P. Putnam's Sons, 1962.

Willey, Gordon R. *An Introduction to American Archaeology—North and Middle America.* Englewood Cliffs, N.J.: Prentice-Hall, 1966.

———. *An Introduction to American Archaeology—South America.* Englewood Cliffs, N.J.: Prentice-Hall, 1971.

Wormington, H. M. *Ancient Man in North America,* 4th ed. Popular Series no. 4, Denver: Denver Museum of Natural History, 1957.

Periodicals

"An Indian Epic." *Newsweek,* April 16, 1979, p. 86.

"A Pre-Columbian Mystery—The Fat Boys." *Time,* September 3, 1979, p. 63.

"Are Placebos Magic or Real?" *Time,* July 30, 1979, p. 70.

Ascher, Robert. "Recognizing the Emergence of Man—Specific Courses Necessary for Utilizing the Early Traces of Man." *Science,* 147, January 15, 1965, pp. 243–250.

Bada, Jeffrey L., and Helfman, Patricia Masters. "Amino Acid Racemization Dating of Fossil Bones." *World Archaeology,* vol. 7, no. 2, 1975, pp. 160–175.

Bada, Jeffrey L., Helfman, Patricia Masters, Schroeder, R. A., and Carter, G. F. "New Evidence for the Antiquity of Man in North America Deduced From Aspartic Acid Racemization." *Science,* 184, May 17, 1974, pp. 791–793.

Barnes, Alfred S. "The Differences Between Natural and Human Flaking on Prehistoric Flint Instruments." *American Anthropologist*, no. 41, Spring 1939, pp. 99–112.

Berger, Rainer. "Advances and Results in Radiocarbon Dating: Early Man in America." *World Archaeology*, vol. 7, no. 2, 1975, pp. 174–184.

"Brazilian Tree Pours Pure Diesel Fuel." *Science News*, vol. 116, no. 111, September 15, 1979, p. 182.

Breternitz, D. A., Swedland, A. C., and Anderson, D. C. "An Early Burial From Gordon Creek, Colorado." *American Antiquity*, vol. 36, no. 2, April 1971, pp. 170–181.

Bryan, Alan L. "Developmental Stages and Technological Traditions." *Annals of the New York Academy of Sciences*, vol. 288, February 28, 1977, pp. 355–367.

———. "Early Man in America and the Late Pleistocene Chronology of Western Canada and Alaska." *Current Anthropology*, vol. 10, no. 4, October 1969, pp. 339–365.

———. "The Problems of Finding Early Man in the Northeast." *Annals of the New York Academy of Sciences*, vol. 288, February 28, 1977, pp. 160–164.

Canby, Thomas Y. "The Search for the First Americans." *National Geographic*, vol. 156, no. 3, September 1979, pp. 330–363.

Carter, George F. "Early Man in America." *Anthropological Journal of Canada*, vol. 10, no. 3, 1972, pp. 2–9.

———. "Evidence for Pleistocene Man at La Jolla, California." *Transactions of the New York Academy of Sciences*, vol. 2, no. 7, May 1949, pp. 254–257.

———. "Evidence for Pleistocene Man in Southern California." *The Geographical Review*, vol. XL, no. 1, 1950, pp. 84–102.

———. "Man in America: A Criticism of Scientific Thought." *The Scientific Monthly*, vol. XXIII, no. 5, November 1951, pp. 297–307.

———. "On the Antiquity of Man in America." *Anthropological Journal of Canada*, vol. 15, no. 1, 1977, pp. 2–19.

———. "On Pebble Tools and Their Relatives in North America." *Anthropological Journal of Canada*, vol. 4, no. 4, 1966, pp. 10–19.

———. "Uhle's Mastodon." *Anthropological Journal of Canada*, vol. 16, no. 2, 1968, pp. 21–24.

Childers, W. M. "Preliminary Report on the Yuha Burial, California." *Anthropological Journal of Canada*, vol. 12, no. 1, 1974, pp. 2–9.

Douglas, J. H. "The Origins of Culture." *Science News*, vol. 115, April 14, 1979, pp. 252–254.

"Early Man Confirmed in America 40,000 Years Ago." *Science News*, vol. 111, March 26, 1977, p. 196.

Emiliani, Cesare. "The Great Flood." *Sea Frontiers*, September-October 1976, pp. 259–270.

Evans, Tom. "Yuha Man Pushes Back Frontier of Knowledge." *Our Public Lands*, Fall 1972, pp. 4–5.

"Extra Continent May Have Existed." *Science News*, June 18, 1977, p. 389.

Fladmark, K. R. "Routes: Alternate Migration Corridors for Early Man in North America." *American Antiquity*, vol. 44, no. 1, January 1979, pp. 55–69.

"Florida Burial Site: Brains to Boomerangs." *Science News*, vol. 112, August 6, 1977, p. 90.

Frazier, Kendrick. "Stars, Sky and Culture." *Science News*, vol. 116, August 4, 1979, p. 91.

Genoves, Santiago T. "Some Problems in the Physical Anthropological Study of the Peopling of America." *Current Anthropology*, vol. 8, October 1967, pp. 297–312.

"Golden Discovery: Oldest Bering Man?" *Science News*, vol. 115, May 12, 1979, p. 311.

Gould, R. A., Koster, D. A., and Sontz, A. H. "The Lithic Assemblage of Western Desert Aborigines of Australia." *American Antiquity*, vol. 36, no. 2, April 1971, pp. 149–169.

Greenman, E. F. "The Upper Paleolithic and the New World." *Current Anthropology*, vol. 4, February 1963, pp. 41–91.

Gruhn, Ruth. "Earliest Man in the Northeast: A Hemisphere-Wide Perspective." *Annals of the New York Academy of Sciences*, vol. 288, February 28, 1977, pp. 163–164.

Haynes, Vance C. "The Calico Site: Artifacts or Geofacts?" *Science*, vol. 181, July 27, 1973, pp. 305–309.

———. "The Earliest Americans." *Science*, vol. 166, November 7, 1969, pp. 709–715.

———. "Elephant-hunting in North America." *Scientific American*, vol. 214, no. 6, June 1966, pp. 104–112.

Hindley, Keith. "Reviving the Food of the Aztecs." *Science News*, vol. 116, September 8, 1979, pp. 168–169.

Hopkins, D. M. "Cenozoic History of the Bering Land Bridge." *Science*, vol. 129, 1959, pp. 1519–1528.

Irving, W. M., and Harrington, C. R. "Upper Pleistocene Radiocarbon-Dated Artifacts From the Northern Yukon." *Science*, vol. 179, January 26, 1973, pp. 335–340.

Keeley, L. H. "The Functions of Paleolithic Flint Tools." *Scientific American*, vol. 237, no. 5, November 1977, pp. 108–126.

Krieger, Alex P. "The Calico Site and Old World Paleolithic Industries."

Quarterly of the San Bernardino County Museum, vol. XXVI, no. 4, Summer 1979, pp. 69–74.

Leakey, L. S. B., Simpson, R. E., and Clements, T. "Archaeological Excavations in the Calico Mountains, California: Preliminary Report." *Science*, vol. 160, March 1, 1968, pp. 1022–1023.

Lee, Thomas E. "Editorial Comments on the Antiquity of Man in America." *Anthropological Journal of Canada*, vol. 15, no. 1, 1977, pp. 2–4.

———. "Editorial Comments on Pebble Tools and Their Relatives in North America" *Anthropological Journal of Canada*, vol. 4, no. 4, 1966, pp. 18–19.

———. "Sheguiandah: Workshop or Habitation?" *Anthropological Journal of Canada*, vol. 2, no. 3, 1964, pp. 16–24.

MacNeish, R. S. "Early Man in the Andes." *Scientific American*, vol. 224, no. 4, April 1971, pp. 36–46.

———. "Early Man in the New World." *American Scientist*, vol. 64, May–June 1976, pp. 316–327.

Marshack, Alexander. "Exploring the Mind of Ice Age Man." *National Geographic*, vol. 147, no. 1, January 1975, pp. 62–89.

Martin, Paul S. "The Discovery of America." *Science*, vol. 179, March 9, 1973, pp. 969–974.

Martin, Paul S., and Mosimann, J. E. "Simulating Overkill by Paleoindians." *American Scientist*, vol. 63, no. 3, May–June 1975, pp. 304–313.

Meggers, Betty J. "The Transpacific Origin of Mesoamerican Civilization: A Preliminary Review of the Evidence and Its Theoretical Implications." *American Anthropologist*, vol. 77, March 1975, pp. 1–28.

"Modern Man: Mid-East Origins?" *Science News*, vol. 115, March 3, 1979, p. 132.

"Mormon Mystery." *Time*, July 11, 1979, p. 69.

Nelson, Ian. "Temples, Turtles and Fat Boys—On the Origins of the Mesoamerican Mother Culture." *Dartmouth Alumni Magazine*, vol. 72, no. 1, September 1979, pp. 36–38.

Neumann, George K. "The Upper Cave Skulls From Choukoutien in Light of Paleo-Amerind Material," abstract. *American Journal of Physical Anthropology*, vol. 14, 1956, p. 380.

Newman, Marshall T. "Aboriginal New World Epidemiology and Medical Care." *American Journal of Physical Anthropology*, vol. 45, no. 3, November 1976, pp. 667–672.

———. "Geographic and Microgeographic Races." *Current Anthropology*, vol. 4, 1963, pp. 189–207.

"New World Archaeology: A 70,000 Year Old Site." *Science News*, vol. 103, May 26, 1973, p. 337.

Odell, George Hamley. "Micro-Wear in Perspective." *World Archaeology*, vol. 7, no. 2, 1975, pp. 225–240.

Puttkamer, W. J. von. "Man in the Amazon: Stone Age Present Meets Stone Age Past." *National Geographic*, vol. 155, no. 1, January 1979, pp. 60–82.

Raemch, B. E., and Vernon, W. W. "Some Paleolithic Tools From Northeast North America." *Current Anthropology*, vol. 18, no. 1, March 1977, pp. 97–99.

Richards, Douglas. "Poseidon 76: A Progress Report." *The A.R.E. Journal*, vol. XII, no. 3, May 1977, pp. 95–104.

Schiller, Ronald. "Who Were the First Americans?" *Reader's Digest*, June 1979, pp. 92–97.

Schuiling, W. C., ed. "Pleistocene Man at Calico." *Quarterly of the San Bernardino County Museum*, vol. XXVI, no. 4, Summer 1979, pp. 1–112.

Schultes, Richard Evans. "The Ethnotoxicological Significance of Additives to New World Hallucinogens." *Plant Science Bulletin*, vol. 18, no. 4, 1972, pp. 34–40.

Singer, Clay A. "A Preliminary Report on the Analysis of Calico Lithics." *Quarterly of the San Bernardino Museum*, vol. XXVI, no. 4, Summer 1979, pp. 55–64.

Stalker, A. McS. "Geology and Age of the Early Man Site at Taber, Alberta." *American Antiquity*, vol. 32, no. 4, 1969, pp. 425–428.

Stanford, Dennis. "Bison Kill by Ice Age Hunters." *National Geographic*, vol. 155, no. 1, January 1979, pp. 114–121.

Steen-McIntyre, Virginia. "Hydration and Superhydration of Tephra Glass—A Potential Tool for Estimating Age of Holocene and Pleistocene Ark Beds." *Quarternary Studies*, 1975, pp. 271–278.

Szabo, Barney J., Malde, Harold E., and Irwin-Williams, Cynthia. "Dilemma Posed by Uranium Series Dates on Archaeologically Significant Bones From Valsequillo, Puebla, Mexico." *Earth and Planetary Science Letters*, vol. 6, no. 4, July 1969, pp. 237–244.

Tobias, Phillip V. "Calico Mountains and Early Man in North America." *Quarterly of the San Bernardino County Museum*, vol. XXVI, no. 4, Summer 1979, pp. 97–98.

Tringham, Ruth, and others. "Experimentation in the Formation of Edge Damage: A New Approach to Lithic Analysis." *Journal of Field Archaeology*, vol. 1, 1974, pp. 171–196.

Weathers, D., and Huck, J. "A Fight for Rites." *Newsweek*, April 9, 1979, p. 98.

Witthoft, John. "Technology of the Calico Site." *Quarterly of the San*

Bernardino County Museum, vol. XXVI, no. 4, Summer, 1979, pp. 47–54.
————. "Texas Street Artifacts." *New World Antiquity,* vol. 2, no. 9–12, 1955.

Newspapers

Allen, Paul. "Digging Up the Past With Help From a Psychic." *Olé-Tucson Citizen Magazine,* August 22, 1977.
"America Born Much Earlier?" *Tucson Daily Citizen,* January 3, 1976.
"Ancient Artifacts Are Found." *Arizona Republic,* March 2, 1978.
"Ancients Here Charted the Skies—Archaeologists Investigate Tortolita Stonehenge." *Tucson Daily Citizen,* June 19, 1979.
"Artifacts Place Man in New World 250,000 Years Ago—Conventional Views Contradicted." *Denver Post,* November 13, 1973.
"Coca Leaf Medicinal Value Cited—Effects Differ From Cocaine." *Tucson Daily Citizen,* February 20, 1978.
"Date of Man's U.S. Debut Disputed—12,000 or 250,000 Years Ago?" *Tucson Daily Citizen,* November 14, 1973.
"Evidence Puts Humans in California 40,000 Years Ago." *Arizona Republic,* May 14, 1975.
"Fred's Skull May Alter Man's Past—Found in Ecuador." *Chicago Tribune,* March 16, 1973.
"Fossil Study Surprise—Man's New World Age Put at 50,000 Years." *Arizona Daily Star,* March 15, 1974.
"Government Finally Gives Indian Religions a Break." *Tucson Daily Citizen,* March 15, 1979.
"Have Russians Found Atlantis?" *Tucson Daily Citizen,* August 12, 1979.
"Herb's Cure Cancer." *Tucson Daily Citizen,* August 17, 1979.
Hines, William. "Theory Traces Indian Origins to Lost Continent in Pacific." *Arizona Daily Star,* December 18, 1978.
Holstein, William J. "Digs Around the World Shed New Light on Man's Origin." *New Haven Register,* November 5, 1976.
Holton, Felicia A. "One of the Most Important Archaeological Digs in America." *The New York Times,* July 15, 1973.
"Indian Experts Polarized—Arrival Time in Question." *Tucson Daily Citizen,* December 10, 1976.
"Indian Site Frozen in Time Is Now Revealing Secrets." April 22, 1976.
"Man Got to America Earlier Than Believed." *Tucson Daily Citizen,* May 11, 1977.
"Man Uncovers Mastodon Hit With Spearhead." *Tucson Daily Citizen,* August 23, 1977.

"Pompeii of West Reveals Indian Life." *Tucson Daily Citizen*, May 13, 1975.

Rensberger, Boyce. "Bones in Venezuela Hint at Culture 13,000 Years Ago." *The New York Times*, May 17, 1978.

―――. "Coast Dig Focuses on Man's Move to New World." *The New York Times*, August 16, 1976.

―――. "Pennsylvania Site Yields Clue to Life of Stone Age Man." *The New York Times*, July 1975.

Satchell, Michael. "These Battles the Indians Are Winning." *Parade Magazine/Arizona Republic*, May 17, 1979.

"Seafaring 11,000 Years Old." *Tucson Daily Citizen*, October 28, 1978.

"Sioux-U.S. Settlement in the Millions." *Tucson Daily Citizen*, June 14, 1979.

Smith, Cliff. "New Test Shatters Theory on Age of American Man." *San Diego Union*, May 15, 1974.

"Stone Tools Estimated at 100,000 Years Old." *Arizona Republic*, April 23, 1977.

"Sunken Continent Found, Soviet Feels." *Arizona Republic*, April 3, 1979.

Specialized Publications

Angel, J. Lawrence. "Early Skeletons From Tranquility, California." *Smithsonian Contributions to Anthropology*, vol. 2, no. 1, Washington, D.C., 1966.

Bordes, Francois. "Feuille de Laurier Solutreene Rappelant Les Sandia Points des Etats Unis." *Bulletin de la Société Préhistorique Francais* 52, no. 7, 1955.

Bryson, Reid A., and Wendland, Wayne M. "Radiocarbon Isochromes of the Retreat of the Laurentide Ice Sheet." *Technical Report #35*, Department of Meteorology, Madison, Wisconsin, 1967.

Cottevieille-Giraudet, R. "Les Paux-Rouges dolichociphales de l'est américain, Caractères, Caractères Physiques Affinités Palecuzopilnes." *XV Congrès International d' Anthropologie et d'Archaeologie Préhistorique*, Portugal, 1930 (Paris: Librairie E. Nowry, 1931) pp. 265–277.

―――. "Les Races et le Peuplement du Nouveau Monde: Comment l'Europe y a Participe." *III Session Institut International d'Anthropologie*, Amsterdam, 1927 (Paris: Librairie E. Nowry, 1928) pp. 268–273.

―――. "Les Relations Probables de l'Europe et de l'Amérique du Nord à l'âge du Renne." *XV Congrès International d'Anthropolo-*

gie et d'Archaeologie Préhistorique, Portugal, 1930 (Paris: Librairie E. Nowry, 1931) pp. 318–326.

Crabtree, Don E. "An Introduction to Flintworking." Idaho State University Museum Occasional Papers, #28, 1972.

Heizer, Robert F. "Observations on Early Man in California." Reports of the University of California Archaeological Survey, no. 7, (Berkeley: 1950) pp. 5–9.

Prest, V. K. "Retreat of Wisconsin and Recent Ice in North America." Map 1257A, Geological Survey of Canada, Ottawa, 1969.

Rainey, Froelick. "The Significance of Recent Archaeological Discoveries in Inland Alaska," in Asia and North America: Transpacific Contacts, ed. Marian W. Smith, Memoir No. 9, Society for American Archaeology, vol. XVIII, no. 3, pt. 2, 1953, pp. 43–46.

Roberts, Frank H. Jr. "A Folsom Complex." Smithsonian Miscellaneous Collections, 94, no. 4, Washington, D.C., 1935.

Rogers, Spencer L. "An Ancient Human Skeleton Found at Del Mar, California." San Diego Museum Papers, no. 7, San Diego, July 1974.

————. "An Early Human Fossil From the Yuha Desert of Southern California—Physical Characteristics." San Diego Museum Papers, no. 12, San Diego, Calif., August 1977.

————. "The Physical Characteristics of the Aboriginal La Jollan Population of Southern California." San Diego Museum Papers, no. 4, San Diego, Calif., July 1963.

Unpublished Reports and Papers

Austin, Janice. "A Test of Birdsell's Hypothesis on New World Migrations." Paper presented at the annual meeting of the Society for California Archaeology, April 1976.

Berger, Rainer. "New Finds at Santa Rosa Island, California." Informal paper presented at the annual meeting for the Society for American Archaeology, Tucson, Ariz., May 1978.

Beal, James B. "Electrostatic Fields and Brain/Body/Environment Interrelationships." Paper presented at the Rhine-Swanton Interdisciplinary Symposium "Parapsychology and Anthropology," American Anthropological Association 73rd Annual Meeting in Mexico City, November 1974.

————. "Field Effects, Known and Unknown, Associated with Living Systems." Paper presented at the Institute of Electrical and Electronics Engineers Convention and Exposition, March 26–29, 1974.

Dobkin de Rios, Marlene. "Is Science Catching Up With Magic? A Look at the Content, and NOT the Structure of Belief Systems."

Paper presented at the Rhine-Swanton Interdisciplinary Symposium "Parapsychology and Anthropology," American Anthropological Association 73rd Annual Meeting in Mexico City, November 1974.

Goodman, Jeffrey. "Psychic Archaeology: Methodology and Empirical Evidence from Flagstaff, Arizona." Paper presented at the Rhine-Swanton Interdisciplinary Symposium "Parapsychology and Anthropology," American Anthropological Association 73rd Annual Meeting in Mexico City, November 1974.

Reeves, Bryan O. "Early Man at Mission Valley, San Diego." Paper presented at the Annual Meeting for the Society for American Archaeology, Tucson, May 1978.

Steen-McIntyre, Virginia, Fryxel, Roald, Malde, Harold E. "Age of Beds Exposed at Archaeological Sites—Tephro Hydration Dating May Give Approximate Age." Report to U.S. Geological Survey, August 1975.

Steen-McIntyre, Virginia, Fryxel, Roald, Malde, Harold E. "Age of Deposits of Hueyatlaco Archaeological Site, Valsequillo, Mexico." Rough draft of revised paper, March 1975.

————. "Unexpectedly Old Age of Deposits at Hueyatlaco Archaeological Site, Valsequillo, Mexico, Implied by New Stratigraphic and Petrographic Findings." Paper presented at the annual meeting of the Geological Society of America, Dallas, Texas, November 1973.

Index

About the Author

Jeffrey Goodman, Ph.D., has degrees in geological engineering, business, anthropology, and archaeology from the Colorado School of Mines, Columbia University Graduate School of Business, the University of Arizona, and California Western University. He is accredited by the Society of Professional Archaeologists, and he is the Director of Archeological Research Associates, Inc., of Tucson, Arizona. Goodman has presented a number of scientific papers on archaeology and this is his second book on the subject.